"John de Gruchy's lifelong immersion in South Africa's struggle for a just society has been deeply formed by his engagement with the life and thought of Dietrich Bonhoeffer. In these reflections he helps us see how Christian faith demands a risky wrestling with the realities of this world—whether its science and technology, its twisted histories of oppression and liberation, or our own ambiguous responses to the mysteries of death, love, and transcendence."

—WILLIAM JOHNSON EVERETT
Andover Newton Seminary at Yale Divinity School

"From local to global level, our age is beset by formidable challenges for humanity's future. With Bonhoeffer as major interlocuter, de Gruchy presents a wide-ranging and rigorous argument that Christian faith can and must engage creatively with these uncomfortable realities. Soaked in his experience as a South African theologian but with a vision reaching beyond familiar national and religious boundaries, this is an unflinchingly honest book that opens our eyes to both crisis and hope."

—KEITH CLEMENTS
Former general secretary, Conference of European Churches

"John de Gruchy writes like Bonhoeffer himself. Reflection on their own social and political contexts, and shared sufferings, analyzed through the prism of Christian theology. Just as Bonhoeffer did, so de Gruchy shows that theological reflection offers a distinctive lens on the world's problems. A book for any time but especially for our times."

—TERENCE LOVAT
University of Newcastle, Australia

"*Faith Facing Reality* will challenge its readers anew not to settle for lazy thinking and cheap consolations in light of our contemporary realities. As it stirs up discussion in dialogue with Bonhoeffer on the persistence of colonialism, racism, imperialism, anti-Semitism, oppression, and other threats to our common life, this book combines moral outrage with theological wisdom to stir, above all else, our imaginations towards justice and hope. This is vintage De Gruchy!"

—ROBERT VOSLOO
Stellenbosch University

Faith Facing Reality

FAITH FACING REALITY

Stirring Up Discussion with Bonhoeffer

John W. de Gruchy

CASCADE *Books* • Eugene, Oregon

FAITH FACING REALITY
Stirring Up Discussion with Bonhoeffer

Copyright © 2022 John W. de Gruchy. All rights reserved. Except for brief quotations in critical publications or reviews, no part of this book may be reproduced in any manner without prior written permission from the publisher. Write: Permissions, Wipf and Stock Publishers, 199 W. 8th Ave., Suite 3, Eugene, OR 97401.

Cascade Books
An Imprint of Wipf and Stock Publishers
199 W. 8th Ave., Suite 3
Eugene, OR 97401

www.wipfandstock.com

PAPERBACK ISBN: 978-1-6667-3680-9
HARDCOVER ISBN: 978-1-6667-9562-2
EBOOK ISBN: 978-1-6667-9563-9

Cataloguing-in-Publication data:

Names: De Gruchy, John W., author.

Title: Faith facing reality : stirring up discussion with Bonhoeffer / John W. de Gruchy.

Description: Eugene, OR: Cascade Books, 2022. | Includes bibliographical references and index.

Identifiers: ISBN 978-1-6667-3680-9 (paperback). | ISBN 978-1-6667-9562-2 (hardcover). | ISBN 978-1-6667-9563-9 (ebook).

Subjects: LSCH: Theology. | Bonhoeffer, Dietrich, 1906–1945. | Racism. | Israeli-Palestinian conflict.

Classification: BX4827 .B57 D390 2022 (print). | BX4827 (ebook).

VERSION NUMBER 101822

Dietrich Bonhoeffer, *Letters and Papers from Prison*, translated by Eberhard Bethge, © SCM Press, 1971. Reproduced by permission of Hymns Ancient & Modern Ltd. rights@hymnsam.co.uk

Dietrich Bonhoeffer, *Ethics*, SCM Press 1955 © SCM Press. Used by permission of Hymns Ancient & Modern Ltd. rights@hymnsam.co.uk

Unless otherwise indicated, Scripture quotations are taken from the New Revised Standard Version Bible, copyright © 1989 National Council of the Churches of Christ in the United States of America. Used by permission. All rights reserved worldwide.

Scripture quotations marked (NIV) are taken from the Holy Bible, NEW INTERNATIONAL VERSION®, NIV® Copyright © 1973, 1978, 1984, 2011 by Biblica, Inc.® Used by permission. All rights reserved worldwide.

In Memory of
Jaap Durand
(1934–2022)
Theologian, Mystic & Mensch

and

Suellen Shay
(1961–2022)
Extraordinary Friend
Hopeful, Joyful, Compassionate

CONTENTS

Acknowledgments | ix

Prologue: Stirring Up Discussion on the Important Issues in Life | 1

1 FAITH
   & the Nature of Reality | 8

2 CONVERSION
   & the Persistence of Colonial Racism | 31

3 TRANSCENDENCE
   & the Will to Power | 56

4 WISDOM
   & the Threat of Scientism and Soulless Technology | 79

5 SOLIDARITY
   & the Palestinian Question | 104

6 RESPONSIBLE FREEDOM
   & the Threat to Bodily Life | 127

Epilogue: LIVING IN HOPE
& the Inevitability of Dying and Death | 150

Bibliography | 155
Index | 169

ACKNOWLEDGMENTS

I AM INDEBTED TO many people who have stirred up discussion with me over the years on issues related to the writing of this book. Some I remember well and still count as companions on the journey of life and, above all, in reflecting on its meaning and purpose. Many others have crossed my path, including many students and colleagues who became friends. I may have forgotten all your names and might not recognize you if I saw you today—or you me—but at one time or another you contributed to my life and the development of my thought. If you happen to come across this book, please accept this acknowledgment as meant for you, for each of you has made some contribution to the lifelong process that has resulted in this slender volume.

It would be very remiss of me, however, not to thank those who read and commented on earlier drafts of the book: Robert Vosloo, Keith Clements, Larry Rasmussen, William (Bill) Everett, as well as others who, in addition, have endorsed it, and whose names are mentioned elsewhere. I must also thank K. C. Hanson, my editor at Cascade Books/Wipf and Stock Publishers, for his unfailing support and encouragement, and others of the Cascade Books team who make the task of publishing an enjoyable experience. Of course, my colleagues at Stellenbosch University and members of the Volmoed Community and the Rondebosch United Church must as always be thanked for their support, as must my immediate and wider family both in South Africa and abroad.

What, then, can I say about Isobel, my soulmate over the years that has not already been said? Well, I could acknowledge her ability to stir up discussion in a gentle but firm manner and take a stand on the issues of the day. But let me rather once again express my immense gratitude for her support, but only this time add my congratulations. I think it must also

ACKNOWLEDGMENTS

be something of a record that we both completed books on the same day, and for the same publisher. Her book, *Psalms Now*, a wonderfully fresh paraphrase of the Psalter, published by Resource Publications (an imprint of Wipf and Stock), and this volume, were both finished this afternoon, and sent on their way.

March 30th, 2022
Volmoed

PROLOGUE

Stirring Up Discussion on the Important Issues in Life

> Come now, let us reason together,
> says the Lord.
> —Isaiah 1:18 (NIV)

> The church must get out of its stagnation . . . out into the fresh air of intellectual discourse with the world. We also have to risk saying controversial things, if that will stir up discussion of the important issues in life.
> —Bonhoeffer[1]

> In Christ we are invited to participate in the reality of God and the reality of the world at the same time, the one not without the other.
> —Bonhoeffer[2]

I HAD JUST STARTED working on this new book when, suddenly, on two occasions, I collapsed while walking up the hill from the Volmoed chapel to our house. The cardiologist diagnosed a faulty heart valve. A few weeks later I was in the hospital to receive a new one. The procedure, named TAVI (transcatheter aortic valve implantation), is one of the marvels of modern

---

1. Bonhoeffer, *Letters and Papers from Prison*, 498.
2. Bonhoeffer, *Ethics*, 55.

medicine. Instead of open-heart surgery, a new valve is inserted through the groin using a catheter placed in a large blood vessel. Since then, I have also received a pacemaker, so I am wired up to go. I am in awe of medical science and its ability to save and enhance life. But I am privileged. I have access to medical aid funds and excellent physicians beyond the reach of many. Yet privileged or not, our bodies have a limited life span, and no amount of medical science can prevent the inevitable. And though medical technology is a boon in the meantime, not all technology is benign either to humanity or to our habitat.

The day I began writing this Prologue, I received the news that Jaap Durand, one of my close friends of many years and a stalwart of the antiapartheid struggle, died the previous day. His health had been failing for some time, so his passing was expected. But I am sad even as I celebrate his remarkable life of Christian commitment and the struggle for justice. In the end, death remains the ultimate reality we must all face, whether we have faith or not. But in the penultimate there are other realities that stretch our faith in God to the limit. This book is about some of these realities that I have reflected on over the past twelve years since the tragic drowning of our son Steve, aged forty-eight, in February 2010. He, too, was a pastor and a theologian, with an uncanny ability to stir up discussion.[3] Steve had already achieved much before his death and had much more to give with his life. But you never know what to expect around the next corner, for life is uncertain even at the best of times.

In the first Steve de Gruchy Memorial Lecture in 2012, Archbishop Desmond Tutu, like Job long before, pondered why God sometimes seems to be God's own worst enemy.[4] My attempt to answer that question led me to write *Led into Mystery* soon after Steve died.[5] The realities I consider in this book may be different, but the reality of death and dying remains omnipresent. Irrespective of what the other realities happen to be at any given moment, in the end they are about our hopes and fears, and our journey of faith together or alone into the mystery we name God. Nothing has brought this more sharply into focus than the fact that I began writing this book in 2021 during the second wave of the COVID pandemic and brought it to a conclusion as the horrendous war erupted in Ukraine following the Russian invasion in February 2022. How that will end and change global reality

---

3. See Cochrane et al., eds., *Living on the Edge*.
4. Tutu, "God Is God's Worst Enemy."
5. De Gruchy, *Led into Mystery*.

on the ground we do not yet know; we only know that it will. Much of what follows is, I believe, relevant to what is unfolding, even if not directly addressed.

The chapters that follow originated over the past decade in response to invitations to write essays or give lectures on some burning issues of the day. They were not written with a book in mind. But they cohere because they are all about faith filtered through my experience and reflection as I have faced the realities that daily confront us all. It is at this interface that reality is defined, and faith tested and tried. Also binding the book together is my ongoing dialogue with the legacy of Dietrich Bonhoeffer, the German theologian who died a martyr's death in 1945 aged thirty-nine. Following his example and in conversation with him, I am wanting to "stir up discussion on the important issues of life," in the hope that this will strengthen our faith and resolve in these uncertain times.

IN DISCUSSION WITH BONHOEFFER

Some readers might be forgiven for thinking that this book reveals more of a lifelong passion with Bonhoeffer's legacy than simply a discussion. That may well be true. But it is not primarily a book about Bonhoeffer's theology, for that you need to turn to his own writings or to one of the many accounts of his legacy. But it is certainly a discussion, and that inevitably means that it is also an interpretation filtered through my own experience and reflections on the issues discussed. It is also doing what he suggested we should be doing as the quotation at the beginning of the Prologue reminds us. Writing from prison, he said that sometimes we have "to risk saying controversial things if that will stir up discussion of the important issues in life." I have taken that challenge to heart.

My discussion with Bonhoeffer began in 1963–1964 when, at the height of the civil rights movement in the United States, I was a student in Chicago and used his writings as a resource for my Master of Theology dissertation, "The Local Church and the Race Problem in South Africa." It was then that I also became interested in the German *Kirchenkampf* or Church Struggle against Nazism. That early engagement with Bonhoeffer informed my decision to work for the South African Council of Churches (1968–1973), where I was daily directly involved in the church struggle against apartheid. This gave me the incentive, the subject, and the opportunity for writing my doctoral dissertation, "The Dynamic Structure of the

Church," which was a comparative study of the ecclesiologies of Karl Barth and Dietrich Bonhoeffer, with a concluding chapter on their implications for the church in South Africa. Looking back, I can now see how formative that dissertation was for the development of my theology and engagement with reality over the years that followed.

But what can we still learn today from a White male German theologian who lived in the first half of the twentieth century? It is a question that I have often asked myself and been asked by others. In response, I would begin by saying that it is a mistake to think that Bonhoeffer has only found resonance among a handful of other White theologians. Black and feminist theologians have also engaged and appropriated his legacy and been inspired by his courageous witness, some of them also South Africans.[6] There are several reasons for my own preoccupation with his legacy. The most obvious is the similarity between the German *Kirchenkampf* and the church struggle against apartheid in South Africa. Another is the fact that I continue to discover fresh resources in his writings that help me address the issues of the day, even though some of them he did not directly consider. And, existentially, I have always been challenged by his struggle to overcome personal privilege as a follower of Christ and to maintain hope in the most desperate of situations. The truth is, Bonhoeffer helps me to see things differently, challenges me to act differently, and stirs up debate on the realities that face us all. And he does so because of his family background, his faith and courage, his formation in Christ, and his conviction that the church should be Christ existing as a community of people for the sake of the world.

In 1984 I published a little book of essays titled *Bonhoeffer and South Africa* based on lectures I had previously given. The first of those lectures was given at the Second International Bonhoeffer Congress in Geneva in 1976, and the last in the book was given in Seattle in 1984 at a conference celebrating the fiftieth anniversary of the publication of the Barmen Declaration, which launched the German *Kirchenkampf*. Each of the essays in *Bonhoeffer and South Africa* arose out of doing theology during the struggle against apartheid. That was *the* omnipresent reality that faith faced at the time in my home context. The method I developed for doing so has shaped my theological work ever since then.

---

6. See Williams, *Bonhoeffer's Black Jesus*; Young, *No Difference in the Fare*; Boesak, "Church Racism and Resistance"; Jenkins and McBride, eds., *Bonhoeffer and King*; McBride, "Bonhoeffer and Feminist Theologies." See de Gruchy, ed., *Bonhoeffer for a New Day*; *Journal of Theology for Southern Africa*, No. 127, March 2007.

For that reason, I have thrown academic modesty out the window in what follows and have not hesitated to include personal anecdotes where appropriate or to reference my own work where necessary. As is true for many others, my theology is linked to my own narrative and includes working on and writing about Bonhoeffer over a long period of time. So I think I owe it to readers to indicate where and when I have previously written about his legacy in relation to the issues discussed in this book. I have also referenced the work of my late son Steve whose contribution to theology has been documented by others, and from whom I learned much over the years until his death in 2010.

Perhaps my South African colleagues who have also written about Bonhoeffer and I have had an advantage over those elsewhere because of the parallels between Bonhoeffer's historical context and apartheid South Africa. This was noted by Eberhard Bethge, Bonhoeffer's friend and biographer, during a visit to our country in 1973, and over the years that followed as he mentored and encouraged me in my task.[7] Bethge, I must also mention, cautioned me against the dangers of misusing Bonhoeffer's legacy in contexts other than his own, and I have tried to heed his polite but firm warning.[8] This, then, to belabor the point, is not a book *about* Bonhoeffer; it is a discussion *with* Bonhoeffer. So a very brief word about method, that is, how I have sought to do this, is appropriate.

In doing theology in discussion with Bonhoeffer in our own respective contexts, we must first consider whether there are trajectories in his legacy that relate to them, consider how he responded to them in his, be mindful that he always drew from the wells of the Bible and Christian tradition in doing so, and retain a critical distance. Doing theology in discussion with Bonhoeffer is different from writing a monograph on his theology in much the same way as biblical exegesis is different from hermeneutics and requires a different set of skills. Exegeting Bonhoeffer's theology is not the same as trying to fuse his horizon with our own and engage in contemporary interpretation. Yet Bonhoeffer would surely expect us to do both, for that is how he did theology as he demonstrated in his 1932 lectures on Christology.[9] To answer the question "who is Jesus Christ really for us today?" we must first consider the testimony of the New Testament and Christian tradition. But the point of doing this is not antiquarian but to

---

7. See de Gruchy, "Bonhoeffer in South Africa."
8. See de Gruchy *Daring, Trusting Spirit*, 158–67.
9. Bonhoeffer, *Berlin 1932–1933*, 299–360.

discern the significance of Jesus as the Christ for us here and now, as I have described more systematically in *Bonhoeffer's Questions: A Lifelong Conversation*. But it is about more than discerning significance; it is about expressing that significance in ways that, like the ancient Hebrew prophets, were controversial, stirred up heated discussion, and challenged his hearers' assumptions and prejudices. After all, in his own ministry, Jesus was continually engaged in doing that, not least in his many encounters with the Pharisees and other religious leaders of his day.

The Christocentric character of Bonhoeffer's theology does not mean that it is narrow in scope, for the "narrow gate" through which we enter in faith opens out into wide spaces in which life in all its fullness waits to be explored. As he says in his prison letters, with Christ as our *cantus firmus* the "polyphony of life" becomes possible.[10] Not only is this evident in his involvement in the politics of his day, but it is also expressed in the way his musical talent and aesthetic sensibility influenced his theology, and likewise in the way his interest in science shaped his later thinking in prison. Bonhoeffer was a Christian humanist, and his interest in the reality of the world in all its dimensions is everywhere apparent.[11] But it is undoubtedly Bonhoeffer's Christology that gives his theology its coherence, and it likewise gives coherence to the chapters in this book. This inevitably means that certain christological emphases and insights will recur in the chapters that follow, but each time they will take us one step further in discovering their relevance for the issues that now confront us.

THE CHAPTERS

All the specific essays and lectures that provide much of the content of this book, with the exception of Chapter 1, were previously published, but they have been thoroughly rewritten, enlarged, and brought into relationship with one another. So I have included fresh material and clarified my arguments where necessary. But I have not engaged issues that I have not previously examined with the thoroughness required. And I confess, I have implied much but said little about three of the most challenging and critically important of these: the environmental crisis, the economic systems that create huge disparities between the rich and the poor, and gender-based violence. Bonhoeffer's theology has much to contribute to the discussion of

---

10. Bonhoeffer, *Letters and Papers from Prison*, 394.
11. De Gruchy, "Dietrich Bonhoeffer as Christian Humanist."

each of these, even if they were not at the center of his theological inquiries or have been of mine.[12]

There is, however, a great deal in his legacy that relates to the issues that I do explore: the meaning and significance of faith in facing reality (Chapter 1); Christian conversion in responding to the persistence of colonialism and racism (Chapter 2); the desire for transcendence and the will to power as seen in the contemporary threat of resurgent aggressive nationalism and imperialism (Chapter 3); the need for wisdom in dealing with the challenge of scientism and life-threatening technology (Chapter 4), anti-Semitism and oppression in Palestine today (Chapter 5); and the recurring threat of tyranny, terror, and the plague (Chapter 6). An Epilogue on hope in facing the reality of death and dying brings the volume to completion.[13]

Each of these essays was written in a specific historical context, so I have briefly attempted to sketch its background as and when appropriate. In some instances, especially in Chapter 2, I have been mindful that readers other than South Africans might need more information, and I have provided that as succinctly as possible. But the issues discussed are as global as they may be local. Obviously much more could be said, but hopefully enough has been provided to locate the discussion in its context. If not, the bibliography will point readers to additional resources that will help fill the gaps.

---

12. See Rasmussen, *Earth-Honoring Faith*, 65–67, 82–86; Rayson, *Bonhoeffer and Climate Change*.

13. The details of the original versions of my chapters are—chapter 2: "Can a White South African Male Enter the Kingdom of God?" Steve de Gruchy Memorial Lecture, Rondebosch United Church, Cape Town, South Africa, March 2019; chapter 3: "The Search for Transcendence in an Age of Barbarism: Bonhoeffer, Beethoven, Mann's *Dr Faustus* and the Spiritual Crisis of the Present Time," published in *Polyphonie des Lebens* (2019); chapter 4: "Reality and Mystery: Science, Humanism, and Ethics," a lecture at the University of the Free State in Bloemfontein during a conference on Radical Orthodoxy in May 2015, published as "Reality and Mystery: Scientific Understanding, Christian Humanism, and Defining Moral Imperatives" in the *Journal of Theology for Southern Africa* 157 (March 2017) 59–70; chapter 5: "Bonhoeffer's Legacy and *Kairos-Palestine*," *Journal of Theology for Southern Africa* 143 (July 2012) 67–80; and chapter 6: "Playing God during the Pandemic: Courage, Responsibility, and the Ethics of Necessity," *Ecumenical Review* 72.3 (July 2020) 660–72.

1

FAITH

&

the Nature of Reality

Faith is the assurance of things hoped for, the conviction of things not seen.
—Hebrews 11:1

Faith is nothing less than developing the bold vision of a new reality and mobilizing the needed resources to make it happen.
—Mitri Raheb[1]

For me the love of God is, both in a direct and in an inverse sense, incommensurable with the whole of reality.
—Søren Kierkegaard[2]

The attempt to escape ideological and utopian distortions is . . . a quest for reality. These two conceptions provide us with the basis for a sound scepticism, and

---

1. Raheb, *Faith in the Face of Empire*, 105.
2. Kierkegaard, *Fear and Trembling*, 45.

> they can be put to positive use in avoiding the pitfalls into which our thinking might lead us.
>
> —Karl Mannheim[3]

> Only in the act of faith as a direct act is God recognized as the reality which is beyond and outside of our thinking, of our whole existence. Theology . . . is the attempt to set forth what is already possessed in the act of faith.
>
> —Bonhoeffer[4]

WE LIVE IN APOCALYPTIC times, some say, on the brink of a Third World War. Even if today's global calamities are nothing new, their scale is terrifyingly different, as Niall Ferguson demonstrates in his aptly named book *Doom*.[5] Together, they threaten our existence in complex and converging ways we have only begun to grasp. It is not only fundamentalist Christians who tell us that we are living in the "end times"; many others believe that as well. Intelligent young people I know think it is immoral to procreate and condemn another generation to life in a world hastening to its destruction.[6] As Larry Rasmussen, a foremost ecotheologian, tells us in *The Planet You Inherit: Letters to My Grandchildren,* the only certainty is uncertainty.[7] Ideological and utopian claims to the contrary, including those made by Christian faith, are thus treated with skepticism by an informed new generation. But what if we do accept that the world is in deep trouble, perhaps terminally ill, yet live by faith, work in love for justice, and labor in hope for its redemption? Are we simply blind to reality and living in a dreamworld?

Facing reality honestly, recognizing the power of evil and the inevitable decay of material reality, and struggling with the temptation to doubt and lose hope is, however, a necessary ingredient to living by faith. Doubt is not the opposite of faith but the shadow side of a living faith, its constant companion. Sin is faith's nemesis, not doubt. But if faith is dishonest or

---

3. Mannheim, *Ideology and Utopia*, 98.
4. Bonhoeffer, *Barcelona, Berlin, New York*, 454. Slightly modified by author.
5. Ferguson, *Doom*.
6. See de Gruchy, *The End Is Not Yet*.
7. Rasmussen, *Planet You Inherit*.

serves self-interest or the grasp for power at the expense of others, it too becomes sinful.

Conversion to Christ, if it is not an ongoing process of growth and formation in Christ, can also become a way of escape from reality or can be abused to rationalize prejudice, arrogance, and injustice. The desire for transcendence then becomes a desire for power. No longer a true desire for God, it becomes a desire to *be* God. If evil is the absence of goodness, sin is the corruption of what is good and is too often rationalized by religion and ideology. We humans are prone by nature reinforced by nurture to justify our self-interests instead of subjecting them to critical inquiry. We shall encounter a great deal of this going forward, because the realities that confront us are generally instances of individual, national, gender, or ethnic self-interest. This is the reality we face if we seriously and therefore honestly believe. It is not reality as a philosophical concept or even broadly in a historical context, but reality that faces us, as we colloquially say, "on the ground," for it is there that it confronts our faith.

THE REALITY WE FACE

I was born a few months before the Second World War and recall that everything in my early childhood was overshadowed by its threatening reality. It may seem bizarre now, but in 1940, the year after I was born and when we were living in Pretoria, we feared an attack by Japan after its forces captured Singapore and raced westwards towards India. My parents also told my older sister, Rozelle, and me about what it had been like living through the First World War, which claimed the life of one of my uncles and seriously affected the mind of another. They told us about the Great Influenza Epidemic (which, apparently, was first reported in Kansas, not in Spain) that raged across the globe in 1918, followed by the Great Depression. To make sure we ate our vegetables, they also told us about starving children in famine-stricken China. For my parents, the offspring of British colonial settlers in South Africa, this was the global reality that shaped their lives just as it did millions of others of their generation.

The reality that was omnipresent as I finished high school and entered university was apartheid. I experienced it differently from Black South Africans, but it overshadowed and affected all our lives. Apartheid was *the* omnipresent reality that shaped my theological studies, my early ministry as a pastor, and eventually my work as an ecumenical activist and theologian. It was also *the* reality that determined my wife Isobel's life as a teacher and social volunteer, and the education and future of our three children, Steve, Jeanelle, and Anton. Travel abroad and the news made us mindful of other realities that shaped the lives of people elsewhere: the decolonization of Asia and Africa, the Cold War, the civil rights movement, and the Vietnam War. But irrespective of where we were, apartheid was the inescapable backdrop reality and the greatest challenge to our faith as South African Christians.

The most threatening reality facing us today, irrespective of where we live, is the future of the planet itself. Global warming casts its expanding shadow over the earth and threatens to bring everything we have cherished to a frightful end. Dystopian reality seriously challenges whatever utopian longing we may cherish. This is now *the* framework within which all the other life-threatening realities confront us. Their relationship to each other has been demonstrated and heightened by the COVID-19 pandemic that has changed our lives and livelihoods and continues to rage in multiplying variants even as I write. Like all plagues, we assume it will pass, yet we fear it will inevitably return in some new form. In the meantime, the pandemic has highlighted other realities that have long been part of our social fabric but are now more apparent and challenging than perhaps the privileged and powerful previously thought. Among the most obvious are global inequality and poverty, the cycle of war and terror, the refugee crisis, gender-based violence, human trafficking, failed states, the rise of totalitarianism and right-wing nationalism, and the persistence of systemic racism. Singly they test our faith; together they push it to the limit.

Those who are informed about twentieth-century theology and especially theology as it engages politics and society may see some resonance between what follows in this book and what has generally been referred to as Christian realism. The major exponent of Christian realism was Reinhold Niebuhr, who was also one of Bonhoeffer's professors during a study year in New York. On several occasions I had the privilege to discuss South African politics with Niebuhr late in his life, and I eagerly devoured many of his books and came under his spell. Then, our son Steve wrote his doctoral dissertation on Niebuhr, which played a major role in his theological development,[8] and there was much family discussion on how his theology could be meaningfully appropriated in the South African context. But we

---

8. De Gruchy, "Not Liberation but Justice."

agreed. Niebuhr's Christian realism had to be mediated through the lens of Bonhoeffer's theology.

No one, to my mind, has better described how Bonhoeffer's thought reshapes Christian realism than Robin Lovin in *Christian Realism and the New Realities*. Lovin wrote his book early in the new millennium in response to the "new realities" that faced global society after the end of the Cold War. The world is undoubtedly different now even after this short period of time, for much has happened to refigure its contours since 9/11, the War in Iraq, and now the COVID pandemic and the war in Ukraine. But Lovin's interpretation of Bonhoeffer remains as relevant as ever. So let me acknowledge my indebtedness to his account at the outset and indicate that though I will not discuss his work, much of what follows is informed by his insights into Bonhoeffer's legacy. Christians are called to be visionaries, even utopian in our hopes for a more just and peaceable world, but we must always be sufficiently realistic in relating to reality as we experience it on the ground. Or, as Bonhoeffer said, not quixotic, that is, fighting reality with blunt swords.[9] And we do so by continually asking, "who is Jesus Christ for us, today?" In sum, in facing the realities that confront faith at any time and in any place, the tension between what Bonhoeffer called the ultimate and the penultimate is fundamental, as is his "theology of the cross" and his inclusive understanding of Christ as the human being who exists for others.

The nature of reality has long been debated by seminal thinkers. Whatever we may learn from them, or by whatever name it is known, for most of us reality is what stares us in the face day by day if we open our eyes and are not blinded by ideological opinion, religious fundamentalism, or utopian illusions. Reality challenges whatever faith in God we may have if we still have any. Bonhoeffer faced such reality in the raw. We have only to read his *Letters and Papers from Prison*, written as Germany was hurtling to its destruction, to sense his foreboding. But despite his moments of intense doubt, bouts of deep depression, and thoughts of suicide, somehow his faith sustained him in hope, not least for the sake of future generations and, of course, because of his desire to be reunited with his fiancée and family. Reality for Bonhoeffer was life-threatening, but it was also theologically speaking a sacrament, that is, a means of grace through which we may discern by faith God's will for the world.

---

9. Bonhoeffer, *Ethics*, 51.

REALITY AS SACRAMENT

I recall the day the penny dropped in my early attempt to understand Bonhoeffer's theology. In a word, it had to do with *Wirklichkeit*, that is, "reality." From the moment I discovered its importance for Bonhoeffer, the word jumped out from every page I read of his writings. He was truly a "theologian of reality," as André Dumas described him.[10] Indeed, to use Bonhoeffer's own words written from prison, his theological journey itself was a turning "from phraseology to reality (*Wirklichen*)" prompted by his early travels abroad and his first conscious awareness of his father's influence.[11] That journey did not end until at the last he had to face the reality of his death at the hands of the Gestapo. But it was in facing reality that Bonhoeffer's faith was nurtured and became authentic.[12] For good reason Heinrich Ott refers to Wirklichkeit as the "one theme of his life's history and life's work." Indeed, the uncompromisingly honest endeavour to face the concreteness of reality "without subtraction, without speculative addition, without self-deception."[13]

Bonhoeffer reflected on *Wirklichkeit* in his 1927 dissertation, *Sanctorum Communio* and in *Act and Being*, his 1931 *habilitation* (a second dissertation, written to qualify as a university lecturer). Both works greatly influenced his theological development.[14] But that was academic. His existential turn from "phraseology to reality" occurred during his year of study at Union Theological Seminary in New York in 1931–32. This came about as a result of his friendship with two fellow students, the saintly French pastor and pacifist Jean Lasserre, who challenged his German nationalism, and the African American, Franklin Fischer, who challenged his Whiteness.[15] From then on, Bonhoeffer's life became a journey of discipleship shaped by the Sermon on the Mount and a rejection of violence and war, nationalism and racism.

---

10. See Dumas, *Dietrich Bonhoeffer: Theologian of Reality*.
11. Bonhoeffer, *Letters and Papers from Prison*, 358.
12. See Tödt, *Authentic Faith*.
13. Ott, *Reality and Faith*, 19.
14. Bonhoeffer, *Sanctorum Communio*; Bonhoeffer, *Act and Being*.
15. Following a June 2020 update to the seventeenth edition of *The Chicago Manual of Style* I capitalize words for racial identity. Like national identity (American, South African) they identify the self and the "other" even though race as distinct from ethnicity is an unscientific category.

Bonhoeffer's turn to reality was already evident when in July 1932, a year after he returned from New York, he gave a lecture at a youth conference in Czechoslovakia organized by the World Alliance for Promoting International Friendship through the Churches. This prophetic call urged the churches to stop passing resolutions enunciating principles and to take a bold categorical stand against war. At the time few Christians in Germany shared Bonhoeffer's newly gained ecumenical and pacifist convictions. But for Bonhoeffer, preaching the gospel was not about proclaiming eternal principles; it was about discerning God's will in facing reality and declaring what God demanded in response. The gospel was not about timeless truths that applied to reality in general, but about the truth that spoke to the reality facing us today. "For that which is 'always' true," he declared, "is precisely not true 'today': God is for us 'always' God precisely 'today.'"[16]

Those who heard Bonhoeffer could be forgiven for thinking that his was the voice of presumptuous youth, much like today when youthful environmentalist protesters call for decisive action in brash tones and uncompromising words. But there was theological substance and political realism in what he said. Indeed, he struck a distinctly biblical-prophetic chord: "Today, if you will hear his voice, harden not your hearts."[17] While he acknowledged that no one had all the information and knowledge necessary to have a complete grasp of reality, this did not mean that the church could avoid responsibility by remaining silent or uttering platitudes. The church, he said, cannot honestly proclaim the commandment: "Love your neighbor" without saying what this specifically means here and now. Not to do so would reduce God's commandment to a moral principle instead of an imperative requiring concrete action.

In driving home his point, Bonhoeffer made the evocative statement that gave his political challenge theological depth: "what the sacrament is for the proclamation of the gospel," he said, "the knowledge of concrete reality is for the proclamation of the commandment. *Reality is the sacrament of the commandment.*"[18] Reality not only faces us, it is also the means whereby we discern God's will and purpose for our lives. Just as the sacraments of baptism and the eucharist are concrete in their proclamation of the gospel of God's grace and forgiveness, so the knowledge of material reality is

---

16. Bonhoeffer, *Ecumenical, Academic, and Pastoral Work*, 359–60.

17. See Bonhoeffer, *Discipleship*, 191. The words of Ps 95:7, quoted in the Letter to the Hebrews 4:7, were underlined by Bonhoeffer in his copy of Luther's Bible.

18. Bonhoeffer, *Ecumenical, Academic, and Pastoral Work*, 359–62 (italics original).

necessary for us to proclaim God's justice. From then on, this "sacramental worldliness," as Barry Harvey calls it, became fundamental to Bonhoeffer's theology.[19] God's real presence revealed in the Incarnation, that is, in the "Word become flesh," confronts us in the harsh reality of the world with both a demand and a promise. The demand is justice, the promise is peace.

Although God's presence is *in* the world, it is not *of* the world, that is, it is not obvious to sight or controlled by the world but hidden, and therefore beyond all our attempts to capture it for our own designs. We can only discern what God is doing in the world by faith, just as we can only discern God's presence in Christ crucified on the cross, and in the bread broken in the eucharist, by faith. Faith is necessary to grasp what is hidden from sight in worldly reality. Jesus spoke in parables precisely to enable his hearers to discern the reign of God beneath the surface of appearances, because, as he said to his followers, people see but do not perceive; they hear but do not listen or understand (Matt 13:13).

Bonhoeffer had already explored the christological connection between the reality of God and the realities facing us in the world in a masterful lecture much influenced by Karl Barth, which he gave at Union Seminary in 1931, titled "Concerning the Christian Idea of God."[20] Theology, he declared, "starts with the statement of the reality of God," which gets us thinking about what that means. In doing so, we soon discover that it requires an act of faith which recognizes that God is the reality "beyond and outside of our thinking"—indeed, "our whole existence." We also recognize the limitations of our thinking, which requires that we "leave room for the reality of God, which can never be conceived by theological thinking." Indeed, he went on to say, God "is absolutely free of all theoretical generalization." Even saying "God is love" is meaningless without saying what this requires of us.

Moreover, said Bonhoeffer, to speak of the "transcendence of God" as if God can be described in philosophically abstract terms, fails to understand that it refers to the "personality of God" who cannot be talked about in general terms. God is Subject, the "Thou" who confronts us in the reality of Jesus the Christ, not an object waiting to be examined. That is why all Christian God-talk is a response of faith to God's self-revelation in history mediated through Christ. Or, as he would later write shortly before his imprisonment, faith overcomes "fear of the future," because "God is no

19. Harvey, *Taking Hold of the Real*, 19–57.
20. Bonhoeffer, *Barcelona, Berlin, New York*, 451–61.

timeless fate but waits for and responds to sincere prayer and responsible actions."[21] We do not read God's will in the events of history (or the news), except through the eyes of *such* faith. This is the prophetic vision of the great Hebrew prophets as fulfilled in Christ.[22]

The Christian response to the reality of the world, and therefore to the realities we now face, cannot then be based on general moral principles. As Bonhoeffer wrote in the opening paragraph of his *Ethics*, those who focus on Christian ethics are faced "with an outrageous demand." Instead of asking how we can be good, or do the good, we "must ask the wholly other, completely different question: what is the will of God?" This demand, Bonhoeffer, continued, "is radical precisely because it presupposes a decision about ultimate reality, that is, a decision of faith." Which leads him to conclude: "Of ultimate importance, then, is not that I become good, or that the condition of the world be improved by my efforts, but that the reality of God show itself everywhere to be the ultimate reality."[23] Concrete worldly obedience to God's commandments in the penultimate, the here and now, prepares the way for the ultimate coming of God's grace. Faith saves us because through faith we discern both the judgment and the redemptive reality of God in the world and are enabled to obey God's will for the world. Such faith is not trust in a principle, however lofty, but in a person who is alone fully trustworthy.

FAITH AS TRUST

Census statistics tell us that many people believe in God, but that does not tell us much unless we probe further. Who (or what) is the God they believe in and trust, and how does this help them face reality honestly? Answers, when forthcoming, will undoubtedly vary greatly, some detailed and offered with conviction, others vague and incoherent. They also often reveal what some people do not believe. During the COVID-19 pandemic, trusting God has meant, for some, not trusting scientists, especially medical ones. But the question, who can we trust? is, nonetheless, fundamental in responding to the realities that face us.

We learn the importance of faith as trust in everyday life as we grow towards maturity. James Fowler describes this in his *Stages of Faith* in

21. Bonhoeffer, *Letters and Papers from Prison*, 46.
22. De Gruchy, *Bonhoeffer's Questions*, 59–76.
23. Bonhoeffer, *Ethics*, 47–48.

relation to the life cycle of human development.[24] Trust may be inbred, but its healthy development cannot be taken for granted, and it can easily be undermined or even extinguished. Our experience of loving parents should enable us to learn what it means to trust others, but if our childhood is marred by parental neglect or worse, then the formation of faith as trust will be stunted. The consequences can be severe. When trust is broken, life can fall apart. But this does not negate the claim that we are born to trust, that we flourish through trusting, and that we struggle to trust when the odds are against us, because we need to do so. Without developing trust, building good relationships becomes difficult if not impossible, and life is scarred and may become intolerable. But then, our trust needs to be placed in what is trustworthy.

During the pandemic I reread Umberto Eco's book of essays, *Faith in Fakes*. In his youth, the celebrated Italian writer was a committed Catholic, but as the years passed, he became a critical outsider. The institutional church was no longer trustworthy. Yet he retained his respect for authentic—an important qualification—Christianity until his death in 2016. Indeed, his writings convey a good knowledge of the Bible, medieval theology, and Catholic tradition. But he achieved fame as an agnostic postmodern philosopher deconstructing holy cows, and a semiotician—that is, a specialist in the interpretation of signs and symbols. For him words were important even when abused by propagandists and the purveyors of fake news, values, medicines, prophets, and gods.

At one time many of us trusted Father Christmas and believed in the omniscience of parents and teachers, but the day dawned when we discovered that we had been conned and naïve. We had been childish and appropriately so. If we were to mature, we had to learn who we could truly trust (hopefully this included our parents and mentors in a new way) and therefore to distinguish between truth and error, and not be taken in by fake news and charlatans. And, for many people who are taught to pray as children, asking God for help and a blessing or two, the day comes when they lose faith in the God they had previously trusted. *Such* faith could not honestly face the reality of experience, the challenge of reason, or expanding knowledge. Indeed, when our faith fails to help us face reality, above all the reality of suffering, it cannot save us from despair and hopelessness; on the contrary, it is prone to manipulation by those who profit from our weakness and unthinking trust. While reflecting, in prison, on the fact

---

24. Fowler, *Stages of Faith*. 106–10.

that in our time science and secularism had pushed God out of our lives, Bonhoeffer acknowledged that for many "there still remain the so-called ultimate questions—death, guilt—which only 'God' can answer, and for which people need God and the church and the pastor." But, he then asked, "what happens if some day they no longer exist as such, or if they are being answered 'without God'?"[25]

While we may be dismissive of childish trust, we should not confuse this with what Jesus called *childlike* trust. If it were not for such faith, many of the most poor, oppressed, and vulnerable people living on the planet would lose all hope and resign themselves to inevitable fate. So, whether we are trained theologians or not, learning to become childlike, "being born anew," or reaching the stage of what the philosopher Paul Ricoeur called a "second naiveté," is essential on the journey of faith. In a letter to Eberhard and Renate Bethge from prison Bonhoeffer writes about such naiveté as a gift of faith in comparison to simplicity, which can "be attained by education." Naiveté, he says, "implies wholeness," which is akin to "purity," and we can only receive it through faith.[26]

This is the context in which Bonhoeffer also writes about the need to recover "aesthetic existence" in the life of the church, for without a sense of beauty and the use of our imagination which evokes wonder, faith becomes soulless and confined to ethics.[27] There is an important relationship, then, between the naiveté of faith and the imagination that enables faith to express itself in the creative arts, especially in music, as we shall see in Chapter 3 in exploring the human desire for transcendence. But, of course, the imagination can also run riot and lead us to put our trust in false images or what Eco calls fakes. Bonhoeffer would have agreed, then, with Eco's aesthetic judgment and sharp critique of inauthentic faith that cannot save us or make us whole.

So, when Bonhoeffer said in his 1931 lecture in New York that the "basis of all theology is the fact of faith,"[28] he did not have every or any kind of faith in mind. Indeed, if we are to speak about "faith facing reality," especially in dialogue with Bonhoeffer's legacy, we need to clarify what kind of faith we are talking about. Is it faith that faces reality in a way that discerns

---

25. Bonhoeffer, Letter to Bethge, June 8,1944, in *Letters and Papers from Prison*, 427.

26. Bonhoeffer, *Letters and Papers from Prison*, 294–95.

27. Bonhoeffer, *Letters and Papers from Prison*, 268. See de Gruchy, *Christianity, Art and Transformation*, 136–68.

28. Bonhoeffer, *Barcelona, Berlin, New York*, 45.

the demand and promise of God, or is it a pious means of escape that avoids all responsibility for the world? For Bonhoeffer, authentic, saving faith was undoubtedly biblical in character. But what precisely does that mean given the diverging faith trajectories in the Bible? There is a qualitative difference between the faith of Job in the face of great suffering and that of his comforters; between the faith of Israel in trusting God to crush its enemies, and that of Isaiah, whose messianic hope embraced all nations in a vision of peace and justice; or between the faith placed in the golden calf in the wilderness, and that of Abraham, who journeyed into the unknown trusting God alone.

We humans have a propensity to put our faith in fakes in responding to reality. But alas, such faith is a placebo at best and a dangerous delusion at worst, as many critics of religious faith have long and correctly argued. We can be totally committed to ideologies that are destructive, and to dictators who are evil. For this reason, the content or subject of our faith matters. Not all faith saves us. What, then, is the nature of Christian faith, the faith by which, as Saint Paul says, "we are justified"? (Rom 5:1). Or, stated differently, what is biblical faith?

BIBLICAL FAITH

Just as the COVID-19 pandemic heightened our awareness of the many fault-lines that divide societies and nations, so it has dramatically shown how divisive and even politically explosive faith in the God of the Bible is among Christians. But let us be clear: trusting the Bible is not the same as trusting God. The Bible is a witness to faith in God, not a substitute. Like misguided patriotism that claims one's own country is always right even when it is patently wrong, believing in the Bible without qualification because we want to defend its authority does exactly the opposite. There are too many biblical passages that can be quoted in support of attitudes and actions that are as abhorrent as those propagated by ISIS based on its reading of the Qur'an—stoning women caught in adultery or homosexuals to death are two; brutally slaying unbelieving enemies, including women and children, are others. If we believe that such practices are justified because some text in the Bible says they are, then I would not give the Bible much authority or credibility. Likewise, if we use the Bible in support of nationalism, racism, and war—and there are texts that are quoted in doing so—then, at least from a Christian perspective, we are misusing the

Bible. Such texts remind us how the will of God was often misunderstood in biblical times and subsequently used to justify conquest, slavery, and the subjugation of women. Biblical faith is not the same as an ill-informed trust in the Bible as though every statement and text has been crafted by God.

But the fact that I do not trust every word the Bible contains as "God-inspired" does not mean that I do not take the Bible seriously. I do not take it literally in believing that the universe was created in seven days; neither did the poet-prophet who first wrote the creation narrative. But I do take it literally when it tells me that God requires me to do justice, care for the earth, and love my neighbor, as Jesus and the prophets insist. To take the Bible seriously requires an awareness of its character and of the various genres employed in its many varied parts; it also means listening carefully to what the Spirit is saying to us today as we learn to live our lives by faith in God.

The biblical account of faith begins with Abraham's mysterious call to go out into the unknown trusting the promise of the One who was as unknown as Abraham's destination (Gen 12). Moses's experience at the burning bush of the One who IS (YHWH) clarified God's identity as the Wholly Other in contrast to the idols of the nations, which prompted Moses to hide his face from God in awe (Exod 3:1–6). The journey of the liberated Hebrew slaves through the wilderness en route to the promised land depicts their struggle to learn not to trust fake gods, for it was YHWH who set them free from bondage and gave them reason to live in hope of inhabiting the land of promise. In sum, as Walter Brueggemann says, faith in YHWH became "a critical principle" that de-absolutized "every other claimant to ultimate power." YHWH refused to "be recruited or used for any social or human agenda."[29]

Speaking specifically as a Christian, for me the Bible is a trustworthy necessity because it tells the story of the Word who was "with God from the beginning," the Word who at a particular time in human history "became flesh and lived among us" (John 1:1–14). For this reason Christians believe that the reality of God and the reality of the world are connected not only in creation but also in redemption, and therefore by faith we "participate in the reality of God and the reality of the world at the same time, the one not without the other."[30] Christian faith is, therefore, a way of being and acting in the world informed by God's self-disclosure in Jesus Christ, and

---

29. Brueggemann, *Theology of the Old Testament*, 184.
30. Bonhoeffer, *Barcelona, Berlin, New York*, 454.

that means living and acting differently from those who trust in fakes. Such faith is more than trust: it is a commitment—or to quote Bonhoeffer's trenchant aphorism: "*only believers obey,* and *only the obedient believe.*"[31]

Faith in Christ is not then primarily an acceptance of a set of propositions about who Christ is but a response to Jesus' call to follow him. However, critical reflection on faith inevitably leads to the articulation of what that faith means both in practice and in understanding. Christian praxis thus leads to the formulation of tradition, including teaching or doctrine, which continues to shape Christian commitment over time. In the process, faith is reformulated as it faces reality in changing historical contexts. Such faith may not be based on reason, but from earliest times and with few exceptions Christian theologians have argued that it is reasonable and therefore needs to give an account of why there is good reason for placing their trust in the biblical God and living in hope for a more just world. For them, if not for all, faith and reason are not polarities.

A REASONABLE FAITH

When I first studied philosophy, the curriculum included metaphysics, and Kant's idealism was taken seriously. By the time I studied theology, only theologians on the faculty still referred to Kant, but Ludwig Wittgenstein and A. J. Ayer reigned supreme in the philosophy department. For them, the task of philosophy was not to explore reality but to clarify concepts and unpack the language used to describe it. If that could not be done, then it was non-sense. As a theological student attending seemingly endless lectures and discussions on the relationship between faith and reason, epistemology, and analytical philosophy, I recall that several of my fellow students, among them some of the brightest, gave up theology and pursued other career paths. For them, "God was dead" not simply because Christendom had "killed him," as Friedrich Nietzsche insisted, or because faith in God was irrational—how could an all-powerful and all-loving God allow suffering?—but because to say "I believe in God" was a meaningless, unscientific proposition. To resort to the language of mystery, as theologians do, only obfuscated matters further. God-talk was indulging in a mystical sleight of hand; it was unreal, quite literally unthinkable. Science reigned or, more correctly, the scientific method was the only basis of all knowledge. Philosophy had become symbolic logic. This is still largely the considered

31. Bonhoeffer, *Discipleship*, 63.

opinion of the secularized intellectual West today even though many philosophers have become less positivist and more nuanced in describing reality.

Steven Pinker, the Harvard professor of psychology, who I will engage again in Chapter 4, concludes his recent book *Rationality* with words that are worth pondering for people of faith in a world that has become increasingly irrational and, in some quarters, insane:

> Sound arguments, enforcing a consistency of our practices without principles and with the goal of human flourishing, cannot improve the world by themselves. But they have guided, and should guide, movements for change. They make the difference between moral force and brute force, between marches for justice and lynch mobs, between human progress and breaking things.[32]

Yes, indeed, such "sound arguments," as Pinker says, help us detect moral failures, help us find remedies that might work, and so foster "moral progress" today just as they did in the past. The "power of rationality" helps us to choose wisely, just as it awakens us to ideas and exposes us "to realities that confound our intuitions but are true for all of that."[33]

No Christian theologian in her or his right mind would disagree with Pinker's eloquent defense of reason as fundamental to moral and material progress. Indeed, in reflecting on the heritage of Western Christendom and the achievements of the age of reason that followed the wars of religion in the seventeenth century, Bonhoeffer spoke of the need for intellectual honesty on questions of faith and declared that any contempt "for the age of rationalism" was "a suspicious sign of a deficient desire for truthfulness." He went on: "Just because intellectual honesty does not have the last word on things and rational clarity often comes at the cost of the depth of reality, we are not absolved from our inner duty to make honest and clean use of ratio."[34] Indeed, ratio is an essential tool in pursuit of the truth and discerning God's will.[35] Faith requires reason to understand and explicate its claims, and some of the greatest minds have engaged in the task. But reason is not infallible, nor does it necessarily lead to wisdom, a subject to which I will return in Chapter 4. That is why Christian theology, in acknowledging the indispensability and power of reason, insists that it needs to be informed

---

32. Pinker, *Rationality*, 340.
33. Pinker, *Rationality*, 340.
34. Bonhoeffer, *Ethics*, 115–16.
35. See Bonhoeffer, *Ethics*, 324.

by justice, driven by love, and inspired by a hope that is sustained by faith. Faith "born of love is not irrational," writes Matthew Lamb, but what "is profoundly irrational is the continued heroic efforts of humankind to make it on its own in the face of distorted, biased world history."[36] And it is this ideological distortion of reality that biblical faith challenges, not the need for rationality.

No Christian philosopher of my generation has better argued the case for a creative relationship between faith and reason in the formulation of theory or doctrine than Nicholas Wolterstorff, already in his short but cogently argued *Reason within the Bounds of Religion*. Christian faith is not blind or irrational, nor is it a rejection of our ever-expanding knowledge of reality through reason and science. But it is a praxis of love and hope that arises out of commitment to Christ and shapes the way we understand God, ourselves, and the world in which we live. In trying to express what this commitment means, and to keep us honest, faith seeks to understand and explain itself with the aid of reason, and on that basis engages with others who believe differently or not at all. So, in a world mired in religious and ideological irrationality, captivated by fake news, and subjected to unethical technologies, I endorse both Pinker's and Wolterstorff's pleas for rationality.

Yet Pinker himself admits that rational arguments alone cannot do what is needed. If reason really ruled, we would not be mired in mindless wars claiming to be just or even holy; we would fight pandemics with greater success; and we would not be destroying planet Earth, perpetuating racism, poverty, and violence against women and children. But that is clearly not the case because reason is too often compromised by self-interest. So Pinker adds an important qualification to his conclusion. Rationality, he writes, "emerges from a community of reasoners who spot each other's fallacies."[37] No person can change the world alone because our individual reasoning is subject to error and requires constant critique. Science is not infallible, and technology can destroy us if we are not careful. The question then arises: What informs that critique? If reason is not absolute or infallible, as seems self-evident, is there anything that can keep it in check? And who keeps a critical eye on the "community of reasoners"? How do we overcome self-interest or what the Bible calls sin?

---

36. Lamb, *Solidarity with Victims*, 9–10.
37. Pinker, *Rationality*, xvi.

Just as Pinker sees the need for a community who reason together, so Christian faith is not simply the faith of individuals but of a community we refer to as the church. From the time he wrote his doctoral dissertation *Sanctorum Communio* onwards, Bonhoeffer spoke of "Christ existing as a community of persons" in relationship to each other through their faith in Christ. To believe in Jesus Christ not only means participating in the reality of the world but also in the "body of Christ," as "members one of another." And it is there that the praxis of faith is meant to be accountable and kept under critical scrutiny. This is a major task of its theologians, but it is also a corporate responsibility of the community, made implicit in the practice of acknowledging guilt and confessing our sins, about which Bonhoeffer has a great deal to say.[38] This alone indicates that the church is not infallible; it is as much a community of sinners as it is meant be a community of saints. It therefore also needs to be accountable to reason and to its prophets. Furthermore, the church cannot tackle the challenges facing global society on its own—certainly not if driven by an irrational faith, or if it compromises its values and surrenders its prophetic role in society. Not only is the church too often part of the problem; the challenge is too great.

Christians, then, can and must be engaged with other faith communities and with secular humanists in responding to the realities facing us. Indeed, in his *Ethics*, Bonhoeffer writes about "one of the most astounding experiences" he had "in the face of the deification of the irrational powers of blood, of instinct, of the predator within human beings," namely, the "alliance between the defenders" of humanist values, not least rationality, "which until recently had served as battle cries against the church, against Christianity, even against Jesus Christ, now surprisingly found themselves in very close proximity to the Christian domain."[39] Surprisingly, this happened in Germany at a time "when everything Christian had been driven into a tight corner as never before, when the central Christian tenets were being emphasized in their sternest, most uncompromising, and most offensive form to humanist values." Bonhoeffer is here referring to the Christocentric theology, so strongly influenced by Barth, that declared German Christian theology a heresy and guided the Confessing Church in its struggle against Nazism. Yet it was precisely within that circle of opposition to the irrationalism and inhumanity of National Socialism that some humanists and some Christians found common cause in shared values that

---

38. See Bonhoeffer, *Life Together*, 108–14; Bonhoeffer, *Ethics*, 134–45.
39. Bonhoeffer, *Ethics*, 339–41.

had "become homeless." "Reason, justice, culture, humanity, and other concepts like these sought and found new meaning and new strength in their origin."[40]

What happened in Nazi Germany occurred again in the struggle against apartheid. Inspired by Barth and Bonhoeffer, we declared that the Christian attempt to legitimate apartheid was "nothing but a heresy."[41] Such language did not endear us to apartheid apologists, but neither did it appeal to secular humanist colleagues or those of other faith traditions who shared with us in the struggle against apartheid. But we found common cause with them in the struggle for justice and human dignity and learned to respect each other irrespective of whether we were believers or not. Indeed, the more we confessed Christ as Lord, the more open we became to people of other faiths or none. We did so because for us Christ embraced all of us in the struggle in the same way that he embraced all victims of oppression. So, faith and reason came together in a common justice praxis informed by a humanism rooted in Christian tradition.

Bonhoeffer's contribution to this understanding is well-described by Jens Zimmermann, who says that his "insistence on religion's respect for the intrinsic rational laws of things (*Wesengesetze*), exemplifies the Christian humanist heritage of integrating faith and reason." For Bonhoeffer, Zimmermann continues, "the unity of the world in the incarnate Logos has to be realized through interpretation in a reciprocal correlation of sacred and secular." That is why any "fundamentalist retreat into an unworldly bubble is unreasonable and un-Christian. Trying to think only within the artificially erected confines of a pure Christian theology, inevitably *falls prey to unnaturalness, irrationality, presumption and arbitrariness.*"[42] But this does not imply compromising the gospel; it means recovering commitment to the reality of God revealed in the "Word made flesh." What, then, does it mean to say, with Bonhoeffer, that "in Christ we are invited to participate in the reality of God and the reality of the world at the same time, the one not without the other"?[43]

---

40. Bonhoeffer, *Ethics*, 341.
41. Bosch, "Nothing but a Heresy."
42. Zimmermann, *Humanism and Religion*, 338–39 (italics added).
43. Bonhoeffer, *Ethics*, 55.

FAITH IN CHRIST

In a lecture he gave at Union Theological Seminary in 1931 Bonhoeffer, at the height of his Barthian phase, insisted that theology starts with the "reality of God." However, he admitted, we cannot grant God's reality without thinking about what we have just said and being pulled into a circle of reasoning and the debate about how we know certain things to be true. The problem for us Christians and all who believe in a personal God, is that our knowledge is based on faith in God's revelation, yet God is "the reality . . . which is beyond and outside of our thinking, of our whole existence."[44] If theology is "God-talk," this means that theology is about the unthinkable! In that case, the skeptic in us suggests that we immediately stop the conversation, for of what use is theological discussion if its subject matter is beyond any intellectual grasp or formulation?

But Christian theology, when you think about it, is not simply about the "unthinkable"; its basic premise is that the "unthinkable" happened; it became embodied in world history at a specific time and place: first-century Palestine. It therefore became "thinkable," that is, part of worldly reality. Our faith is not in what philosophers sometimes name "ultimate Reality," or in a general sense of the transcendent or numinous, but in the particular, admittedly outrageous conviction that "the Word that was there in the beginning became flesh and dwelt among us" (John 1). This means that a specifically Christian theology is not about an Idea, Principle, Concept, or an Abstract Reality, however rational or ultimate, but in a person and a life lived in human history, that is, in Jesus of Nazareth, who was crucified by the Romans. Not many religious creeds are as specific as the Christian confession that this happened under an official of the Empire, thus dating the event with precision. But daily we Christians confess that Jesus Christ was "crucified under Pontius Pilate"; in other words, his death is empirically verifiable and presents a radical critique of imperial power. Moreover, in the struggle between Christian faith and Gnosticism, the early Christian community insisted that the Word could be touched, seen, and handled (1 John 1:1). In this way, the unthinkable becomes and remains part of worldly reality, but always in tension with its claims to ultimacy or its tendencies to escape responsibility for its faults.

But, of course, the claim that this Word was "God incarnate" is a faith claim and as such beyond empirical verifiability. *Who* Jesus as the Christ

---

44. Bonhoeffer, *Barcelona, Berlin, New York*, 454.

is for us today, is always a question addressed to faith. When Saint John, among the first Christian theologians, answers that Jesus is "the way, the truth, and the life" (John 14:6), he is claiming neither that this can be empirically proved, nor that the Christian religion has all the truth; he is making a faith claim that Jesus embodied the truth about God, showed the way to live according to God's rule, and lived the life that expressed God's love for the world. Jesus as the Christ is, in sum, the "Word of God" revealing who God is from the beginning.

Christians cannot escape the challenge posed by reason, including that of critical biblical scholars, to such astounding faith claims. As I have already said, in response the first Christian theologians, with a few notable exceptions, attempted to give a reasoned account of their faith to their skeptical peers. They did not reject reason, not only because faith required reason in defending its claim and in explaining its meaning, but also because they claimed that Christ was the embodiment of truth. But then the argument became circular, for the only way they could explain *how* this was possible was to say that God alone knows, or that "Jesus was born of the Holy Spirit and the Virgin Mary"—that is, it was an act of God, something transcendental, something extraordinary. That is why Bonhoeffer insists in his lectures on Christology (1933) that the question "who is Jesus Christ?" is the question of transcendence. This is distinct from the *how* question of immanence, or *how* it is possible for God, the infinite One, to become incarnate in a finite human being. Unlike the *how* question, the *who* question, that is, the question of faith, at this point "dethrones reason" and does so "by pushing us to the boundaries of our existence."[45]

I will return to this in Chapter 3, where I discuss the nature of transcendence, and in Chapter 4, where I will further discuss the limitations of reason. But if it is true that the reality of God (transcendence) and the reality of the world (immanence) meet in the reality of Christ, as Bonhoeffer insists, then how we respond to the question "who is Jesus Christ really for us, today?" will determine how our faith responds to the worldly reality that confronts us.

LIVING WITHOUT GOD, BEFORE GOD

In seeking to answer the question "who is Jesus Christ?" while in prison, Bonhoeffer was acutely aware that the future of Christianity hung in the

---

45. Bonhoeffer, *Berlin 1932-1933*, 302-3.

balance. He was equally aware that for millions of people in what was left of Western Christendom, the question of God had become irrelevant. Most Western Europeans faced reality without faith and had already begun to do so back in the seventeenth century when Grotius, the Dutch scholar, said that while it might be impious to live without faith in God, there was no alternative but to do so. We had to face reality *etsi deus non daretur*—as if God is no longer available. Bonhoeffer sums it up: "As a working hypothesis for morality, politics, and the natural sciences, God has been overcome and done away with." So. "it is a matter of intellectual integrity to drop this working hypothesis or eliminate it as far as possible." Is there, then, any room left for God, asks Bonhoeffer? Not if we are honest. We must live without the "working hypothesis" of God, but, he tantalizingly adds, we must do so "before God!" Indeed, it is God who compels us to manage our lives as if God were absent. The paradox is that we are called to live "before God, and with God" and yet, at the same time, to "live without God."[46]

There has been much discussion about what Bonhoeffer meant when he wrote these seemingly contradictory statements. For how can we live with God and without God at the same time? To put it starkly, is it honest for us to go to the doctor when we are sick, that is, to put our trust in medical science, and at the same time pray to God for healing? But what Bonhoeffer is pressing us to do is to get rid of false notions of God, that is, notions based on assumptions about divine omnipotence, and to learn to trust in the reality of God revealed in Christ. In other words, we must live without the omnipotent God we have believed in for so long and trust the God who "consents to be pushed out of the world and onto the cross." This God, Bonhoeffer says, "is weak and powerless in the world and in precisely this way, and only so, is at our side and helps us." While human "religiosity directs people in need to the power of God in the world, God as *deus ex machina*, the Bible directs people toward the powerlessness and the suffering of God," and does so "because only such a God can help."[47] That is crucial to understanding what Bonhoeffer means when he says that the reality of God and the reality of the world meet in the reality of Christ. The crucifixion radically redefines the God in whom we believe. And that is why, as Bonhoeffer says, if we follow Christ we can "no longer see God without the world, or the world without God."[48]

46. Bonhoeffer, *Letters and Papers from Prison*, 478–79.
47. Bonhoeffer, *Letters and Papers from Prison*, 479.
48. Bonhoeffer, *Ethics*. 82.

To believe in the God who is revealed in Jesus Christ thus means facing and engaging reality from the perspective of the cross. The resurrection does not change this; the resurrection confirms that the message of the cross is the truth, vindicating Jesus and dethroning triumphalism of every kind. It is the "suffering God" who reigns supreme, not the gods of empire, war, and criminal wealth. For this reason, Jürgen Moltmann, undoubtedly influenced by Bonhoeffer, ends his opening chapter on the "Identity and Relevance of Faith" in his seminal book *The Crucified God* by saying that the "epistemological principle of the theology of the cross can only be this dialectic principle: the deity of God is revealed in the paradox of the cross."[49] He then concludes his later discussion of the resurrection by saying that this event does not change the fact that Christ was crucified but turns his suffering and death into a "saving event." In other words, "his resurrection expresses the significance of his death."[50]

The Christian life of faith, then, is all about participation in the reality of God and the reality of the world by becoming conformed to Christ's death and resurrection. By that Bonhoeffer means participating in the suffering and struggles of the world with courage and redemptive hope. Christian formation, to quote Bonhoeffer, is about being "drawn into the form of Jesus Christ, by *being conformed to the unique form of the one who became human, was crucified, and is risen*." This happens "as the form of Jesus Christ himself so works on us that it molds us, conforming our form to Christ's own (Gal. 4:9)." Christ is not just the one who teaches us to be good, but "the one who has become human, who was crucified, and who is risen, as confessed by the Christian faith."[51] Christian conversion, in other words, means becoming transformed into the image of Christ, for only then can we discern God's will and do it (Rom 12:1–2). So Bonhoeffer concludes his classic book *Discipleship* by saying that as disciples of Christ, we "bear the image of the incarnate, crucified, and risen Jesus Christ"; indeed we "have been transformed into the image of God" and "are called to be 'imitators of God.'"[52]

Such faith in Christ is only possible through conversion, the subject of Chapter 2—that is, being transformed through Christ "into the image

---

49. Moltmann, *Crucified God*, 27.
50. Moltmann, *Crucified God*, 182.
51. Bonhoeffer, *Ethics*, 93–94 (italics added).
52. Bonhoeffer quotes Eph 5:1 in Bonhoeffer, *Discipleship*, 288. See also Burridge, *Imitating Jesus*, 224.

of God." However, we describe it, and however it occurs, this is what happened to the first disciples who came to believe in the crucified Jesus as the risen Christ, as have countless others across the centuries. For all of them, the cross of Christ was not a sign of divine weakness or foolishness, as it appeared to be, but the power and wisdom of God (1 Cor 1:16). It also happened to Bonhoeffer during his year of study in New York in 1930–31 when, he says, he, the theologian, became a Christian.[53] And that, as I shall argue in the next chapter, is neither a one-off event nor unrelated to reality; it is an ongoing transforming process directly related to the challenges that face us in the world. And one of the most challenging of these, as Bonhoeffer discovered and I have experienced, is the legacy of colonialism and the persistence of racism.

---

53. See Bethge, *Dietrich Bonhoeffer*, 202–6.

2

CONVERSION

&

the Persistence of Colonial Racism

No one can see the kingdom of God without being born from above.

—John 3:3

Racism [is] . . . a litmus test or a barium meal, which reveals other disorders and injustices within the body politic. It therefore provides a vital area of self-scrutiny and self-criticism for religious communities and traditions.

—Kenneth Leech[1]

My share in the sin against Africa or Asia for the last hundred or fifty years may be very remote or indirect, but would Europe be what it is, and would I be what I am, if that expansion had never happened? . . . I did not take it from anybody, but simply inherited it by law.

—Karl Barth.[2]

---

1. Leech, "Racism," 711.
2. Barth *Ethics*, 164–65.

> It remains an experience of incomparable value that we have for once learned to see the great events of world history from below, from the perspective of the outcasts, the suspects, the maltreated, the powerless, the oppressed and reviled, in short from the perspective of the suffering.
>
> —Bonhoeffer[3]

In July 1985, James Cone, a pioneer of Black theology in the United States, and Cornel West, the prophetic philosopher of the Black socialist Left and currently Dietrich Bonhoeffer Professor at Union Seminary in New York, visited South Africa. Cone later described it as a visit that had more impact on his theological perspective than any other experience outside the US. But both commented on the startling contrast between the spectacular landscapes and the affluence of White society alongside the squalor of the living conditions and the suffering of Black society.[4] Today, the scenery remains spectacular but so does much of the racial inequality despite the dramatic political changes that occurred in 1994. There is now a Black government in power and a growing Black middle class, but the material conditions for many have not changed. Cone and West would probably say that the same is true in the US despite the Civil Rights Act of 1964, except, of course, the demographics are different. In the US, African Americans are a minority; in South Africa, Whites are the minority. But racism persists, it infects the church as much as society, and it confronts faith head-on.[5]

I helped arrange the visit of Cone and West, and no one was more surprised than I that it happened, except perhaps they themselves. Not only because they received visas to visit South Africa, especially during a national state of emergency, but because they were permitted to move freely across the country, meet whomever they chose, and participate in anti-apartheid protests and discussions. At one three-day event in Cape Town, a handful of Black and White theologians spent most of the time discussing the urgent need for the church to participate in the liberation struggle as called for in the *Kairos Document*, which had only recently been published. The *Kairos Document* was a "call to conversion" specifically aimed at White Christians and churches.

---

3. Bonhoeffer, *Letters and Papers from Prison*. 52.
4. Cone, *Speaking the Truth*, 157–67; West, *Prophetic Fragments*, 109–11.
5. On the connections between the narratives, see Fredrickson, *Black Liberation*.

CONVERSION & THE PERSISTENCE OF COLONIAL RACISM

Conversion inclusive of repentance is the way in which the Greek biblical word *metanoia* is usually translated into English. It literally means a change of heart and mind. The four Gospels all begin with a call to conversion. Like the great prophets of Israel, John the Baptist declared that the *kairos* (God's time) had come for the people to change their hearts and minds (*metanoia*) and obey God's will. However, my introduction to the word "conversion" came when I "gave my life to Christ" as a young teenager and joined the ranks of the born-again. I had little idea what I was doing, but I was informed that I had now become a "real Christian." It has taken me a lifetime to discover what that means, for what happened back then at a high school camp was only the beginning—and it was that—of a long journey.

I have learned over the years that conversion is a process of formation that occurs every day, with inevitable setbacks along the way. The Gospels describe this as they recount the journey of the disciples with Jesus from Galilee to Jerusalem. Saint Paul described it when he exhorted the Christians in Rome to be "transformed by the renewing of their minds" (Rom 12:2), for only then would they discern God's will and be able to do it. It was what Saint Benedict in his famous monastic *Rule* called the "conversion of manners," that is, the daily transformation of our minds and actions as we journey into the mystery of God.[6] In other words, Christian conversion has to do with the whole of life, and therefore with our response to the realities that confront us in the context in which we live. Conversion is not a religious event; it is becoming a new person, a truly human being in Christ. And that is a journey.

In 1989, the theologians who drafted the *Kairos Document*, in cooperation with colleagues from other so-called Third World countries, published *The Road to Damascus*, which highlighted something the *Kairos Document* failed to mention, namely, the colonial roots of systemic racism. Racism in South Africa, it declared, was one "of the most serious and lasting legacies of colonialism."[7] This is true wherever colonialism has ruled, and it is now painfully true in Europe where the modern-day colonial story originally began. Colonialism was also closely connected to the planting of the church and the expansion of Christianity in South Africa, both as ally and critic.[8] Responding to this reality requires, then, both a personal and an

---

6. See de Gruchy *This Monastic Moment*, 81.
7. *The Road to Damascus*, art. 5, par. 1.
8. De Gruchy, *Christianity and the Modernisation of South Africa*, 1–51.

ecclesial *metanoia*, and that in turn requires that we understand the legacy of colonialism and the way it has conditioned our personal and social lives.

No one has better described the challenge facing those of us who are Whites than the South African economic historian Sampie Terblanche, whose observations set the agenda for this chapter:

> Without a clear understanding of the systemic nature of the exploitation that has taken place, it would also not be possible for the beneficiaries (i.e., mainly Whites) to make the necessary confession, to show the necessary repentance, to experience the necessary conversion and to be prepared to make the needed sacrifices.[9]

That an economic historian can call for repentance and conversion is not only remarkable; it is also a reminder that Christian conversion does not take place in a vacuum but in a historical context that gives substance to the way we understand what it means to be converted to Christ. So, we must begin, as Terblanche tells us, with an attempt to understand "the nature of the exploitation that has taken place" if we are going to understand what conversion means in a South African context or in any other context in which racism persists. I can also only understand my own White narrative within that framework.

FROM COLONIALISM TO APARTHEID

In their extensive study of the connection between Christianity and colonialism, Jean and John Comaroff refer to "the divisions within colonizing populations" that were related to distinctions of "class, gender, and nation" back home and in South Africa. These, they say, "played across the racial line between ruler and ruled, creating new affinities and alliances that blurred the antimonies of the colonial world," adding to the complexity of the colonial narrative.[10] They also speak about how the gospel proclaimed by the missionaries (they have Protestants especially in mind) "gave rise to novel forms of consciousness and action," eventually fueling "Black nationalist politics with both causes of complaint and a rhetoric of protest" that "foreshadowed other forms of Black consciousness and struggle." The

---

9. Terblanche, *Western Empires*, xv.
10. Comaroff and Comaroff, *Of Revelation and Revolution*, 10.

result was "a complex dialectic of challenge and riposte, domination and defiance."[11]

Clearly, the story of church complicity in colonial racism and participation in the struggle for justice is as complex as the colonial narrative itself. That remains the case even now, well after the completion of the formal process of decolonization that began in India after the Second World War and ended with the birth of the "new" post-apartheid democratic South Africa in 1994. Yet the legacy of imperialism and colonialism, which prospered on slavery and racist exploitation and gave birth to apartheid, too often legitimized by Christianity, continues. Despite aid and many assistance programs, developing countries remain pawns in the global trade and violent conflicts between powerful nations as they fight to control the world's resources. This is the neocolonial reality that faces us today.

The church struggle against apartheid, which seemingly ended rather abruptly in 1994, has therefore had to begin anew, but now Christian faith must confront realities that were previously kept on the back burner. As Steve de Gruchy identified them in 2004, some of these were the need for national reconciliation and reparations, poverty, the HIV/AIDS pandemic, gay rights, gender violence and justice, and the neocolonial challenges of globalization.[12] Now, almost twenty years later, these realities have been further exacerbated by the COVID-19 pandemic, demonstrating how colonial racism continues to influence global politics and determine the fate of millions of people. The prophetic task of the ecumenical church is clearly as necessary today as it ever was in the struggle against apartheid or, Cone and West would add, during the Civil Rights Movement in the US.

For many centuries, going back into Greco-Roman antiquity, Africa south of the Sahara was for Europeans a dark, alien space inhabited by an inferior species of humans without culture or religion. At best, Black Africans were exotic inferiors in need of paternal care, conversion, and instruction; at worst, threatening enemies—either way, they were "the other." When, in the sixteenth century, intrepid Portuguese explorers traveled down the west coast of Africa and rounded the Cape of Storms in search of India, the indigenous Khoi and San peoples at the tip of the African continent were useful trading partners. But when the Dutch East India Company established a permanent settlement at the Cape a century later, the inevitable happened. Company employees took root and were soon supplemented by

---

11. Comaroff and Comaroff, *Of Revelation and Revolution*, 11–12.
12. De Gruchy and de Gruchy, *Church Struggle in South Africa*, 223–60.

others arriving from Holland, as well as French Huguenots fleeing persecution. This led to a need for more land—and as the Indigenous peoples, as far as the settlers could (or wanted to) ascertain, did not seem to have any sense of ownership or, in European law, any right of occupation, the land was waiting to be possessed. It was a God-given gift much the same as the land of the Philistines waiting to be occupied by the Israelites after their arduous journey from slavery in Egypt. More to the point, the Europeans also had the firepower to possess the land without too much of a struggle. So, the Indigenous people became indentured laborers or slaves and were soon joined by others imported from East Africa and the Far East. But the question of land ownership, which was central to the colonial project, did not go away. Indeed, racism and land dispossession went hand in glove, which is why it is central to the political debate today in post-apartheid South Africa or wherever Indigenous peoples clash with the descendants of colonials.

By the nineteenth century the Cape Colony had become British, and in 1834 when slavery was outlawed across the empire, statutory slavery—but by no means all its practices—ended at the Cape. In reaction, many farmers (*Boers*) of Dutch or French origin began their Great Trek into the interior where, through conquest whenever necessary, they established their Afrikaner Republics of the Orange Free State and Transvaal. Meanwhile the Cape Colony was expanding along the eastern seaboard into territory long occupied by various Nguni nations collectively known as the amaXhosa. A contingent of English settlers who, after the Napoleonic Wars, were unemployed, were literally dumped in the Eastern Cape in 1820 by the British government to act as a buffer between the Cape Colony and the amaXhosa. The result was a lengthy series of brutal frontier wars, the Wars of Dispossession, until the amaXhosa capitulated to the might of imperial forces.

Further north, the British also began to colonize the amaZulu Kingdom and eventually, after bloody but indecisive conflicts, established the Colony of Natal. Beginning in 1860, but especially from 1874 to 1897, the British government imported indentured laborers from India to work on the burgeoning sugar plantations, further complicating the already complex demographics of the region. Their plight would later be highlighted by a young lawyer, Mahatma Gandhi, who arrived in 1893 and, a year later, established the Natal Indian Congress to fight for the rights of Indian laborers. It was then that he developed strategies of nonviolent protest that he later perfected back in India in the struggle against British colonialism. As we shall see, Gandhi's example would later have an important influence on Bonhoeffer.

The discovery of rich diamond deposits at Kimberley in the northern Cape in the 1860s and then gold in the Transvaal, where Johannesburg is now situated, attracted more European settlers to South Africa, who came to make their fortunes through mining and related skills. The scene was set for the Anglo-Boer War (1899–1902), fought over who should control the land and its resources and determine the future of the region. British propaganda said that the war was waged to set Africans free from Boer oppression, but they became unwitting pawns in the conflict. And then, once the war was over, they were further oppressed as Europeans united to form the Union of South Africa in 1910. Talk about reconciliation back then had little to do with Black and White race relations; the primary goal was the uniting of the English and the Afrikaners in one country within the British Empire.

My grandparents, who came to the Cape Colony in the late nineteenth century, lived through the Anglo-Boer War. They also witnessed the formation of the Union of South Africa in 1910, composed of the British colonies and Boer Republics. The Union was based on a racist constitution approved by the British government despite considerable protest from African leaders, who were ignored by Westminster. The formation of the African National Congress (ANC) in 1912 was a response to this consolidation of White power and the notorious Land Act of 1913, which put 87 percent of the land under the control of White South Africa. This became the cornerstone of later apartheid legislation. However, the mineral wealth of the country remained under the control of British imperial or colonial companies, such as De Beers and Consolidated Gold Fields, founded by Cecil John Rhodes. Rhodes, an Oxford graduate, the prime minister of the Cape from 1890 until 1896, and the founder of Rhodesia (now Zimbabwe), symbolized British colonial power and racial exploitation.

The African population, still largely rural but subdued by conquest and rendered largely landless, provided the cheap labor needed to work on the mines in Kimberley and the Witwatersrand Reef on which Johannesburg was being built. The rapid Black urbanization and White immigration that followed indelibly shaped the social contours of the country and led to legislation to control the influx and movement of rural migrant laborers. Black shanty townships and labor compounds soon dotted the landscape around White urban and suburban areas. To further complicate the demographic mix, wars and pogroms in Europe created waves of additional settlers, many of them Jewish refugees from Lithuania and Latvia. All came to find employment, and a better life in a sunny environment. And all were privileged because of their skin color despite their ethnic diversity and the prevalence of anti-Semitism. But they were Europeans and generally, if sometimes reluctantly, welcomed to the newly born Europeans-only country. South Africa thus became a temporary solution to problems in Europe to the ongoing disadvantage of Africans themselves.

My grandparents, all of them of Methodist working-class stock, came from England. My maternal grandfather was a grocer from London who settled with his wife in the Eastern Cape and later became the mayor of Walmer; my paternal grandfather was a sea captain from Jersey who settled in Cape Town where he administered the Seamen's Home.[13] Their combined children numbered eighteen. This was an indicator that English-speaking South Africans were rapidly growing in number, though never to the same extent as the Afrikaner and Black African communities. We would always be a minority. But my grandparents were citizens of the empire, and so protected and privileged. They could purchase land and build houses, and gradually improve their status. Like original sin, this privilege was transmitted from one generation of settlers to the next, and therefore to my parents and to us, their grandchildren in turn. Our own children were the first generation to have no sense of belonging to the empire; indeed, as a family we regarded ourselves as White Africans. We could not change the color of our skin, and colonial privilege was in our shared DNA. But we could find ways to distance ourselves from the empire.

Many Afrikaners had been impoverished by the Anglo-Boer War, and many had suffered severely from incarceration in British concentration camps. They were not generally as privileged as the English settler community. But being White in the Union meant that they had the vote, they could organize, they could improve their economic prospects, and they could fight for their rights—not least their evolving language, Afrikaans. And they did so with the strong support of the Dutch Reformed Church, without which their eventual rise to power would not have been possible. Afrikaner nationalism was in the making founded on the conviction that the Afrikaner nation had a covenantal relationship with God, for which their theologians provided the rationale. In 1938 the anniversary of the Great Trek was celebrated countrywide, and the foundations laid for the

---

13. See de Gruchy, *I Have Come a Long Way*, 20–28.

Voortrekker Monument in Pretoria. My father, who was a telephone technician at the time, was one of the few English speakers present that day, but his participation was strictly professional.

Nine years later, despite Afrikaner opposition, the British Royal family headed by King George VI visited South Africa. Those of us of British origin, myself included, celebrated being part of the empire "on which the sun would never set." But in the same year, 1947, India gained its independence, and in 1948 the Afrikaner National Party was voted into power in South Africa on the promise of implementing apartheid. Many in the National Party had supported the Nazis during the Second World War and its leaders were influenced by its fictional views on racial purity. Those on the right wing were also anti-Semitic, but the roots of anti-Semitism in South Africa were as much British as Afrikaner; indeed, many Afrikaners identified theologically with the biblical people of Israel. In South Africa there has always been, as Milton Shain remarks, "a persistent strain of philosemitism" acting as a "counterweight to crass anti-Jewish bigotry."[14]

Black-White segregation was always the dominant issue in South Africa, not anti-Semitism. Apartheid was attractive to the White electorate in South Africa because many feared the *swart gevaar*, that is, the danger of a growing Black majority in the land. And though we English speakers disliked Afrikaner nationalism, apartheid was to our immediate advantage, and it was, after all, entrenching segregation policies already embedded in the 1910 constitution approved by the British Parliament. What counted was skin color; whether we were Black, Colored (descendants of slaves, the Khoi San, or mixed marriages), Indian, or White. There was no scientific basis for such discrimination, though some tried to provide one. But racism was real and systemic. White supremacy reigned.

Apartheid organized reality for everyone, whether you benefitted from it or suffered under it, or whether you made friends across the racial barriers. For apartheid was not just about personal relationships, even though those were proscribed to prevent miscegenation; it was about the way society was structured. Being White, Black, or Colored determined your status and fate. Certainly, there were "poor Whites" when I grew up, but being White, and especially being male, normally meant that you got a good education, used good sporting facilities, and more easily rose to positions of power and influence in the workplace or public arena.

---

14. Shain, *Roots of Anti-Semitism in South Africa*, 152.

In 1961, the year I was ordained and began my ministry in Durban, the year in which our son Steve was born, South Africa left the British Commonwealth and became a republic. By now African opposition to apartheid had intensified, but so too had the power of the security forces. By 1963 internal resistance was virtually eliminated, and Nelson Mandela along with many other leaders, including Robert Sobukwe of the Pan-Africanist Movement, were imprisoned on Robben Island. The armed liberation struggle had begun, largely led by exiles.[15] At the time, Isobel, Steve, and I were living in Chicago, where I was studying for the academic year, 1963–1964. It was at the height of the Civil Rights struggle. Seeing and reflecting on what was happening back home from that perspective was one of the defining experiences of our lives and my ongoing conversion.

The major downside to being a White male under apartheid as the armed struggle intensified was that you could be conscripted into the army to defend Christendom against Communism, according to the metanarrative employed by the apartheid regime to galvanize support both within the country and abroad. The psychological, social, and economic consequences of that senseless war are still part of the problem we face today. But there was another cost to being White and privileged if you had a moral conscience, recognized that your privilege came at the expense of others, and identified with the struggle against apartheid. Your White skin helped to mitigate the cost, but many suffered social ostracism, banning, imprisonment, or exile. But still, we did not live inside Black skins, that would have forced us to live with the brutality of racism; we did not live in a shack or shanty.

In 1968 we moved from Durban to Johannesburg where I started working for the South African Council of Churches, which was helping to lead the church struggle against apartheid. But even if we did oppose apartheid, as Steve Biko, the leader of the Black Consciousness Movement in the late 1960s, told us, we had to accept that Blacks had to liberate themselves without our interference, though hopefully with our support. To claim that we Whites had some good Black friends, while undoubtedly commendable, as was our opposition to apartheid, being White did not give any of us the right to call the shots. So we began to talk about the need for the awakening of a "White consciousness" and the need for "White liberation."[16] Then, dramatically, just as the external armed liberation struggle was running out of steam, the student Soweto uprising erupted in 1976, ushering in a new

15. See Karis and Gerhart, *From Protest to Challenge*, 3–18.
16. Karis and Gerhart, *From Protest to Challenge*, 414–96.

phase in the struggle against apartheid inspired by Black Consciousness.[17] The reaction of the state was brutal, but a new dynamic had been injected into the resistance against apartheid from within the country.[18]

When James Cone and Cornel West visited South Africa ten years later, the final stage in the struggle had begun. This was why there was a declared state of emergency at the time of their visit. Internally, the struggle was now spearheaded by the United Democratic Front led by, among others, church activists, including Allan Boesak, Frank Chikane, and Desmond Tutu, as well as by the trade unions, many progressive organizations, and faith communities. Externally, the liberation movement, still led by the ANC, was supported by, among others, many countries and organizations, and many churches around the world associated with the World Council of Churches and its Program to Combat Racism.[19] Western governments and the US, which criticized apartheid, were cautious in their support of the liberation struggle, some even listing the ANC as a terrorist organization. Many European countries benefitted economically from apartheid, and the South African story fitted well with the colonial narrative that had shaped the European understanding of history and justified the plunder of resources.

Apartheid was finally outlawed in 1994, and since then democratic South Africa has been governed by the ANC. South Africa today is at a very different period in its torturous history toward justice and equity for all, and the land question remains a central contentious issue. So, despite many changes for the better, the legacy of colonialism and apartheid persists, in the same way that racial injustice persists in the US. It has become systemic—that is, built into the fabric of society. This is but one of the striking similarities between the plight of Black people in the US and South Africa, which has been highlighted again during the present COVID pandemic by the Black Lives Matter movement, the concerted effort to deconstruct colonialism, and the intense debate about reparations in both countries. All of this is symptomatic of the systemic and persistent racism that confronts Christian faith today long after Nelson Mandela walked to freedom and Martin Luther King Jr. had his dream.

There is a footnote to my narrative, one that grows longer as time passes. The adage that absolute power leads to absolute corruption is true

17. Karis and Gerhart, *From Protest to Challenge*, 551–95.
18. Karis and Gerhart, *From Protest to Challenge*, 736–66.
19. De Gruchy and de Gruchy, *Church Struggle in South Africa*, 101–222.

irrespective of ethnicity, and the rise to power and the domination of the ANC since 1994 has proved its truth. Liberation often leads to the abuse of power. So, the diagnosis of racism in South Africa and my analysis of its current ills cannot be dealt with in purely Black-White terms, not least because apartheid was never just a racial matter; it was economic at its core. Hence the struggle for justice today includes fighting rampant corruption that afflicts all of us whether Black or White. How to attract much-needed foreign investment and at the same time to avoid becoming beholden to neocolonial investors, how to secure loans without incurring enormous debt—these are challenges yet to be resolved. Hence the struggle for racial justice today is also a struggle against postcolonial economic injustice and the militarism that defends it. When financial markets collapse in the US, Europe, China and Japan, the so-called developing countries suffer more than they do; when their environmental policies fail to curb carbon emissions sufficiently, it is the same countries that bear much of the brunt of the consequences; and when they go to war to protect their interests, everyone suffers.

BONHOEFFER, COLONIALISM & RACISM

Count von Bismarck, the chancellor who reshaped Germany in the nineteenth century with Prussia as its powerhouse, was initially not enthusiastic about overseas colonization.[20] He was too aware of the difficulty of competing with Britain and France. But then, in a surprising turnabout in 1884, he convened a conference in Berlin during which the major European powers carved up much of Africa and divided it among themselves. In the process, many artificial national boundaries were drawn that have plagued Africa ever since. Germany gained South West Africa (SWA), an enormous, sparsely populated territory on the northwestern border of South Africa, known today as Namibia.

German interest in the region increased when in 1900 Bismarck gave German support to the Boers in their war against the British in South Africa, a classic example of a European struggle for power being fought elsewhere at the expense of the natives. German participation in the Anglo-Boer War was sparked by an incident involving a German ship off the South African coast. But irrespective of that, German sympathies were with the Afrikaner Republics, both because German settlers had identified with them, and

20. See Carr, *History of Germany*, 95–362.

because Germany regarded Britain as a threat to its own interests. Then, after the Anglo-Boer War, Germany agreed not to enlarge its navy if Britain did not interfere with its overseas colonies. But during the Second World War, South African forces invaded SWA, defeated the German army, and took control of the country. After the war, SWA was made a South African protectorate by the League of Nations and, in effect, became part of South Africa and subject to apartheid legislation. Namibia only gained its independence after a long liberation struggle in March 1990.

There is no evidence that as a child Bonhoeffer had read the popular children's books of the time that recounted tales about German colonial exploits in SWA. But if he had, he would have read Gustav Freensens' *Peter Moors Fahrt nach Südwest*, published in 1906, which praised the brave German soldiers and justified the genocide of the Herero people.[21] Certainly, in much of the literature published during the time Bonhoeffer was in school, Africans were described as wild animals, subhuman, dogs, murderers, and black devils. That Bonhoeffer was aware of German colonialism, though not necessarily its dark side, is evident from an essay he wrote in high school in February 1920 on "Germany's situation before the First World War."[22] That he was also aware of German colonialism specifically in SWA is clear from the semiautobiographical novel he wrote in prison during 1943. Renate's statement that she was "homesick for South Africa" reflects the view of Helmuth von Moltke, a member of Bonhoeffer's resistance circle with whom he traveled in Scandinavia in 1942, and who had previously lived in South Africa.

The young Bonhoeffer who went to study in New York in 1930 was a German nationalist who, like many of his illustrious teachers in Berlin, blamed Britain for starting the First World War. His attitude changed, however, after he met Jean Lasserre and they went together to see the 1930 American movie *All Quiet on the Western Front*, based on Erich Maria Remarque's German novel with the same title, as part of a course requirement at Union Seminary.[23] For the first time, Bonhoeffer saw the war through French eyes and, to say the least, was deeply embarrassed by German aggression. Indeed, a year after he returned to Germany Bonhoeffer gave a

---

21. See Tötemeyer, "Problematik der Kinder- und Jugendliteratur Namibias," 57. See also Frenssen, *Peter Moors Fahrt nach Südwest*.
22. Bonhoeffer, *Young Bonhoeffer*, 191–97.
23. See Introduction to Bonhoeffer, *Barcelona, Berlin, New York*, 26n126.

stirring lecture in Czechoslovakia on the need for the ecumenical church to take a stand against war.[24]

If Lasserre helped Bonhoeffer to break with German nationalism and embrace pacifism, Franklin Fischer, one of the few Black students at Union, helped open his eyes to the plight of African Americans. He did so first when he introduced Bonhoeffer to young Black leaders in Washington DC, and then to the Abyssinian Baptist Church in Harlem. Bonhoeffer decided that he could no longer worship in White churches, and so for the last six months of his stay in New York he participated in the life of the Harlem church community, enthusiastically embracing the evangelical preaching and social activism of African American Christianity and becoming aware of the plight of the Black community.[25]

Bonhoeffer supplemented his experience by intense conversation with some of his professors, including Reinhold Niebuhr, as well as extensive reading and reflection on the "race question."[26] He read about the lynching of a Negro and later said he would never forget seeing a "photograph of the burning schoolhouse and the lynch mob." He "learned about the infamous Scottsboro case, in which nine young Black men were hastily convicted and condemned to death." He described this as a "terrible miscarriage of justice," something that was still fresh in his mind when he wrote his *Ethics* ten years later.[27] Bonhoeffer was learning to see reality "from below," preparing him for the rapidly approaching time when he would have to speak out on behalf of Jews, who were becoming the victims of Nazism. His turn from "phraseology to reality" was both a theological and existential shift that required action. But each element in his turn to reality over the next few years, can be traced back to his experience of the plight of Black Americans—especially his opposition to National Socialism, war, and anti-Semitism.

Bonhoeffer was not only appalled by the racism he observed in American society, reinforced by his experiences when he later toured the Deep South, but he was equally appalled by the racism he observed in the life of the church. This was so deeply embedded that it had led to a schism he considered as grave as any other in the history of Christianity. For him, the church was meant to be ethnically inclusive; it was unthinkable that it could

---

24. Bonhoeffer, *Ecumenical, Academic and Pastoral Work*, 356–69.
25. See Young, *No Difference in the Fare*.
26. Bonhoeffer, *Theological Education Underground*, 421.
27. Bonhoeffer, *Ethics*, 295.

be racially segregated. This was the gist of what he wrote in his report on his American visit after he returned to Germany in 1932:

> For American Christendom the racial issue has been a real problem from the beginning... The fact that today the "Black Christ" of a young Negro poet is pitted against the "White Christ" reveals a destructive rift [Zerstörung] within the church of Jesus Christ. It cannot be overlooked that many White Christians through influential organizations do whatever they can to improve the relations between the races and that discerning Negroes recognize the serious difficulties. But today the general picture of the church in the United States is still one of racial fragmentation.[28]

The racial issue in the church, Bonhoeffer wrote further, could be traced back to the beginning of slavery when "the first larger transports of Negroes—who had been stolen from Africa as slaves—arrived in America."

To justify slavery and provide a reason why slaves should not be evangelized, their Christian owners cited African paganism, but the truth was their fear that baptism would call "into question the legitimacy of slavery" and give "undesirable privileges and rights to the Negroes." It was only when the bishop of London reassured them "that nothing whatsoever had to change in the outward conditions of the slaves who were baptized," and that it would give their owners more control over them that they relented. Negroes could become Christians but had to sit in the balconies during worship, the ecclesiastical equivalent of the "back of the bus," and take communion only after all the Whites had done so. The die was cast. It was inevitable, Bonhoeffer wrote, that the church of Jesus Christ had to endure another great schism, one that separated White and Black Christians. So, he concluded: "The issue of the Negro is one of the most decisive future tasks for the White churches."[29] For Bonhoeffer, as noted earlier, it was inconceivable that the church of Jesus Christ could be racially segregated; that was nothing but a heresy. This was not just expressed in personal relations between Black and White Christians; it was structural and systemic, "a sociological and theological way of imagining difference as part and parcel of the way in which the world has come to be organized and thus known."[30] This is the reality that still faces Christian witness.

---

28. Bonhoeffer, *Theological Education*, 456.
29. Bonhoeffer, *Theological Education*, 456–58.
30. Harvey, *Taking Hold of the Real*, 180.

If it was in New York that Bonhoeffer "the theologian became a Christian," it was earlier in Rome on his "first visit abroad" that Bonhoeffer as a young theological student discovered the reality of the church as an inclusive, catholic community. Recording his attendance at Mass in Saint Peter's Basilica on Psalm Sunday, he describes the scene at the altar as illustrating the "universality of the church . . . in a marvelously effective manner. White, black, yellow members of religious orders—everyone was in clerical robes united under the church. It truly seems ideal."[31] That might be far from adequately inclusive for us today, but for Bonhoeffer it was an eye-opening experience. He could not help contrasting it with the Prussian Protestant church back home, which, in Bethge's words, "struck him as provincial, nationalistic, and narrow-minded."[32] In Rome, Bonhoeffer discovered the reality of the church as universal, united in its global diversity.

Bonhoeffer's experience of the church in Rome was one of the motivations for writing his doctoral dissertation, *Sanctorum Communio* (1927) when he returned to Germany. The church, he argued, is nothing less than the bodily representative of the "new humanity" that God had brought into being through the life, death, and resurrection of Christ and made actual through the Holy Spirit.[33] This is the critical passage in *Sanctorum Communio*:

> God established the reality (*Wirklichkeit*) of the church, of humanity pardoned in Jesus Christ—not religion, but revelation, not religious community, but church. This is what the reality (*Wirklichkeit*) of Jesus Christ means.[34]

This means that the church is not just a means to an end, but also an end in itself; it was meant to embody the new humanity "established in reality in Jesus Christ."[35]

Sanctorum Communio provided the theological basis for my dissertation on the church and racism, which I wrote in Chicago, because it addressed, without Bonhoeffer saying so, the problem of systemic and structural racism in the church. If the church is understood as a religious community of like-minded individuals or "born-again" believers, related to

---

31. Bonhoeffer, *Young Bonhoeffer*, 88.
32. Bethge, *Dietrich Bonhoeffer*, 59.
33. Bonhoeffer, *Sanctorum Communio*, 145.
34. Bonhoeffer, *Sanctorum Communio*, 153.
35. Bonhoeffer, *Sanctorum Communio*, 147.

each other because of their faith in Christ, then it is their piety that connects them. But if the church is understood as "Christ existing as community," as Bonhoeffer insisted, then its existence as the "new humanity" precedes individual faith. That is, its given structure is an inclusive and dynamic reconciling structure because it is actualized by the Holy Spirit in the life of the world as I later argued in my doctoral thesis.

Bonhoeffer grew increasingly disillusioned with the Protestant church in Germany, including the Confessing Church, as he had previously become disillusioned with the White church in New York. But he never gave up on the church as such, for that would have meant giving up on Christ. The *Kirchenkampf*, for Bonhoeffer, was not primarily a struggle against Nazism but a struggle for the soul of the Protestant church in Germany: a struggle for the church to be the church of Jesus Christ rather than the church of a particular nation, ethnic group, or religious clique. And finally in his "Outline for a Book" drafted in prison, having insisted that Jesus is always the One who exists "for others," and that our "relationship to God is a new life in 'being there for others,'" Bonhoeffer draws the inference that the "church is church only when it is there for others."[36]

In *This Monastic Moment* I have described more fully what this might mean in practice for the church today, following Bonhoeffer's proposal for a "new monasticism," which could lead the way.[37] But at the very least, the church can only be recognizably the church of Jesus Christ when it transcends ethnic barriers and strives to embrace all sectors of humanity. So, when the Protestant Church in Nazi Germany excluded Jewish-Christians from membership, Barth and Bonhoeffer immediately recognized that a *status confessionis* had arrived. For the same reason we in South Africa followed suit, declaring that an apartheid church, even though it included many devout believers, was heretical.[38] This was the core message of the Barmen Declaration adopted by the Barmen Synod of the Confessing Church in May 1934, and the Belhar Confession adopted by the Dutch Reformed Mission Church in South Africa in 1984.[39]

But no sooner had the *Kirchenkampf* begun, than Bonhoeffer, much to Barth's dismay and disapproval, accepted an invitation to become the pastor of two German-speaking congregations in London. He began his

---

36. Bonhoeffer, *Letters and Papers from Prison*, 501, 503.
37. De Gruchy, *This Monastic Moment*, 125–32,148–51.
38. See de Gruchy, *Aparthef\id Is a Heresy*; Cloete, *Moment of Truth*.
39. See Cloete and Smit, eds., *A Moment of Truth*.

ministry there in November 1933, so he did not attend the Barmen Synod and witness the birth of the Confessing Church. But this did not mean that he withdrew from the *Kirchenkampf*, not in the least. In London he ensured that his two congregations would side with the Confessing Church and began to develop ecumenical support for the cause with the assistance of George Bell, the bishop of Chichester, a great supporter of the Confessing Church, and Joe Oldham, the progressive general secretary of the International Missionary Council.[40] Although there seems to be no evidence that Bonhoeffer read Oldham's pioneering book, *Christianity and the Race Problem*, first published in 1926,[41] they must surely have discussed both colonialism and the race problem, which were then beginning to take center stage in missionary discussions. Bonhoeffer would have been particularly interested in what Oldham had to say about the situation in India as the subcontinent was much on Bonhoeffer's mind at the time. Indeed, with the help of Oldham he began to explore the possibility of going to India to learn from Mahatma Gandhi about passive resistance to British colonial oppression.[42]

In a letter to Gandhi explaining this desire, Bonhoeffer told the Indian leader that the "great need of Europe and of Germany" was not political or economic but spiritual. "Europe and Germany," he wrote, "are suffering from a dangerous fever and are losing both self-control and the consciousness of what they are doing." It sounds frighteningly contemporary! Bonhoeffer then went on to say that Christianity could help "western people to a new and spiritually sound life," but only if it was "reborn on the Sermon on the Mount" and learned from Gandhi "what realization of faith means, what a life devoted to political and racial peace can attain."[43] Bonhoeffer never did visit India or Gandhi; instead when he left London in April 1935 he returned to Germany to direct the new Confessing Church seminary in Finkenwalde. But he had already learned from Gandhi that the way to peace was through the struggle for justice, and that nonviolent protest was the means to that end.

---

40. See Clements, Introduction to Bonhoeffer, *London*, 6–10.

41. Oldham, *Christianity and the Race Problem*; see Clements, *Faith on the Frontier*, 208.

42. Bonhoeffer, *London*, 152, 136–37; see Oldham, *Christianity and the Race Problem*, 108–25.

43. See Green "Dietrich Bonhoeffer's Letter to Mahatma Gandhi"; see also Bonhoeffer, *Ecumenical, Academic and Pastoral Work*, 251.

RACIAL SCHISM IN THE SOUTH AFRICAN CHURCH[44]

The racial schism in the American church that confronted Bonhoeffer during his study year in New York bears striking resemblance to the rise and rapid proliferation of the African Independent or Indigenous Churches in the nineteenth and early twentieth centuries in southern Africa. Their separate existence, now many in number and representing the vast majority of Christians in South Africa, is as significant as all the other major schisms that have divided the church through the centuries. It was a response to the European control of missions and denominations, mainly Protestant.[45] Indeed, even when these became more multiracial in character, local congregations were invariably racially exclusive, just as, for example, the theological education of ministers and priests was segregated. The same applied within the Roman Catholic Church despite its catholicity.[46] Even when most denominations had a Black-majority membership, they were often controlled by their White constituency. They were trapped in varying degrees in a colonial and paternalist mindset if not by naked apartheid.[47]

The situation was more rigid and systemic in the Dutch Reformed Church (NGK). Already in 1857, the Cape Synod agreed, against its better judgment, that congregations could be segregated at the celebration of the Lord's Supper. But in due course, a theological rationale was provided that led to the segregation of the NGK as a Whites-only church, and the eventual formation of "daughter" mission churches serving Africans, Coloreds, and Indians. Racial discrimination was thereby structured into the life of the church. It became ecclesiologically systemic. This segregation within the NGK contributed to the formulation of what became government policy and gave it theological legitimacy. Indeed, all leading proponents of apartheid belonged to either the dominant NGK or its two sister White Afrikaans-speaking Reformed Churches. Among its members were not only the theological apologists for apartheid but also prime minister Hendrik Verwoerd, its chief architect. The NGK continues to struggle to overcome its apartheid legacy.[48]

---

44. For a comprehensive social history, see Elphick and Davenport, eds., *Christianity in South Africa*.

45. Elphick, *Equality of Believers*; Cochrane, *Servants of Power*.

46. See Prior, ed., *Catholics in Apartheid Society*.

47. See Villa-Vicencio, *Trapped in Apartheid*; de Gruchy and de Gruchy, *Church Struggle in South Africa*, 51–100.

48. See Plaatjies–Van Huffel and Vosloo, eds., *Reformed Churches in South Africa*.

The *Kairos Document* thus rightly described the church in South Africa as a "site of struggle" during the years of apartheid, irrespective of denomination. It was a struggle to be the church of Jesus Christ, an alternative structure in society that exists for the sake of the world by not conforming to it (Eph 2:11–22). It is insufficient for the church to evangelize and "win people for Christ" if it is not "Christ existing as a community of people," to use Bonhoeffer's definition—that is, becoming a new, inclusive humanity that transcends ethnicity.

This is the significance of Pentecost and the subsequent expansion of the church beyond the confines of Judaism embracing people of every tongue and nation; this is the ecumenical character of the church without which the church is not the church of Jesus Christ. Tim Hartman rightly speaks, then, of the "false narrative" of European Christendom that has "left many Christians (again, predominantly white) asking questions about how the church and Christian theology can survive."[49] The realities of colonialism and systemic racism are a challenge to the faith, integrity, and witness of the Christian church. The stark reality is that it is very difficult for White Christians to overcome racism if it is structured into the church. An anti-Semitic church will produce anti-Semites, just as a racist church will produce racist Christians, or else it will eject those who betray their social and ecclesial location.

BETRAYING OUR SOCIAL LOCATION

In 1973, at a Congress on Mission and Evangelism held in Durban, Manas Buthelezi, a leading Black theologian back then gave a powerful address in which he said that the time had come for Black Christians to evangelize and convert Whites.[50] His words still ring in my ears, as they did when he uttered them and brought the Congress to a sudden halt. One of those attending the Congress was Dr. Beyers Naudé, the director of the ecumenical anti-Apartheid Christian Institute (CI), a colleague of Buthelezi and the most prominent leader of church opposition to the apartheid state.

Naudé's story is iconic.[51] He was a Dutch Reformed minister, part of the Afrikaner elite, and eventually moderator of the Transvaal Synod. Some spoke of him as a future prime minister of South Africa. But, like

49. Hartman, *Theology after Colonization*, 8.
50. Buthelezi, "Six Theses on Evangelism."
51. See Hansen, ed., *Legacy of Beyers Naudé*.

Bonhoeffer, Naudé had a remarkable conversion following the Sharpeville Massacre in March 1960 when police killed sixty-seven Pan-Africanist protesters against the Pass Laws. At the Cottesloe Consultation convened in response by the member churches of the World Council of Churches, which included the Dutch Reformed, in December that year, Naudé, then still a moderator of his Church, played a major role. But his church's rejection of the outcomes of that Consultation precipitated Naudé's decision to establish the Christian Institute to fight apartheid, and that led in turn to his dismissal as a minister of the Church.

The Christian Institute was in the same building in Johannesburg as the SACC, where I worked from 1968 to 1973. For us younger White ministers and theologians Naudé was a challenging mentor and inspiration. He embodied what "White liberation" meant. Eberhard Bethge once referred to him as South Africa's Bonhoeffer and, indeed, he had been greatly influenced by Bonhoeffer's legacy.[52] It was Naudé who encouraged me to work on Bonhoeffer's significance for the church struggle in South Africa. Two of my published outcomes, following the 1976 Soweto uprising, were a paper I presented at the Second International Bonhoeffer Congress in Geneva on "Providence and the Shapers of History," and a year later, another presented at the American Academy of Religion, on "The Liberation of the Privileged," both of which anticipated this chapter.[53]

Naudé's "conversion" also influenced our son Steve during his student years and contributed to his own liberation from racism. When I was invited to give Steve's memorial lecture in 2016, as the debate about colonialism and gender-based violence was reaching fever pitch, I had both Naudé and Steve in mind.[54] Yes, it was possible for White male South Africans to enter the kingdom of God—but they had to be "born all over again" as Jesus told Nicodemus. Understandably Nicodemus was perplexed. How is that possible? Can I get out of my skin or change my DNA? Can prodigal sons break from male privilege and find their way to join the human family as equals rather than superiors?

The story of Nicodemus was the favorite Bible passage of the fundamentalist-evangelical mentors who helped nurture my adolescent faith. But over time I came to see that they did not understand the social significance

---

52. De Gruchy, "Beyers Naudé"

53. De Gruchy, *Bonhoeffer and South Africa*, 47–90.

54. See de Gruchy, *Keeping Body and Soul Together*; and Cochrane, ed., *Living on the Edge*.

of the story because they refused to challenge apartheid as evidence of "original sin," and misunderstood what Jesus meant by the "kingdom of heaven." If racism is sinful, then being born again must mean a change that is more fundamental than simply shifting religious gears by "accepting Jesus as Savior." That might well lead to a further process of conversion, but it is only the beginning of the journey, and if that journey does not confront racism, it is unrelated to reality. For if the "kingdom of heaven" is about the reign of God, then spiritual rebirth is not a ticket to heaven but a commitment to living differently from the values that shape the prevailing culture. In short, being "born again" is not what most White Christians think it is. It means starting life again on a new basis, a *metanoia*, and therefore breaking the genetic code that predetermines us to act in a way that is contrary to God's rule of justice. To recall Terblanche's comment quoted at the beginning of this chapter, we Whites not only need a "clear understanding of the systemic nature of the exploitation that has taken place," but "we also need to confess our sins, show the necessary repentance, experience the necessary conversion, and be prepared to make the needed sacrifices."[55]

In an essay written in memory of Steve, his colleague and friend Gerald West at the University of KwaZulu-Natal describes how he and Steve had struggled over the years with the question of White identity in the struggle for liberation and justice. The title of his essay "White Theology in a Black Frame: Betraying the Logic of Social Location," goes to the heart of the matter. Betraying our social location means breaking the genetic code. This is precisely what Bonhoeffer did when he broke with German nationalism, identified with the Black community in Harlem, became a pacifist, sided with the Jews in Germany, and joined the Resistance. The "crime" that led to his death was labeled treason (Naudé was also regarded as a traitor by Afrikanerdom), and only many years after the war did the German government pardon Bonhoeffer. But he betrayed his people for the sake of saving them. That is what true patriotism might require, as it did of Naudé and other White South Africans who identified with the Black liberation struggle and were vilified by the "White tribe," including the White church. This is nothing unusual in the history of Christianity. Jesus himself was condemned to death as a traitor, as were most martyrs who followed him.

Gerald West wrote more concretely of this process of conversion as a threefold movement. The first stage is becoming aware of and owning one's social location; that is, our Whiteness, and acknowledging how this works

---

55. Terblanche, *Western Empires*, xv.

itself out in practice. The second is becoming open to the interrogation of others; that is, to listen to the Black narrative. And the third is "forging strategic alliances and coalitions across our partially reconstituted social locations and their respective resources around the particular contextual issues that confront us."[56] Those of us who are White cannot get out of our skin, nor can we easily get out of our social location, but we can become critically aware of what our "Whiteness" means, we can interrogate our privileged status, and if we are Christians we can also interrogate the theologies that legitimate White racism and supremacy. But to do so we must listen carefully to those who are the victims of racism in order to see reality from their perspective. We must be evangelized, as Buthelezi said, by Black Christians, and so learn with Bonhoeffer to see things from below; that is, from the perspective of the powerless and the oppressed and all who suffer.[57] But how do we learn? I think that Steve's story provides some clues.

REFLECTIONS ON THE LIFE OF STEVE

Steve grew up in a historically White local church that belonged to a majority-Black denomination, both of which were committed to the struggle against apartheid informed by solid biblical and theological leadership. His exposure to the teaching of the Bible in a way that not only made sense to him as a student but also offered an alternative understanding of reality, who he was, and what it means to be a Christian living fully in the world, was critical. You are not going to break with White privilege if you read the Bible in ways that reinforce its assumptions, and you cannot easily listen to the Black voice in a segregated denomination or congregation.

As a high school student, Steve was introduced to the legacy of Bonhoeffer by the youth pastor at the church and soon became excited about "doing theology" alongside his growing involvement in the Student Union for Christian Action and the wider life of the ecumenical church. In the process young Black Christians both befriended and challenged him. He was one of 144 young South Africans of all races invited to join Archbishop Tutu's Pilgrimage of Hope to the Middle East and the Taizé Community in 1980, a journey that set the direction for the rest of his life, as Tutu noted in giving the first Steve de Gruchy Memorial Lecture in April 2012.[58]

56. West, "White Theology," 72.

57. Bonhoeffer, *Letters and Papers from Prison*, 52.

58. Tutu, "God Is God's Worst Enemy," x.

In 1977, during a sabbatical year with his parents in the US, Steve was exposed to the Mennonite peace tradition, which eventually led him to become a conscientious objector back home. On two occasions he was arrested by the police during protest marches against apartheid and imprisoned for several days. He later became involved in the struggle for gender and gay justice both as a student and within the life of the church. His graduate theological studies at the University of Cape Town and Union Theological Seminary in New York were informed by academic rigor and social critique. He chose to do his doctoral studies at the Black University of the Western Cape; his first pastorate was a Black congregation; he then spent several years as director of the Kuruman Mission on the edge of the Kalahari Desert before becoming a professor in theology and development at the University of KwaZulu-Natal, where many of his students came from across Africa.

Not everyone has the opportunities that changed and formed Steve's life and ministry, but the opportunities came because others were committed to making it possible for the next generation to continue the legacy of leaders like Naudé in the struggle for justice and peace. If the White church is to be transformed and overcome racism and patriarchy, then it needs leaders and members who have been liberated from privilege and equipped for that task. And this does not happen without mentoring and multicultural and ecumenical exposure, combined with critical reflection and spiritual formation.

The question, then, is not *can* a White male South African enter the kingdom of God, but *how* can he do so? A genuine commitment to Christ such as Bonhoeffer and Naudé made is undoubtedly a first step, but only that. The second is getting rid of the idea that we cannot change, that we are who we are by birth and there is nothing we can do about it. This is patently not true because some have broken free, refused to conform to the patterns imposed by the dominant and prevailing norms and skewed values of society, and have thereby betrayed their social location and overcome the strictures of their DNA. But this will not happen if we do not listen to the voice of the victims of oppression, for it is only when we hear their stories and begin to participate in their struggles, however inadequately, that we begin to change and face reality in a redemptive way. You cannot become a champion of justice if you do not see injustice, as best you can, through the eyes of those who experience it; you cannot become a worker for liberation if you do not experience something of the pain of oppression and are yourself liberated from prejudice. You cannot overcome fear of the other if you never meet and listen to her story.

Not all White males, even South African ones, are the same, and some are undoubtedly more privileged than others. If you were White, male, and gay you would have benefitted from apartheid, but if you did not play by the homophobic rules of the time, you were ridiculed and excluded. Steve was not gay, but he had a deep concern for gay rights because he heard the stories of gay people and did much to express his solidarity with them.[59] For him solidarity with gays was on the same continuum as solidarity with Black people and women. Yes, there are many variables within our White, male tribe—except for the fact that we are all White and male. There were also many variables when it came to Germans in Bonhoeffer's day. His aristocratic background, education, and personal ability set him apart from many others. But he came to see reality through the eyes of the oppressed, and that, for him, was "a great liberation." So, what *must* we do to "enter the kingdom of heaven"? is a pertinent and decidedly uncomfortable question facing White males.

Few of us may be able or willing to follow the example of Saint Francis, who renounced everything to follow and serve Christ. But at the very least we can heed Jesus' words: "From everyone to whom much has been forgiven, much will be required" (Luke 12:48). Bonhoeffer never denied his elite background or rejected his German identity, but he did acknowledge that because he had received so much, he had a great responsibility to use his gifts for the benefit of others. What we do with our inheritance is the challenge we face. And, for Bonhoeffer, as for Saint Peter, the first step *of faith* in following Jesus is invariably "an external deed which exchanges one mode of existence for another." Peter could not convert himself, but he could leave his nets. So, writes Bonhoeffer, in "the Gospels that first step consists of a deed which affects all of one's life."[60] Conversion or *metanoia* is about taking that step daily as we face the reality of racism and gender-based violence. It is also at the heart of our innate human desire for transcendence, to which we must now turn our attention.

---

59. See De Gruchy, *Aliens in the Household of God*.
60. Bonhoeffer, *Discipleship*. 64.

3

TRANSCENDENCE

&

the Will-to-Power

> As a deer longs for flowing streams,
> so my soul longs for you O God.
> My soul thirsts for God,
> For the living God.
>
> —Psalm 42:1

> Come, let us build ourselves a city,
> and a tower with its top in heaven,
> and let us make a name for ourselves.
>
> —Genesis 11:4

When we listen to a superb Beethoven symphony . . . we are often speechless with wonder and awe. Are we not often awestruck . . . when we behold a glorious sunset, or a still, moonlit night with the stars winking in a dark blue sky? . . . I have heard that scientists wax ecstatic and break into poetic utterance because

TRANSCENDENCE & THE WILL-TO-POWER

of the aesthetic qualities of some scientific experiment and the truth that it will have proven.

—Desmond Tutu[1]

Music can be heard as a mode of "secular theology" that exposes some of the major theological issues of our time.

—Daniel Chua[2]

The transcendent is not the infinite, unattainable tasks, but the neighbor within reach in any given situation.

—Bonhoeffer[3]

My friend Jaap Durand, to whom this book is dedicated, was trained as a neo-Calvinist Reformed theologian.[4] Neo-Calvinism has always been skeptical about mystical piety, regarding it as too Romantic, too subjective, and removed from reality. Mysticism was considered a way of escape from the world, not a way of engagement. But towards the end of his life, Jaap told me that he had become something of a mystic, largely under the influence of the Jesuit palaeontologist Teilhard de Chardin and considerable suffering.[5] Like Job, Jaap had come to a fresh understanding of God, an understanding he discovered in the writings of the great mystics who spoke of the "dark night of the soul," and the God "beyond knowing."

What Jaap told me resonated with my own experience as expressed in *Led into Mystery*. But I never considered myself a mystic until one day well on in my academic life a graduate student asked me straight out: "Are you a mystic?" I was nonplussed and had no ready answer to give him. But as I had once taught an undergraduate course on mysticism, I was familiar with the subject. I knew that while it eludes precise definition and

---

1. Tutu, comp., *African Prayer Book*, 5. Amended by the author.
2. Chua, "Music as the Mouthpiece of Theology," 138.
3. Bonhoeffer, *Letters and Papers from Prison*, 501.
4. See Conradie and Lombard, eds., *Discerning God's Justice in Church, Society and Academy*.
5. Durand, *Many Faces of God*; See also Durand, *Evolusie, Wetenskap en Geloof*.

is differently expressed in various religious traditions, it is by no means necessarily escapist or world denying. Indeed today it is not uncommon to speak of prophetic mystics, such as the Trappist monk Thomas Merton, or many of those described by Dorothee Soelle in *The Silent Cry*, appropriately subtitled *Mysticism and Resistance*.[6] If my friend Jaap was a mystic, and I think he was, he was this kind of mystic.

Traditionally across religious traditions, mysticism has been understood by philosophers as referring to our relationship to what they call the "transcendental" as contrasted with what is "immanent," or what theologians call God and the world. The Christian mystical tradition began to develop in the early centuries of the church under the influence of Neoplatonic philosophy and has generally been described in terms drawn from that tradition. But it is primarily and deeply rooted in the biblical narrative. For even though the word *mysticism* does not occur in the Bible, stories and images abound that express what can be called a mystical desire for God, just as a "deer longs for flowing streams."

In the next chapter, where I discuss faith and science, I will use the phrase "there is more to reality than meets the eye" as a colloquial way to describe transcendence. But equally we could say that there is something more ultimate than the penultimate, more infinite than the finite, and more absolute than the contingent. But is the ultimate, the infinite, and the absolute the equivalent of what theists call God? Is our relationship to God, indeed, our desire for God, even if described in mystical Neoplatonic terms, the same as our relationship to the impersonal transcendent of Idealist philosophy? This question has sparked much debate among Christian theologians from earliest times through the Middle Ages to the present as they have engaged philosophy and other religious traditions and have tried to give an account of their faith in response. For can impersonal categories describe a relationship with God if the reality of God revealed in Christ is about absolute love?

Bonhoeffer entered the debate in its modern guise in *Act and Being*, which he wrote to qualify as a university lecturer. Like his earlier dissertation, *Sanctorum Communio*, *Act and Being* left an indelible impression on the development of his theology. But already there, his Christology played a major role in his understanding of transcendence, leading him to speak of a "Christian transcendentalism."[7] That is, a transcendentalism not de-

---

6. Soelle, *Silent Cry*.
7. Bonhoeffer, *Act and Being*, 31.

termined by philosophy but understood in terms of God's embodiment in Jesus Christ. This laid the foundation for his prison formulation that the "transcendent is not the infinite, unattainable tasks, but the neighbor."[8] The tragedy is that this human desire for transcendence, this desire for God, can be subverted and become what the philosopher Friedrich Nietzsche called the "will to power" that can take hold of a nation as cultured as Germany and lead it to destruction. I will examine this tragic enigma through the lens of Bonhoeffer's remarkable understanding of music, which helps us distinguish between a genuine desire for God, or Christian transcendentalism, and the demonic reality of political powermongering that faith must also face in our time, indeed especially in our time.

Nothing better illustrates the connection between our human desire for God and the will to power than the fact that the sexual act of intimate love that brings new life to birth is too often perverted in an act of rape that brings death. Energized by self-giving love or *agape*, erotic love is creative; driven by a self-interested lust to possess what is not its own, it is destructive. So, the desire for God or the transcendent is perverted by the will to power, that is, to *be* God, and inevitably results in destruction. That inevitably happens when we transgress the boundaries and limits of our humanity by wrongly asserting our divinity and wilfully seeking domination. The primordial sin depicted in the biblical myths of the fall and the collapse of the tower of Babel results from such a desire. If human sexuality provides one analogy that helps us understand the connection between the desire for transcendence and the will to power, the power of music is another.

THE WILL TO POWER, AND THE POWER OF MUSIC

Much of Bonhoeffer's most creative theological thinking was a response to the challenge Nietzsche presented to Christian faith.[9] In fact his insistence that the reality of God and the reality of the world are united in Christ, rooted in the earth, is his riposte to both Nietzsche's critique of Christianity as a religion of heavenly-minded weakness and the philosopher's advocacy of the will to power.[10] "There is in the soul of human beings," said Bonhoeffer, in one of his earliest sermons in which he refers to Nietzsche, "something that makes them restless, something that points them toward

---

8. Bonhoeffer, *Letters and Papers from Prison*, 501.
9. See Frick, "Friedrich Nietzsche's Aphorisms."
10. Frick, "Friedrich Nietzsche's Aphorisms," 198–99.

the infinite, eternal . . . It wants to acquire power over the eternal so that it can rid itself of anxiety and restlessness." This restlessness, he continues, has produced "colossal works of philosophy and art," not least "the quartets and symphonies of Beethoven," all of which "were overwhelmed by the idea of something eternal and unchangeable."[11] But such restlessness has also resulted in the desire to *be* God, described in the myth of the fall in Genesis, which shows how the human desire for transcendence becomes a lust for power over others and the resources of the earth, which inevitably leads to violence, war, the suffering of the innocent, and the demise of nations.[12]

Some regard Nietzsche as Germany's "most famous thinker" of the nineteenth century, someone who contributed powerfully "to the mounting sense of impending doom and destruction" out of which "a new world" would be born.[13] But Nietzsche would not have been who he was if he had not come under the spell of the great Romantic composer Richard Wagner. So much was this the case that when Nietzsche listened to Wagner's music, as his biographer Sue Prideaux tells us, "his every fibre quivered, his every nerve vibrated." Indeed, nothing "else produced such a penetrating and lasting feeling of ecstasy . . . the sensation of direct access to the will."[14]

It is not surprising then, that Adolf Hitler found a soulmate in Wagner, for it was Wagner's music that inspired his passion to make Germany great and achieve world domination. This was not, however, an aberration in human history. Tyrants keep grasping power and transgressing boundaries, nations repeatedly go to war, and criminal violence pervades global society, not least in our own time of coups, aggressive invasions, and political gangsterism. This grasp for absolute power and the pursuit of self-interest lies at the center of the destructive global realities we face, including in Russia's war with Ukraine. These same forces previously confronted us in Nazism, and, sadly, just as before, so today Christian faith seems impotent to do much about them.

The often-cited Edward Gibbon famously blamed Christianity for the decline and fall of the Roman Empire. Christianity, he argued, weakened the will of the people to resist the barbarian invaders.[15] We might equally

---

11. Bonhoeffer, *Barcelona, Berlin, New York*, 481–82.

12. Nietzsche, *Will to Power*, 550.

13. Newell, *Tyrants*, 158–59.

14. Prideaux. *I Am Dynamite*, 51.

15. *The History of the Decline and Fall of the Roman Empire* (published between 1776 and 1788).

argue, with Bonhoeffer, that the capture of Germany by the barbarism of Nazism was also due to a failure of the church and Christian faith. But for the opposite reason—the church's support for Hitler's will to power. It was, in any case, a puzzling enigma. For how could it be that the homeland of Bach, Mozart, and Beethoven, one of the most cultured and educated in human history, fell prey to Nazism? And how was it that so many of the heirs of Martin Luther were complicit?

MANN, BONHOEFFER & THE GERMAN ENIGMA

One notable attempt to understand this enigma was Thomas Mann's *Doctor Faustus*, which Terry Eagleton describes as "the most masterly portrait of evil in modern literature."[16] Another attempt was Bonhoeffer's essay "After Ten Years," written as a gift for his close friends shortly before his imprisonment. Victoria Barnett describes this gem in Bonhoeffer's writings as "a synthesis of an ongoing and troubled conversation" between Bonhoeffer's inner circle of resisters, "as they wrestled with their consciences and the diminishing options open to those who sought the end of National Socialism."[17] While Mann was not part of their company (he had fled Germany in 1933), he shared their humanist convictions.

Comparing Mann (1875-1955) and the much younger Bonhoeffer (1906-1945) in trying to resolve the German enigma is, I suggest, a helpful way to proceed. But it must be said that Bonhoeffer had no personal interest in Mann's work, despite the fact that their families were neighbors, and that Dietrich's grandmother had discussed Mann's celebrated writings with him and his siblings.[18] What connects Mann and Bonhoeffer is not Mann's novels or his location but their shared love of music and their rejection of Nazism. Music for them both was a window into the soul of a person or nation, revealing its tensions and ambiguities, and leading to either redemption or destruction. It could empower an enslaved people in their struggle for freedom, but it could also send millions to battle enemies with a frenzied death wish accompanied by the beat of a drum. This powerful emotive capacity of music is not only central to Mann's *Doctor Faustus*; it was also acknowledged and well understood by Bonhoeffer, as we shall soon see.

---

16. Eagleton, *Culture*, 19; See also Jay, *Dialectical Imagination*, 194.
17. Barnett, ed., *"After Ten Years,"* 4.
18. Schlingensiepen, *Dietrich Bonhoeffer*, 9.

Doctor Faustus was inspired by Goethe's *Faust*, the great poetic drama that tells the story of a devout medical doctor who, despairing about the corrupt state of the world, longs for a life of transcendence in unity with nature. Such nature mysticism, we may note in passing, was encouraged and popularized during the Nazi period. Enter the devil, the personification of seductive evil in *Faust*, who promises the admirable doctor his desire, but only if he becomes his loyal servant. Faust accepts the wager, believing that God will help him save his soul. But no self-seeking pleasure or pursuit brings him any solace; instead Faust descends deeper into a hell of his own making.

If Goethe's *Faust* provided Mann with the perfect metaphor for a nation that made a pact with the devil and descended into hell,[19] Mann found an analogical key to unlocking the enigma of Germany in the unresolved tension between its Classical and Romantic musical traditions. The former, represented by J. S. Bach and the latter by Ludwig von Beethoven, who bridged the two traditions, together with Wagner, who, with his devoted acolyte, Nietzsche, is always in the background. If the Classical, which represents the Apollonian in ancient Greco-Roman culture, is about order, stability, and harmony, the Romantic represents the Dionysian, the ecstatic and erotic. Barth aptly described Romanticism as a movement "that holds the universe in thrall . . . reflects ideas in the form of feeling" and "aims at expressing and awakening the passions." It did not aspire to be beautiful, he said, but "enchanting" and, as such, could result in "blessedness and damnation."[20] The question Mann addresses is whether these two powerful cultural currents can coexist in creative "blessed" tension, or must they always clash and end up in damnable disaster?

Already during his Barcelona vicariate sermons in 1928, a young pastor Bonhoeffer quotes Nietzsche that "all joy wants eternity," but then immediately asserts that human joy, beauty, and splendor pass away as do the works of Beethoven, Bach, Goethe, and Michelangelo.[21] Everything is penultimate and therefore subject to death, even if anticipating the ultimate.[22] This early juxtaposing of the penultimate and ultimate with reference to Nietzsche, which anticipates Bonhoeffer's lifelong debate with the philosopher, reaches its climax in Bonhoeffer's theological reflections in prison on

---

19. Travers, *Thomas Mann*, 100.
20. Barth, *Protestant Theology*, 178.
21. Bonhoeffer, *Barcelona, Berlin, New York*, 517.
22. Bonhoeffer, *Barcelona, Berlin, New York*, 518.

the future of Christianity in a "world come of age" and on Christian "aesthetic existence."²³ And it is there that we find Bonhoeffer's observation that we can "go along too easily with Nietzsche's primitive alternatives, as if the 'Apollonian' concept of beauty, and the 'Dionysian,' the one we call demonic nowadays, are the only ones. But that isn't the case at all." Some great landscape paintings, he says, "have a beauty that is neither classic nor demonic, but simply earthly in its own right," and that is "the only sort of beauty," says Bonhoeffer, that speaks to him personally.²⁴ So, for Bonhoeffer, the tension between the Classical and Romantic can be creatively resolved; it need not end in disaster. Responsibility and freedom, stability and change, tradition and innovation, order and justice, need each other, and together give birth to the new. This is the dialectic, represented by the Classical and Romantic musical traditions, that Mann, the secular humanist, and Bonhoeffer the follower of Christ, use to explain what went wrong in Germany with such devastating global consequences—consequences including the rise of apartheid in South Africa.²⁵ If responsibility and freedom are separated, or law and order replaces justice, then society becomes totalitarian or anarchic. On this the theologian and the novelist agreed, and their appreciation of Germany's musical tradition along with their humanist convictions helped them to do so.

THE MUSICAL THEOLOGIAN AND THE HUMANIST NOVELIST

Neither the young Dietrich nor his family were churchgoers, and his father was not very encouraging when his son told him he had decided to become a theologian. Wanting him to make sure that his true vocation was music rather than theology, his parents "arranged for him to play for the pianist Leonid Kreuzer, a virtuoso of the Vienna school."²⁶ The outcome was indecisive, but sometime in March 1921, Dietrich made up his own mind. He would become a theologian. The reason, Bethge says, "was a basic drive for

---

23. See Bonhoeffer, *Ethics*, 106–7; Bonhoeffer, *Letters and Papers from Prison*, 331; Frick, "Friedrich Nietzsche's Aphorisms"; de Gruchy, *Christianity, Art, and Transformation*, 151–53.

24. Bonhoeffer, *Letters and Papers from Prison*, 331.

25. Moodie, *Rise of Afrikanerdom*, 208–33.

26. Bethge, *Dietrich Bonhoeffer*, 37.

independence . . . the need for unchallenged self-realization."[27] Youthful arrogance was at work, a desire to prove to the skeptical members of his family that he could excel in his own chosen field: the science of God. He was not only going to be a theologian but the best theologian possible. As he himself described it, "he plunged into work in a very unchristian way," driven by ambition, turning "the doctrine of Jesus Christ into something of personal advantage."[28] Such was Bonhoeffer's will to power disguised as a desire for God.

Some students at Union Seminary, where Bonhoeffer studied in 1930–1931, found him arrogant. Among them was the future wife of his teacher Reinhold Niebuhr, Ursula Keppel-Compton, who once told me that she found the young German a frightful "know-it-all." Yet it was precisely at Union, as we have previously seen, that this egocentric theologian became, in his own words, "a Christian." He surrendered his will to Christ and turned his back on German nationalism, which was nothing other than the embodiment of a nation's corporate arrogance and egocentricity. Bonhoeffer's later awareness of the strength of his ego has often been noted, but Clifford J. Green has also drawn attention to Bonhoeffer's concomitant awareness "that the dominating power of the individual ego" parallels the "destructive power in society" expressed in the glorification of war and the exploitation of the weak.[29]

Bonhoeffer expressed what this meant in a sermon he preached in London a few years later in which he said that "Christianity stands or falls with its revolutionary protest against violence, arbitrariness and pride of power and with its apologia for the weak." Indeed, he continued, "Christianity has adjusted itself much too easily to the worship of power." To correct this, it "should give much more offence, more shock to the world, than it is doing," and "take a much more definite stand for the weak than to consider the potential moral right of the strong."[30]

Bonhoeffer's conversion in New York changed his views about nationalism but did not alter his love for music. Indeed, while there he was excited by his discovery of the Spirituals that expressed the faith of African Americans in their struggle for justice. Negro Spirituals, he wrote, "represent

---

27. Bethge, *Dietrich Bonhoeffer*, 37.
28. Bethge, *Dietrich Bonhoeffer*, 205–6.
29. Green, *Sociality of Christ*, 126.
30. Bonhoeffer, *London*, 402–3.

some of the greatest artistic achievements in America."[31] They were the means whereby African slaves in the "New World" made Christianity their own while still affirming their African identity, and a means of empowering them in their struggle for liberation through to the present time.[32] Anyone, he said, "who has heard and understood the Negro Spirituals knows about the strange mixture of reserved melancholy and eruptive joy in the soul of the Negro."[33] Bonhoeffer was so affected by the Spirituals that he took a pile of recordings back to Germany to play to his students. He also took a copy of James Weldon Johnson's *Book of American Negro Spirituals*, "with some sixty pieces that he could play on his piano."[34] Later, when Bonhoeffer became director of the illegal Confessing Seminary in Finkenwalde, he introduced the Spirituals to his students and to their bewilderment, spoke of them "as genuine church music."[35] But his enthusiasm for the Spirituals was an unsettling challenge, for it presupposed the kind of *metanoia* or conversion that Bonhoeffer had already experienced in Harlem.

Mann (1875–1955) was thirty and an established author by the time Bonhoeffer was born (1906). He had won the Nobel Prize in Literature in 1929 with his novel *The Magic Mountain* (1924) about the role of music in the rise and fall of Europe before the First World War.[36] Married to a Jewish wife, Mann fled Nazi Germany for Switzerland in 1933, where he had contact with Barth in 1936,[37] before going to the United States in 1938. It was a wise decision. Bonhoeffer was tempted to do the same when he went to New York in 1939 but soon decided to return home for the sake of contributing to the rebuilding of Germany after the war.[38] Their respective decisions determined their destinies and reveal a fundamental difference between them.

The debate about whether to stay or leave Germany was an intensely emotional one for anti-Nazi intellectuals. This was especially the case for those who were Jewish or known for their socialist or humanist convictions

---

31. In a letter to his brother Karl-Friedrich, January 2, 1931, in Bonhoeffer, *Barcelona, Berlin, New York*, 268.

32. See Floyd, *Power of Black Music*, 39–42.

33. Bonhoeffer, *Barcelona, Berlin, New York*, 315.

34. Bonhoeffer, *Barcelona, Berlin, New York*, 30.

35. Green, Editor's Afterword to Bonhoeffer, *Barcelona, Berlin, New York*, 616.

36. Vaget, "'Politically Suspect,'" 123; Mann, *Pro and Contra Wagner*.

37. Busch, *Karl Barth*, 272.

38. Bonhoeffer, *Theological Education Underground*, 210.

such as Thomas Mann, Theodor Adorno, and Paul Tillich, all of them associated with the Frankfurter Schule established at the Goethe University in 1923 for the pursuit of critical philosophy and sociology. Bethge quotes from a postwar speech in which Mann spoke of a "chasm, which yawns between our experiences and those of the people left behind in Germany . . . Any understanding traversing this chasm," Mann concluded, "is completely impossible."[39] It reminds me of the gap between anti-apartheid South African exiles, many of whom returned home after 1990, and those activists who remained in the country throughout the struggle. The tension between them is still evident.

But was it impossible to traverse "the chasm," to use Mann's phrase, whether in Germany or South Africa? Not without difficulty, for the experience of exile, like that of remaining, invariably changes perspectives and alters expectations. And, of course, Mann was a secular humanist in the tradition of Goethe, at home in the lively intellectual and literary life of Weimar Berlin, whereas Bonhoeffer, a young theologian under the influence of Barth, was embedded in the church and Berlin's premier Faculty of Theology, with little if any interest in the Frankfurter Schüle.[40] If Bonhoeffer's opposition to Hitler was motivated by family humanist values and Christian conviction, Mann's opposition was shaped by his intellectual peers and social humanism. Yet Bonhoeffer had grown up in an enlightened humanist household that was opposed to National Socialism from the outset, and he had imbibed humanist values from an early age.[41] Already in February 1933, as Hitler came to power, Bonhoeffer wrote of the need to work for civil liberties to counter the Nazi "barbarization of German culture."[42] His ingrained humanist persona was undoubtedly muted during the intense years of the *Kirchenkampf* (1933–1936), but it reemerged strongly when he joined the Resistance and called "attention to one of the most astounding experiences" Christians had during the struggle against Nazism, "namely an awareness of some kind of alliance" between humanist defenders of "freedom, tolerance, and human rights" and Christians.[43] With this and future generations in mind, Bonhoeffer would later embark

---

39. Bethge, *Bonhoeffer*, 116.
40. Pangritz, *Polyphony of Life*, 10.
41. See de Gruchy "Bonhoeffer as a Christian Humanist."
42. Bonhoeffer, *Berlin 1932–1933*, 94.
43. Bonhoeffer, *Ethics*, 340.

on his project of reconfiguring Christianity in a "world come of age," the world Mann inhabited.

I suspect Mann would have warmed to Bonhoeffer's proposal. He was not anti-Christian like many of his peers, and he respected Christian ethics as a counter to barbarism.[44] He approvingly quoted Goethe, who was otherwise critical of Christianity but spoke of the noble and ethical culture that "glimmers and shines in the Gospels."[45] In a letter to a fellow German immigrant, civil rights activist, and art patron, Mann expressed his dismay about "the realities and dangers in the current trend of American policy toward restriction of entry and investigation (and castigation) of non-conformist opinion in all walks of life," or McCarthyism.[46] He went on to say that "it would be good if out of all our sufferings a new feeling of solidarity for mankind would emerge, a unifying sympathy for man's precarious position in the universe, between nature and spirit," even though these were pious "Christian wishes if you will." For him, "'Christian' in spite of Nietzsche," was "not a term of abuse."[47] In another letter, he speaks of Christianity as "an enormous revolution," indeed "a spiritual event which can never be effaced, unless it be through a complete relapse into a criminal, atavistic state. Such as represented by German National Socialism . . ."[48]

Mann's appreciation of the moral conscience of Christianity, then, may have been different from Bonhoeffer's commitment as a disciple of Christ, but the two shared humanist values when confronted by the barbarism of Nazism[49] and were united in their love for Beethoven; though, as we shall see, they did not share a liking for Wagner.

Bonhoeffer had a good knowledge of Beethoven in his early teens, and despite some reservations he never lost his appreciation for the composer's Romanticism.[50] But in his doctoral dissertation he challenged the notion that values such as the beautiful have a unifying power, and opposed the liturgical use of Beethoven's music because "its great beauty and

---

44. Mann, *Letters*, 2:538.
45. Mann, *Letters*, 1:135, see also Mann, *Letters*, 1:184.
46. Mann, *Letters*, 2:651.
47. Mann, *Letters*, 2:652.
48. Mann, *Letters*, 2:538.
49. See Bonhoeffer, *Ethics*, 140; John A. Moses, "Rejecting Kultur," 23–40.
50. Bonhoeffer, *The Young Bonhoeffer*, 32–33. The letter to Ernst Schmid is incorrectly dated. It should be March 25, 1926.

power" prevent "us from hearing the Word of God."[51] Beethoven's music, Bonhoeffer also said, seemed "to be nothing but the eternal expression of human suffering and passion," thereby glorifying humanity and stirring the passions.[52] But in prison, Bonhoeffer rediscovered the late Beethoven and recognized in his piano sonata Opus 111 music that not only expressed the frenzied destruction of war but also the hope of redemption.[53] At virtually the same time, Mann was writing *Doctor Faustus* with Beethoven in the foreground and Wagner lurking in the shadows.[54]

Bonhoeffer did not share any of Mann's love for Wagner, whose music, he said, was an expression of a "barbarous pagan psychology."[55] It was all about the *Triumph of the Will*, the title of Leni Riefenstahl's famous film of the Nuremberg rallies, which incorporated Wagner's music and stoked nationalist frenzy and anti-Semitic fanaticism. Mann, incidentally, was fully aware of Wagner's anti-Semitism and the way his music was exploited by Nazi leaders, but for him this did not detract from the composer's greatness.[56] Indeed, it is worth remembering that Christoph von Dohnanyi, the famous postwar conductor and son of Hans, Bonhoeffer's fellow conspirator and brother-in-law, said that he could find nothing in Wagner that *had* to lead to Hitler,[57] and Roger Scruton even refers to Wagner's *Parsifal* as an "allegory of the Gospel story."[58] But that was not Bonhoeffer's opinion at the time Wagner was being used to stir German passions against Jews and everything international.

Mann's celebrated lecture on the "Sorrows and Grandeur of Richard Wagner," given in 1933, provides his clearest alternative reading of Wagner to that of Nazi propaganda, and understandably it contributed to his censure and exile.[59] For Mann, Wagner's music revealed the mystery of life[60] and like the great Nordic myths provided a doorway into reality as it expressed

---

51. Bonhoeffer, *London*, 351ff.

52. See Bonhoeffer, *London*, 356.

53. Pangritz, *Polyphony of Life*, 50–51. See Bonhoeffer, *Letters and Papers from Prison*, 333, 336.

54. Pangritz, *Polyphony of Life*, 41–42.

55. Pangritz, *Polyphony of Life*, 851. See Bethge, *Dietrich Bonhoeffer*, 851.

56. Vaget, Thomas Mann's "The Magic Mountain." 123.

57. Ross, *Wagnerism*, 561.

58. See Scruton, *Wagner's "Parsifal,"* 93.

59. See Mann, *Pro and Contra Wagner*, 91–148.

60. Ross, *Wagnerism*, 543–44.

what Carl Jung called the human "yearning for transcendence."[61] Certainly, in *Doctor Faustus,* Wagnerian Romanticism was the "medium through which the German penchant for mystical 'inwardness' and the 'daemonic' found expression."[62] But it is Beethoven rather than Wagner who provides the clue to Mann's *Doctor Faustus.* Indeed, the life of Leverkühn, its central character, mirrors Beethoven's long and torturous internal struggle between the Classical tradition he inherited and the Romantic one he and Goethe helped create. In *Doctor Faustus,* Mann is saying that the creative genius that characterized Germany's cultural achievements, above all in Beethoven, did not lead to the nation's tragic demise as did the Nazi interpretation of Wagnerism. The latter did precisely because Wagner's quest for transcendence had become the demonic will to power. *Doctor Faustus* is, as Mann says, a "Nietzschean novel";[63] its great promise of reaching transcendence ends in tragedy because the quest for transcendence had become a demonic will to power.

THE TRAGIC QUEST FOR TRANSCENDENCE

The story of Leverkühn is told by his friend of many years, Serenus Zeitblom, a humanist scholar as steady as the Classical tradition. Leverkühn, whose quest for transcendence pays little attention to social constraints or personal consequences, began his adult life studying theology within the framework of nineteenth-century Protestantism and the struggles between Enlightenment rationalism and Romanticism, liberalism and orthodoxy, faith and science. It is a world Bonhoeffer knew well, as did Nietzsche, who, like Leverkühn, turned his back on theology only to discover that the "theological virus does not get out of one's blood easily."[64]

Although the virus remains, Leverkühn soon becomes disillusioned with the inadequacies of divinity and turns to music, which is, in any case, a "highly theological business—the way sin is, the way I am." Music, he says, is a "beautiful art"—in fact "the most Christian of all arts," despite being banned by sections of the church as part of the devil's kingdom.[65] The turning point for Leverkühn in his migration from theology to music came as

61. Jung, *Collected Works,* 5:177–78.
62. Travers, *Thomas Mann,* 101.
63. Mann, *Doctor Faustus,* 242.
64. Mann, *Doctor Faustus,* 355.
65. Mann, *Doctor Faustus,* 242.

he listened to a lecture by his music teacher, Kretschmar, who, commenting on Beethoven's final piano sonata (op. 111), elevates the composer "into a Faustian hero of the mind," anticipating Wagner.[66] This anticipates what Leverkühn hears Kretschmar say, that by the time Beethoven wrote this, his last sonata, he had become deaf and "lost in the giddy heights that one might call other-worldly."[67] As Harvey Sachs puts it, "the second movement . . . takes the listener so profoundly into Beethoven's heart and . . . into the heart of the universe that anything that followed it would have been impossibly anticlimactic."[68] In yearning for this transcendent goal, which Leverkühn desires as much as an alchemist desires gold even at the cost of his soul, he is no different from a politician who desires absolute power despite its potential to bring absolute corruption.

Following Kretschmar's lecture Leverkühn and Zeitblom have a lengthy but revealing conversation on the "secularization of art" and its separation from the "liturgical whole" in which it was conceived. While this was part of the cultural change that took place in post-Enlightenment and post-Revolutionary Europe, it must not, argues Zeitblom, lead to the rejection of the cultural framework within which art and music are located, for "the alternative to culture is barbarism." To which Leverkühn responds, yes, but "barbarism is the opposite of culture only within the order of thought which it gives us."[69] That is, it is all relative, a matter of who makes the rules and where we stand in relation to them. One person's culture is another's barbarism! National Socialism might pass its own laws and insist on "law and order" but in doing so trample on the cultural norms shaped by Renaissance humanism and on human rights achieved by the French Revolution.

In seeking to express himself by transgressing the objective constraints of the Classical tradition (order, stability, reason) and entering the realm of the Romantic, Beethoven provides Leverkühn with the "breakthrough" (*Durchbruch*) he needs to satisfy his desire. He must break with tradition and commit moral transgression in an act of defiance. This he does inexplicably by having sex with a prostitute and contracting syphilis. Such reckless madness shocks Zeitblom, for he cannot but see in it a "deeply mysterious longing for daemonic conception."[70] Having sold his soul to the devil,

---

66. Travers, *Thomas Mann*, 102.
67. Mann, *Doctor Faustus*, 51–52.
68. Sachs, *Ninth*, 27.
69. Mann, *Doctor Faustus*, 59.
70. Mann, *Doctor Faustus*, 155.

Leverkühn is hell-bent on self-destruction. But this, as Zeitblom says, is not just the fate of an individual, for Leverkühn's transgression is Germany's rejection of humanist culture and a descent into barbarism.[71] Leverkühn well knows that the human spirit cannot escape a feeling for the uncanny or mystery;[72] but in the end he is a disillusioned theologian cast in the image of Nietzsche whose will to power leads irrevocably to suicide.

An uncanny sense of this will to power at any cost was highlighted for me when during the US presidential election campaign in 2015–2016, I read a reprint of Sinclair Lewis's *It Can't Happen Here*, written in 1935 shortly after Hitler seized power. Hitler did so by taking control of the media, spreading lies, fomenting fear, awakening unquestioning patriotic passion, silencing critics, and gaining the support of large sections of both the Protestant and Catholic Churches. Like Goethe's Mephistopheles, the devil, who tempted Jesus in the wilderness or appeared as "an angel of light," to quote Saint Paul (2 Cor 11:14), Hitler offered a new world of prosperity in exchange for total loyalty and obedience. This is the playbook of all tyrants. While reading Lewis's sobering satire, I sensed that I was not alone in asking whether the unthinkable was unfolding before our very eyes both in the United States, where Trump was grasping for power, and in South Africa, where a young and vibrant democracy shaped by the legacy of Nelson Mandela was being plagued by corruption under the presidency of Jacob Zuma. And now the unthinkable is happening in Russia and the Ukraine. The grasp for absolute power, as Nietzsche knew only too well, leads to death and destruction, for that is the logic of nihilism.

THE LOGIC OF NIHILISM

We misunderstand Nietzsche if we simply regard him as the archenemy of faith in God rather than a prophet challenging contemporary culture and unworthy versions of Christian faith. For Nietzsche, the "death of God" was not the result of philosophical reasoning but of Western European culture. The God who has died is the God of bourgeois conventional Christianity. *This* God has fallen prey to modernity, secularization, and revolution, a cocktail of unstoppable toxic forces that spread across the landscape of Christendom with potentially dire consequences: the death of beauty,

---

71. Mann, *Doctor Faustus*, 59.
72. Mann, *Doctor Faustus*, 90.

goodness, and truth.[73] Nietzsche's words are echoed by Leverkühn when he asks "whether all seeming, even the most beautiful, even precisely the beautiful, has not today become a lie."[74] Or in Nietzsche's words, we feel "the breath of empty space," it has "become colder," and night is "continually closing in on us."[75] All objective standards, all moral and aesthetic judgments, have been dissolved.[76]

If the "God of Christendom" is dead, Nietzsche warns us, we do not worship Nothing (Nihil). We look for substitutes. Gods less worthy of worship and more destructive fill the vacuum like evil spirits in Jesus' parable (Luke 11:24–26). So, the question is not whether God exists, but what do we worship as God? Nietzsche's project is to find the "true, noble God" and therefore a new basis for ethics and aesthetics "beyond good and evil." But what if there is Nothing in that space? Or if, as the logic of "nihilism" suggests, nothing becomes something which leads to an absurd reductionism.[77] Both Nietzsche's and Leverkühn's lives disintegrate, not when they reach out to take hold of transcendence, but when they discover there is no transcendence, only the silence of absence and the fatal attraction of suicide. Leverkühn is the archetype of all who, having lost or renounced their ancestral religious traditions, institutions, and doctrines, are engaged in a frantic search for meaning and purpose to life everywhere and anywhere, but to no avail. Transcendence is as elusive as sexual fulfilment through rape.

As deafness increased and death approached, Beethoven delved deeper into his subconscious, both for his own sake and that of universal harmony. But just when he is about to achieve his desire and experience transcendence—towards the end of his final piano sonata (op. 111)—there is a brief pregnant silence. But it is not the silence of absence. He has entered the prophet's holy ground, and overtaken by awe, he draws back from grasping the infinite to remain in the finite.[78] He refuses to transgress the boundary separating the human and the divine. By contrast, Leverkühn refuses to step back and so plunges headlong into the abyss despite Zeitblom's

---

73. Nietzsche, *Will to Power*, 423.

74. Mann, *Doctor Faustus*, 180.

75. Nietzsche, *Gay Science*, 81–82.

76. Kee, *Nietzsche against the Crucified*, 35.

77. Cunningham, *Genealogy of Nihilism*, xiv.

78. Bonhoeffer, *Letters and Papers from Prison*, 332. See Pangritz, "Point and Counterpoint."

frantic attempt to prevent his fall. But Leverkühn's fate is more than a personal tragedy; it is symbolic of Germany's disintegration, just as Zeitblom's failure represents the inability of Germany's humanist elite to prevent the return of barbarism in the advent of Nazism.

The apocalypse anticipated in Leverkühn's late composition and described in vivid detail by Zeitblom, evokes a "hellish" horror that, in Mann and Bonhoeffer's day, reflected Auschwitz. "There was no doubt that in the future, after we had begun to practice a large-scale elimination of the unfit, the diseased and weak-minded, we would justify the policy by . . . hygienic arguments for the purification of society."[79] The Four Horsemen of the Apocalypse may be held in check but keep on coming. The virus of the will to power keeps mutating and returning. Romantic aestheticism may be able to describe this awful and tragic reality, stoic humanism may provide courage in facing it, and some may still find solace in religious tradition. But in the end, Mann despairs of the world. We now recognize that Zeitblom is Mann himself. "It is finished," he writes. "An old man (*Mann*), bent, well-nigh broken by the horrors of the times in which he wrote," he begins his Epilogue, and ends: "A lonely man folds his hands and speaks: God be merciful to thy poor soul, my friend, my Fatherland!"[80]

In "After Ten Years" Bonhoeffer, on behalf of his compatriots in the Resistance, confesses their failures and asks whether they are still of any use—especially given that they "have been silent witnesses of evil deeds . . . become cunning and learned in the arts of obfuscation and equivocal speech," and often failed to speak the truth. Indeed, they have even become cynical. Nevertheless, he continues, if "we are to be of use for the sake of future generations, we will not need geniuses, cynics, people who have contempt for others, or cunning tacticians, but simple, uncomplicated, and honest human beings."[81] Thus, the question Bonhoeffer poses as his life nears its end is simply this: Will "our inner strength to resist what has been forced on us have remained strong enough, and our honesty with ourselves blunt enough, to find our way back to simplicity and honesty?"[82]

How then does Beethoven avoid Leverkühn's fate, and therefore how do we avoid the fate of the world at large as it falls prey to the will to power that destroys all that is good, loving, and just? How do we remain strong

---

79. Mann, *Doctor Faustus*, 370.
80. Mann, *Doctor Faustus*, 504, 510. See Bergsten, "Musical Symbolism."
81. Bonhoeffer, *Letters and Papers from Prison*, 52.
82. Bonhoeffer, *Letters and Papers from Prison*, 52.

and honest enough? Maybe Barth would say, with reference to Mozart, by creating "music from a mysterious center," that is, by learning to know and observe limits.[83] But Barth would undoubtedly also agree with Bonhoeffer that it is not possible without recovering the *cantus firmus* that holds the disintegrating fragments of life together. But what is this *cantus firmus* in a post-Christendom, secularized yet strangely religiously fanatic world that is falling apart, and in which the "kingdom of heaven" has lost its allure?

THE HUMAN FACE OF THE TRANSCENDENT

Bonhoeffer was imprisoned in Tegel in 1943, suspected of helping Jews escape Nazi Germany. Exposed to the noise of prison, the cries of fearful men and the nearby din of exploding bombs,[84] he listens to Beethoven in the silence of his cell. He enters the contemplative world of the composer's deafness, and in this silent, transcendental moment he discerns, not the absence of God, but the inexpressible mystery of the God revealed in Jesus. As he had said ten years previously when he began his seminal lectures on Christology, we must be silent "before the Word," for our knowledge of God is not something that we grasp, but dependent on God's self-disclosure in Christ, which takes hold of us. In doing so, as he later says in prison, Christ becomes the *cantus firmus* that makes the polyphony of life possible.[85] Beethoven perfected polyphony only because Bach had developed the *cantus firmus* to the point where this became possible. If the center is not firm, everything falls apart. The orchestral instruments create cacophony not symphony.

Significantly, Bonhoeffer introduces the *cantus firmus* into his prison reflections while discussing the relationship between the love *of* God and the love *for* God with earthly, erotic love.[86] They are distinct and not to be confused, but the love of God provides the *cantus firmus* for the flourishing of earthly love. *Eros* needs *agape* to flourish as in the mystical Song of Songs.[87] The two, says Bonhoeffer, are "undivided and yet distinct," as are the divine and human natures of Christ. The Jesus who Bonhoeffer

---

83. Barth, *Wolfgang Amadeus Mozart*, 53.

84. See his poem "Night Voices," in Bonhoeffer, *Letters and Papers from Prison*, 462–70.

85. See Bonhoeffer, *Letters and Papers from Prison*, 394.

86. Bonhoeffer, *Letters and Papers from Prison*, 394.

87. Bonhoeffer, *Letters and Papers from Prison*, 394.

describes as the human being who "exists only for others" is not only the "Jesus of history" but also, and inseparably, "the Christ of faith." This is also fundamental to our understanding of the Christian life and redefines the meaning of transcendence. Transcendence remains divine, the "wholly Other," but it has a human face. Orthodox iconography recognizes this, and I have come to appreciate icons as a "means of grace," that is, as a way into the mystery of God through the face of Jesus, recognizably fully human but equally divine.[88] The face we discern in the neighbor who, in becoming Christ for us, fulfils our desire for transcendence in the love of God for the world (Matt 25:34–40).

The philosopher Roger Scruton speaks to this in his study of Wagner's *Parsifal* when he refers to liminal experiences such "as falling in love, recovering from illness, becoming a parent, and . . . encountering in awe the sublime works of nature." For it is in "these moments we stand at the threshold of the transcendent, reaching out to what cannot be attained or known. And that to which we reach must be understood in personal terms, since only then does it offer an answer to the unspoken question of our being: the question why?"[89] And the question why inevitably leads us back to the question, who then is the transcendent God we desire?

The theological musicologist Jeremy Begbie defines transcendence with reference to music as the art form that enables us to experience it. Echoing Bonhoeffer, and central to his argument, is the rejection of the idea that love of God and neighbor is at odds with the aesthetic desire for transcendence: "The antithesis between desire and love that many assume by default," says Begbie, "needs challenging." And it needs to be challenged because "to desire God's presence does not necessarily entail trying to enlist or manipulate God for our self-constructed purposes."[90] On the contrary, we must understand divine transcendence in terms of a "*transformative relation with God*" which is, in fact, initiated by God. In this way, transcendence comes to be understood in terms of love and grace rather than some philosophical notion.[91] Just as we should avoid applying our notions of justice to God's, which is always tempered by mercy and controlled by

---

88. See de Gruchy, *Icons as a Means of Grace*, 101–5.

89. Scruton, *Wagner's "Parsifal*," 87. Paraphrased by author.

90. Begbie, *Redeeming Transcendence in the Arts*, 70. See also de Gruchy, *This Monastic Moment*, 142, 151–58.

91. Begbie, *Redeeming Transcendence*, 71.

love,[92] so we must not begin with a definition of transcendence that we then apply to the God of Christian faith.

So, Bonhoeffer's last word on the meaning of transcendence, as we noted in Chapter 1, is categorical: "Jesus' 'being-for-others' is the experience of transcendence!" Therefore, "only through this liberation from self, through this 'being-for-others' unto death, do omnipotence, omniscience, and omnipresence come into being." What, then, does faith in God mean? It means "participating in this being of Jesus." Our "relationship to God is no 'religious' relationship to some highest, most powerful, and best being imaginable—that is no genuine transcendence. Instead, our relationship to God is a new life in 'being there for others,' through participation in the being of Jesus." Indeed, Bonhoeffer continues, the "transcendent is not the infinite, unattainable tasks, but the neighbor within reach in any given situation." God is not "the absolute, the metaphysical, the infinite, and so on," but 'the human being for others'! therefore the Crucified One. The human being living out of the transcendent."[93]

Maybe it was this sense of transformative transcendence that attracted Bonhoeffer to the vibrant spirituality of the African American spirituals, which overcame the tension between the Classical and Romantic traditions because it was deeply rooted in the lived experienced of suffering, the struggle for justice and liberation, and therefore in the Bible and the Christ of faith.[94] Or, as Green describes it, in an "authentic" or "a liberating and transforming transcendence" that can make an impact on society.[95] This is the radical message of the incarnation—God present among us in Jesus Christ: the One in whom the reality of God and the reality of the world (and therefore the reality of the "other") are reconciled.

A TIMELY, URGENT POSTSCRIPT

The death of the God of Christendom has resulted in a restless search for transcendence in what is left of Christendom and ended up either in a mystical withdrawal from the world or in political and economic power struggles to control the world. Bonhoeffer and Mann help us probe Nazism,

---

92. Heschel, *Prophets*, 214–15.

93. Bonhoeffer *Letters and Papers from Prison*, 501.

94. Young, *No Difference in the Fare*, 168–69; Feil, *Theology of Dietrich Bonhoeffer*, 196–99.

95. Green, *Bonhoeffer*, 299.

the greatest Faustian tragedy of twentieth-century history, but they also awaken us to the Faustian dangers of our own time so clearly manifest in the Ukrainian war but by no means confined there. The struggle to achieve social order and genuine peace based on justice tempered with mercy is global, just as the will to power is universal.

The notion that the last or the next war will bring all wars to an end has become a stale joke. We are deluded, that is, out of touch with reality, if we think that what happened in Nazi Germany or in any number of other places where dictators determine the fate of millions, cannot happen where we live. Realism should convince us otherwise and prepare us to counter such will-to-power, whether naked or subtle. When the rise and fall of the American empire is finally written, what reasons will be given for its demise? How could it be that the most powerful nation in history, the guardian of the "free world," and a nation in which Christianity is so predominant, is in danger of losing its status? Has it gained the whole world only to lose its soul? One major factor could be the global rise of right-wing White Christian nationalism, which, ironically, regards itself as the protector of freedom and traditional values while eroding its soul and fearing its own demise. But is this impulse toward soul erosion and fear not also present in what remains of Christendom as a whole, as Bonhoeffer argued in his essay "Heritage and Decay," posthumously published in his *Ethics*?[96]

However we look at it, the desire for transcendence and the destructive will-to-power remains central to the human and social struggles of our time. The question is whether our salvation lies with Nietzsche's nihilistic will-to-power or in the recovery of faith in God and our humanity. Christian faith says the latter. But then we must deal with our own egos, as Bonhoeffer discovered, for the will to power, whether expressed in politics, gender relations or in other ways, has its roots in our own innate desires for transcendence. We return, then, to the theme of the previous chapter: without *metanoia* or conversion there is no way forward.

Thomas Merton, the monk and mystical prophet for our day, as he was during the Cold and Vietnam Wars of yesterday, wrote in *Contemplation in a World of Action* that anyone "who attempts to act and do things for others in the world without deepening his own self-understanding, freedom, integrity and capacity to love, will not have anything to give others." On the contrary, we will only communicate our own obsessions, aggressions

---

96. Bonhoeffer, *Ethics*, 103–33.

and "ego-centered ambitions," prejudices and ideas.[97] If the deeply human desire for transcendence is not expressed in a desire to serve God for the sake of others—that is, if it is not a hunger and thirst for a just and more compassionate world—then it will always end up as a will to absolute and destructive power.

The problem goes much deeper, then, than the current crisis, as appalling as this is. Leverkühn's existential plight is symbolic of a contemporary cultural-spiritual hiatus that is greater than previously acknowledged: our very own humanity is being threatened by the amazing success of our own scientific advances. No wonder that the dystopian novel has replaced the myths of redemption. As Yuval Harari says of twenty-first-century Homo sapiens, we are making a determined effort to gain "immortality, bliss and divinity."[98] Such goals are potentially within reach through the advances of biomedical technology, artificial intelligence, and robotics. But such technological breakthroughs unrestrained by the ethical codes of religious traditions or genuinely humanist culture take us into new and dangerous moral territory, the subject of my next chapter. So, we return to where we began. Christian faith seeks to reconnect the mystical desire for God, which is of the essence of our humanity, to a prophetic commitment to justice, without which we will destroy both ourselves and the earth that sustains us.

---

97. Merton, *Contemplation in a World of Action*, 178–79.
98. Harari, *Homo Deus*, 350.

4

WISDOM

&
the Threat of Scientism and Soulless Technology

> Wisdom cries out in the street;
> In the squares she raises her voice.
> At the busiest corner she cries out;
> At the entrance of the city gates she speaks...
> How long... will fools hate knowledge?
>
> —Proverbs 1:20–21

> Science is not the answer to all our needs, and rationality is claiming things it cannot give. Modern technology underlies a series of major problems facing humanity today... Reason by itself cannot provide an ethical basis for living, and indeed a scientifically based outlook can lead to inhumanity just as much as fundamentalist religion can.
>
> —George Ellis[1]

Technology has become an end in itself. It has its own soul; its symbol is the machine, the embodiment of violation and exploitation of nature. A wholly new

---

1. Ellis, "On Rationality and Emotion," 3.

spirit has produced it, the spirit of violent subjection of nature to thinking and experimenting...

—Bonhoeffer[2]

Many Christians, mainly fundamentalists, assume science and reason are enemies of faith. This wariness goes back a long time, but it reached new heights in the controversy over evolution that erupted in the nineteenth century following the publication of Charles Darwin's *On the Origin of Species.* Nowadays few mainline Christians have a problem with evolution, but fundamentalists still have an aversion to science because its growing authority over the last few centuries has undermined their belief in the infallibility of the Bible. "How can we trust people who tell us we have evolved from apes?" they ask. So, during the COVID pandemic many Christians of this persuasion were among those turned their backs on scientific advice and refused vaccines. Yet, ironically, these despisers of science happily use modern technology without any hesitation in other ways, not least digital communication, patriotically supporting the development of military hardware and even taking their technologically sophisticated handguns with them to church. Science is not a problem if it serves your interests. But that is to identify the problem. Personal, ethnic, and national self-interest, not the common good has become normative.

At the other end of the spectrum, whether they are Christians or not, many people have an uncritically exalted view of science and technology. They assume that "scientists know all," even when pontificating on subjects outside their field. And they welcome all advances in technology as progress towards utopia. This uncritical faith in science is the secular equivalent of religious fundamentalism. I call it *scientism*, the equivalent of believing in an infallible Bible. Not God but science and technology can solve all the challenges that face us in the world today. But as George Ellis, a distinguished mathematician and cosmologist, aptly remarks, science alone "cannot provide an ethical basis for living, and indeed a scientifically based outlook can lead to inhumanity just as much as fundamentalist religion"[3]—

---

2. Bonhoeffer, *Ethics*, 116.
3. Ellis, "On Rationality and Emotion," 3.

hence Charles Villa-Vicencio's persuasive invitation to learn how to live creatively "between science and belief."[4]

THINKING THE UNTHINKABLE

In the lecture he gave at Union Theological Seminary in 1931 to which I earlier referred, Bonhoeffer insisted that theology starts with the "reality of God," but he admitted that we cannot make this claim without thinking about what we have just said. We are therefore immediately pulled into a circle of reasoning and the perennial debate about how we know certain things to be true (that is, *epistemology*). The problem for us Christians (and all theists irrespective of their religion) is that our knowledge of reality is *ultimately* based on faith in God, yet God, says Bonhoeffer, is "the reality ... which is beyond and outside of our thinking, of our whole existence."[5] Theology is therefore thinking about the unthinkable! As anyone who has seriously studied theology will know, it is preoccupied with this conundrum just as science is always preoccupied with uncertainty. But surely, you may ask, if it is unthinkable, it cannot be true, or at least in any commonsense way.

When I introduced this conundrum in Chapter 1, I mentioned the time when I first began to study theology and recalled the endless discussion we had on logical positivism and its claim that nothing could be true that was not empirically verifiable. I also recalled that some of the brightest of my fellow students gave up theology (like Mann's Leverkühn and the philosopher Nietzsche, who I discussed in the last chapter) and pursued other careers. For them belief in God was a meaningless proposition. By then, theology had long been dethroned as queen of the sciences, and agnosticism or atheism was the default opinion of the secularized intellectual West. Despite secularism theology has somehow survived, people still believe in God and even attend church, and Christian fundamentalism thrives alongside a great deal of religious quackery. If religion did not persist in such ways, there would have been little reason for Richard Dawkins to write *The God Delusion*. Nor would the late-in-life conversion of Anthony Flew, the leading analytical philosopher during my student days, have attracted much media attention and added unexpected spice to the contest

---

4. See Villa-Vicencio, *Living between Science and Belief*.
5. Bonhoeffer, *Barcelona, Berlin, New York*, 454

between atheism and theism.[6] For Dawkins and his fellow atheists, Flew's conversion was a sellout; for many Christians it was a victory. But in fact it was neither, for faith in God is not contingent on whether some scientists or philosophers believe and others don't, but on whether science alone and its offspring, technology, can save the world. Do science and technology provide a *more* satisfactory understanding of life, one that alone gives life meaning and purpose and enables us to deal adequately with the challenges facing us?

I find it ironical that many intellectual opponents of Christian faith, even when acknowledging rather paternalistically that some believers are more enlightened than others, seldom engage those theologians, who like Bonhoeffer, have taken their critique seriously and employed the canons of scientific inquiry in their work. For the evangelists of atheism, any faith claim in God is irrational, so there is little point in engaging theologians or joining hands in serving the common good together. Yet science is not value-free, and to assume or claim that it is, is disingenuous. It is common knowledge that scientific research is often funded by companies (tobacco, oil, and armaments companies being obvious examples) largely for their own benefit. Collecting and analyzing data is therefore by no means always, if ever, a neutral endeavour. If reason and science is needed to keep faith and theology honest, maybe critical theological and ethical reflection is necessary to keep science humble and honest, and therefore save it from being the servant of self-interest that sustains injustice, and technologies that are dehumanizing and destructive instruments of barbarism rather than life-giving.

The fact of the matter is that neither reason nor science is an enemy of faith. As anyone familiar with the theological controversies on faith and reason during the Middle Ages will know, the debate is nothing new. What is different is that back then theology was the queen of the sciences, not science, and so the advocates of faith had a controlling interest and almost veto powers in the discussion. Today, theology has been relegated to a back seat in public discourse while science reigns. And science reigns supreme not necessarily because it may have won the rational argument, but because of its amazing technological achievements. If the debate is starkly put as one between saving souls for heaven via faith in God or saving the planet from destruction through appropriate forms of technology, most people would put their energy into solar power rather than the power of prayer.

6. Flew, *There Is a God*; See McGrath, *Why God Won't Go Away*.

Following Bonhoeffer, I do not separate working for justice and praying, but all commonsense realists do.

If the issues raised by science and technology facing us today were simply intellectual and academic, like creation versus evolution, we might ignore them or discuss them in our spare time over coffee. But that is no longer the case. If the COVID-19 pandemic has taught us nothing else, it has taught us that the distrust of scientists and their advice can be deadly. And this is only one of many examples of the importance of science and technology in responding to the challenges of living in the world as it is. Of course, sometimes scientists get it wrong; in fact, that is how science progresses, through trial and error. This painstaking process may not be of much interest to others outside the scientific community or laboratory, but it is of great concern to us. It is the reason why, for example, trials and tests for vaccines are so important.

But what is equally important for us is the ability to recognize that not all technological advances are for our own good or that of the planet. Both the development of heart surgery, of which I am a beneficiary, and the atomic bomb, are the outcomes of amazing scientific endeavour, but their consequences for human well-being are obviously incomparable. In keeping a critical eye on science, theology may sometimes challenge some of its theoretical assumptions but its main concern should be whether its technological developments serve the common good. If theology does not challenge these developments, for us as for Bonhoeffer, it becomes technology without soul, dehumanizing and deadly.

SOULLESS TECHNOLOGY

One of the earliest attempts to unpack the impact of technology on civilization was Lewis Mumford's *Technics and Civilization*, written in 1930 and published the year after Hitler came to power. Tracing the rise and influence of modern technology from the thirteenth century to the first half of the twentieth, Mumford showed how it had the power to change the world as much for evil as for good. Mumford was a conversation partner of Reinhold Niebuhr, Bonhoeffer's theological professor in New York in 1930–1931.

As far as I can tell, Bonhoeffer makes no reference to Mumford's writings, but he does comment in much the same vein about the danger of "technological organization" as a "threat to life."[7] And he would undoubtedly concur with Mumford's concluding warning that while science and technology have taught us "that nothing is impossible," left to itself that includes the possibility of destroying civilization and planet Earth. "It would be a great mistake," Mumford wrote, "to seek wholly within the field of technics for an answer to all the problems that have been raised by technics."[8] A decade later, as the Nazi war machine conquered much of Europe and he became aware of the gas chambers, Bonhoeffer was far more pessimistic. In his essay on "Heritage and Decay" he writes: "The technology of the modern West has freed itself from every kind of service." It no longer serves nature but seeks to master it, violently subjecting it to human control and experimentation. In sum: "Technology has become an end in itself. It has its own soul; its symbol is the machine, the embodiment of violation and exploitation of nature." Such technology, says Bonhoeffer, is driven by "a human hubris that would build a world counter to the one God created . . . a technology that conquers time and space" and so "defies God." Its benefits, he adds, "pale beside its demonic powers."[9]

I am personally very grateful for the amazing advances in medical technology that have kept me alive, and for developments in computer technology that have made writing this book more possible than it might have been. I also know that the human genome project holds out great promise in treating disease, and that without major advances in communications technology, life would have been much more difficult for most of us during the COVID-19 pandemic, to say nothing about the development of vaccines. But as I write, I watch monstrous Russian tanks roll into Ukraine, missiles destroying homes, factories, hospitals and schools; lives are shattered, families scattered, and fear spreads across the land. I wonder to myself, Will anyone be attending the splendid Orthodox churches pictured in the TV visuals today, and what will their priest say in Kiev and Moscow? What would I say? All words seem banal. Yet the Ukraine war is not an exception; there are other conflicts taking place as I write, as they have since ancient times. And increasingly more brutal technologies have been developed to wage them. Technology is a terrible two-edged sword, saving and destroying life at the same time.

---

7. Bonhoeffer, *Letters and Papers from Prison*, 500.
8. Mumford, *Technics and Civilization*, 434.
9. Bonhoeffer, *Ethics*, 116.

But from the beginning, humans have been tool makers, so technology is central to our evolutionary story and central to our development for good. From food production to housing, from transport to communication, and from health care to the provision of clean water, we are now all virtually dependent on technology, at least when it works and is available. But that does not mean that science is infallible or that technology can save the world from disaster. On the contrary, technology can destroy both us and this fragile planet. Yet technology is not the problem; people are.

The motives that drive the production of weapons of mass destruction are not the same as those that lead to the betterment of health and the well-being of people and the environment. So, the challenge facing faith as it engages science and technology is clear, even though the issues may be complex, and decisions exceedingly difficult to make. Much, if not everything, depends on human responsibility. This means that science and technology must be held accountable, that boundaries must be respected, and scientific claims scrutinized. Unfortunately, humankind is not always known for either its humility or its wisdom. More often it is known for its stupidity.

STUPIDITY & WISDOM

Bonhoeffer was seldom engaged in the discussion between theology and science until, in prison, he became passionately interested in the subject.[10] But as we have seen, he was bothered by the danger of "technological organization" as he pondered the future of Christianity and the world. He was equally appalled by the fact that a nation as educated, knowledgeable, and scientifically advanced as Germany had fallen prey to Nazism. Of course, many scientists fled Germany in what was a veritable brain drain before the war began. But how ironic it was that the brilliant scientist and close friend of Einstein, Fritz Haber (1868–1934), who won many awards (including a Nobel Prize) for improving agriculture and staving off famine across the world, also developed the gas used to exterminate Jews and others in the death camps of the Third Reich, and his inventions have subsequently contributed to agricultural unsustainability.[11]

---

10. Bethge, "Nonreligious Scientist and the Confessing Theologian"; see also de Gruchy, *Bonhoeffer's Questions*, 110–14.
11. Rasmussen, *Earth-Honoring Faith*, 348–51.

In "After Ten Years" Bonhoeffer identified stupidity as one of the reasons for the capitulation of Germany to the wiles of Hitler. But reading his words today it is as if he were writing for us and our time as well. Stupidity he wrote, "is a more dangerous enemy of the good than malice." We can protest and expose evil, we can also prevent it by force when necessary, but against "stupidity we are defenseless." We become deaf to reason and ignore facts that contradict our prejudices. Indeed, says Bonhoeffer, "the stupid person is utterly self-satisfied and, being easily irritated, becomes dangerous by going on the attack." He even warns us that it is "senseless and dangerous" to try and "persuade the stupid person with reasons," for stupidity is "not an intellectual defect but a human one." There are, he says, "human beings who are of remarkably agile intellect yet stupid, and others who are intellectually quite dull yet anything but stupid." In other words, the appeal to reason to solve problems and prevent conflict, while eminently sensible, is, quite literally, not foolproof. Bonhoeffer also notes that "under certain circumstances, people are made stupid or that they allow this to happen to them."[12]

The widespread distrust of science demonstrated during the COVID-19 pandemic, startlingly evident in the gullibility of people who trust fake news and support the antivax movement across the world, indicates that we are currently living in circumstances when reason seldom seems able to convince everyone, and stupidity flourishes, even in "the household of faith." But Bonhoeffer, who had great confidence in reason, was also caustic about "reasonable people" just as he was about "stupidity." That is, people who naively misread reality and thought that "with the best of intentions" and "a bit of reason" they could "stop Hitler in his tracks" and "patch up a structure that has come out of joint." They were not unintelligent or badly educated, but they lacked the wisdom to recognize evil and take decisive action. Trying "to do justice on every side," they are "crushed by the colliding forces without having accomplished anything at all. Disappointed that the world is so unreasonable, they see themselves condemned to unproductiveness; they withdraw in resignation or helplessly fall victim to the stronger."[13]

Biblical faith is always wary of the "wisdom of this world." The phrase does not refer to wisdom as such, or to knowledge in general, but to ersatz wisdom guided by self-interest, the will to power, and arrogance. Medieval

12. Bonhoeffer, *Letters and Papers from Prison*, 43.
13. Bonhoeffer, *Letters and Papers from Prison*. 38–39.

monks spoke about the seven deadly sins that produced such debased wisdom in contrast to the biblical or theological virtues of faith, love, and hope, along with the cardinal virtues derived from Aristotle: justice, prudence, temperance, and courage. We may be born with intelligence, but true wisdom is not innate; it must be nurtured and informed by vibrant moral and faith communities, informed by lived experience and critical reason. Part of the challenge facing us today is that society, especially Western secular society, has largely lost touch with such virtue formation, and as Alasdair MacIntyre described in *After Virtue*, there is no way to recover that without rebuilding the communities that foster it. MacIntyre's widely quoted conclusion is that in these "dark ages" we are waiting "for another—doubtless very different—St. Benedict."[14]

The material crisis we face is, at heart, a spiritual crisis, a lack of wisdom, discernment, and commitment to the common global good. Perhaps this is a reason why in recent years there has been a renewal of interest in the biblical wisdom tradition. Instead of emphasizing only God's revelation in history, as in the prophetic tradition, the wisdom literature draws on God's revelation in nature and creation. Its data is the "lived experience" of generations that confirms the moral character of the universe, links deeds to consequences, and discerns "the hidden character and underpinnings of all of reality."[15]

If the prophets of ancient Israel warned the nation not to put its trust in weapons of war because this signaled a lack of trust in YHWH, its sages drew on experience, and added that "wisdom is better than weapons of war (Prov 9:18; Isa 36:9). If the proud display of weapons in military parades is condemned by the prophets as an act of national idolatry, the sages note that the reliance on them is simply foolish. The problem is that just as nations and people seldom listen to prophets, they also seldom learn from sages, or from experience, about the futility of bad policies and actions until it is too late to prevent what then becomes inevitable. Practical wisdom, like preventative medicine, anticipates consequences rather than waiting to resolve them after they have happened.

Larry Rasmussen, who has so ably shown us how the biblical wisdom tradition speaks to the environmental challenges facing us today in his *Earth-Honoring Faith*, concludes that "Gaining wisdom" is about "more

---

14. MacIntyre, *After Virtue*, 245. See de Gruchy, *This Monastic Moment*, 140.

15. Brueggemann, *Theology of the Old Testament*, 681. See also Deane-Drummond, *Creation through Wisdom*.

than genes for humans; it is more than brains, too. It's learning, including the collective social learning and cooperation of cultural innovation and adaptation." Gaining wisdom, Rasmussen continues, "requires various angles of vision, some sufficiently askew of the going paradigms so as to supply the breakthrough insight of another way, whether in science or daily living." It is about "thinking outside the prevailing paradigm," which is also necessary for "cultural innovation and adaptation."[16] But is there a specifically Christian perspective that can be included in the mix?

CHRIST AS THE WISDOM OF GOD

In his Christology lectures, which he gave in Berlin in the summer of 1932, Bonhoeffer said that Christ is not only the center of our existence as persons, or the center of history, but also the center of nature.[17] If the reality of God and the world find their focus in the reality of Christ, what exactly does this mean for nature? Unfortunately, Bonhoeffer did not finish his lectures with a promised section on the cosmic Christ. But the wisdom of redemptive and restorative love of God for the world in Christ clearly provides the key. And we also get a glimpse into the direction of his thinking from some brief comments in his *Letters and Papers from Prison* where he writes about the *recapitulation of all reality* in Christ, a remarkable conviction of faith also expressed in the letters to the Ephesians and the Colossians.[18] For Bonhoeffer, this was a "consummately consoling thought" because it meant that everything has meaning, purpose and direction within the economy of God. In other words, both the conception and the summation of the world is to be understood in terms of the self-emptying love of God in Christ, who is the "alpha and the omega." That is why Paul writes to the Romans that the whole of creation is waiting for us to set it free from the bondage of our sinful abuse (Rom 8:21).

This breathtaking cosmic understanding of Christ also connects Bonhoeffer's Christology with that of the scientist-priest Teilhard de Chardin. Instead of the theory of evolution and Christian faith being at loggerheads, Teilhard sees them converging at the Omega or end point of human evolution, bringing both science and faith together in a cosmic understanding

---

16. Rasmussen, *Earth-Honoring Faith*, 356.
17. Bonhoeffer, *Berlin 1932–1933*, 324–28.
18. Bonhoeffer, *Letters and Papers from Prison*, 246. See Eph 1:10; Col 1:20.

of reality as the summation of all things in love.[19] In a secular world, and probably in most scientific circles, all this might sound like mumbo jumbo, but it derives from an understanding that while the reality of God might be overshadowed by the reality of the world, appearing weak and foolish, it is actually a power and wisdom that redeems the world, even if hidden from the worldly-wise and the intelligent (Matt 11:25; 1 Cor 1:18–25). Thus, to speak of the power of God revealed in the weakness of the cross, as Bonhoeffer says, does not mean that God exists only on the boundaries of human existence, nor does it mean that God is only a stopgap to whom we turn when our scientific knowledge fails to explain reality, for then "God too is pushed further away and thus is ever on the retreat."[20]

What, then, is this wisdom that changes the way we look at the world? Self-giving love is the wisdom of nonviolence, of forgiveness, of justice, and of hope. These are some of the characteristics of the wisdom that guides and informs faith in facing the reality of human stupidity and "technological organization," which, as Bonhoeffer said, has "conquered the soul."[21] Wisdom is insight that derives from lived experience and theological and ethical reflection; it is cumulative and practical; it informs attitudes and guides actions that are creative and redemptive. Wisdom builds community in serving the common good. In short, wisdom restores the soul and as such is an adjunct of faith, a fruit of the Spirit without which we cannot face reality. Such wisdom enables us to face the unpredictable, think the unthinkable, and discern the way to life. The world is awash with knowledge; what it lacks is this wisdom that gives us insight into reality and ultimately derives from authentic faith in God whether recognized or not. A faith that respects the boundaries of our humanity and transcends the limits of our rationality, but does so as a critical companion to, not an enemy of, reason or science.

SCIENCE IS OUR CRITICAL COMPANION

As a Christian humanist I am convinced, with Bonhoeffer, that we should be on the same side as science in fighting obscurantism, stupidity, intellectual arrogance, and the abuse of people and power, rather than fighting

---

19. Teilhard de Chardin, *Phenomenon of Man*, 254–72. See Durand, *Evolusie, Wetenskap en* Geloof, 306–7; de Gruchy, *Confessions of a Christian Humanist*, 96–97, 160–61.

20. Bonhoeffer, *Letters and Papers from Prison*. 405–47.

21. Bonhoeffer, *Letters and Papers from Prison*, 500.

each other. Indeed, in the closing chapter of *Rationality* Steven Pinker invites us all to participate in the humanist project by appealing to the legacy of Martin Luther King Jr., a man of prophetic Christian faith. All people of goodwill, whether believers or not, should engage together in the struggle for the common good.[22] But this does not mean we must surrender our faith-convictions in doing so. For not only are those convictions the reason why I affirm so much of what Pinker says, they also raise critical questions that faith must put to science and technology as our companion in serving the world. Some of these I have already raised in this chapter. But now I want to clarify the relationship between science and theology.

I return to the lecture on which this chapter is based. It was prompted by an essay by the Catholic theologian William Cavanaugh titled "Atheism & Scientism, Evolution & Christian Faith." In his essay, Cavanaugh critically engaged Pinker and Leon Wieseltier, the literary editor of the *New Republic*, on the relation between science and the humanities.[23] In doing so he referred to my discussion on science and theology in *Led into Mystery*, suggesting that I offered a "radical alternative" to the way this is generally understood. I do not make that claim myself, but I am delighted that Cavanaugh does. In truth, it did not occur to me at the time.

Pinker's article "Science Is Not Your Enemy,"[24] together with Wieseltier's rejoinder, was published online on August 6th, 2013, the anniversary, as Cavanaugh reminds us, of the dropping of the first atomic bomb on Hiroshima—an important reminder that the debate about science and theology is not merely academic but has to do with moral values and the imperatives that affect public policy and its outcomes for good or ill on a massive, even terrifying scale. So let me begin by emphasizing that while scientific methodology may be beyond reproach, though not beyond perfecting, the pursuit of science is neither ideologically free nor morally innocent, and therefore "scientific understanding" is insufficient as a moral compass.

In his article Pinker acknowledges the bad side of science but launches a strong defense of what he labels "scientism" in a "good sense." It's a pity he uses the word *scientism* in a good and bad sense because for me, and I suspect most people, *scientism*, as I have previously said, means bad science. It is scientific fundamentalism, arrogant in its claims and dangerous in its consequences—among them destructive technologies. It is the threat

---

22. Pinker, *Rationality*, 339.
23. Cavanaugh, "Science and Theology."
24. Pinker, "Science Is Not Your Enemy."

of scientism (not science), and destructive technologies (not technology per se) that confronts faith today. Pinker is by no means a "scientific fundamentalist." He firmly rejects the claim that science is all that matters, that scientists can solve all problems, and that all current scientific hypotheses are true. Good science, the science that Pinker espouses and promotes, does not have, as he puts it, "an imperialistic drive to occupy the humanities" rather, for him, "the promise of science is to enrich and diversify the intellectual tools of humanistic scholarship." Good science, he says, "is not the dogma that physical stuff is the only thing that exists." Scientists, he continues, are "immersed in the ethereal medium of information, including the truths of mathematics, the logic of their theories, and the values that guide their enterprise." Therefore science "is of a piece with philosophy, reason, and Enlightenment humanism."

So far so good. Pinker's position makes him an admirable partner for theology in serving the common good. But as he proceeds, his case becomes a little clouded. Pinker's humanism is not only "inextricable from a scientific understanding of the world," it is also, he claims, "becoming the de facto morality of modern democracies, international organizations, and liberalizing religions, and its unfulfilled promises define the moral imperatives we face today." Despite his inclusion of "liberalizing religions" among the forces for good in the world, Pinker insists that the liberalizing of religion "requires a radical break from religious conceptions of meaning and value." We can no longer, he says, naively accept "the traditional causes of belief" or their moral prescriptions, which come to us from the past. Meaning and values are defined by a scientific understanding of the world.

This is an audacious claim. In a sentence Pinker writes off, unwittingly I suspect, the wisdom of the ages whether religious or otherwise, the virtues whether theological or philosophical that have guided us over the centuries, and has placed morality on the shaky foundation of science. I say shaky because science has no indisputable moral axioms. By its very nature, science is always in flux, correcting previous errors (even positions long regarded as axiomatic), developing in new directions, and sometimes degenerating into scientism. In James Gleick's words, "Professional scientists, given brief glimpses of nature's workings, are no less vulnerable to anguish and confusion when they come face to face with incongruity. And incongruity, when it changes the way a scientist sees, makes possible the most important advances."[25] Science achieves much precisely because in-

---

25. Gleick, *Chaos*, 36. Gleick is paraphrasing Thomas Kuhn.

novation, rather than received wisdom, is built into its structure. But that does not mean that science can function for the common good without wisdom, which, as I have argued, is more than simply relying on reason.

Pinker rejects, as do I, any "two-state solution" to the relationship between science and the humanities whereby they exist in segregated silos. They need to engage each other, but (and here is the rub) Pinker insists that the scientific worldview and empirical investigation *alone* can guide "the moral and spiritual values of an educated person today." How then can science and the humanities truly engage each other as partners? Leaving aside the elitist implication he draws from his position, that science is not able to guide the "uneducated person" (who, to my mind, often demonstrate a great deal of wisdom), what he is saying also implies that science is not really interested in being a partner with the humanities or religion *in serving the common good*. It is science that determines what is of moral value. This echoes Edward Wilson's comment that "science is a continuation on new and better-tested ground to attain the same end . . . science is religion liberated and writ large."[26] Scientific triumphalism, I fear, has replaced religious triumphalism. In doing so it becomes scientism, which is not good science.

By now it should be evident that my rejection of scientism is not a rejection of scientific inquiry or methodology, nor am I, for example, denying the centrality of the brain in the process of finding meaning in life or articulating moral values.[27] Scientific objectivity is something for which we should all strive, but we should not be deluded into thinking that we can achieve it, and in some fields (the fine and performing arts for example) it is not germane even if truth and integrity are regarded as necessary prerogatives. As Iain McGilchrist reminds us, the artificial precision of our language, controlled by the left side of the brain, always betrays us.[28] So while the dominance of the scientific mythos is understandable, it cannot be true "that there is one logical path to knowledge, irrespective of context," or "that science is the only sure foundation for decency and morality."[29] What, then, is the solution to the apparent conflict on the role of science and the humanities in defining morality?

In his 1931 lecture at Union Seminary in New York, which I mentioned previously, Bonhoeffer said that as "far as science is a discovery of

---

26. Wilson *Consilience*, 5.
27. See de Gruchy, *Led into Mystery*, 144–51.
28. McGilchrist, *Master and His Emissary*, 157.
29. McGilchrist, *Master and His Emissary*, 385.

happening facts, theology is not touched (because theology is concerned only with a certain interpretation of facts). If science itself gives its own interpretation of the world, then it belongs to philosophy and is subjected to the critique of theology."[30] But, just as Bonhoeffer increasingly opposed "thinking in two spheres" in other areas of life (for example, the church and politics), he would have opposed keeping science and theology in separate compartments, the first dealing with "facts" and the second with "values," as distinct from interpretation.

In his lively response to Pinker, Wieseltier defends a "two-state solution" in defining this partnership, with clear boundaries between science, and the humanities and religion. In this way the humanities can keep a critical eye on the sciences in providing moral guidance, and science confine itself to facts on the ground even though knowing where to draw the line may be difficult. Wieseltier states his case in his opening paragraph:

> It is not for science to say whether science belongs in morality and politics and art. Those are philosophical matters, and science is not philosophy, even if philosophy has since its beginnings been receptive to science. Nor does science confer any license to extend its categories and its methods beyond its own realms, whose contours are of course a matter of debate.

Wieseltier goes on to say that the very "credibility of physicists and biologists and economists on the subject of the meaning of life . . . cannot be owed to their work in physics and biology and economics, however distinguished it is."[31] Thinking religious people, as Wieseltier says, have long taken science into account in stating their faith convictions but have also insisted that there are differences between the natural sciences and humanities, which have to do with meaning and value. Scientism, he adds, reduces everything to "an underlying sameness" that "can only distort the richness and plurality of lived existence." To the contrary, Wieseltier defends "the irreducible reality of inwardness, and its autonomy as a category of understanding." Boundaries need to be drawn to resist the "totalizing mentality" of scientism.

At this point Cavanaugh and I are on the same side as Wieseltier. But neither of us is satisfied, any more than is Pinker, though for different reasons, with the "two-state solution," and certainly not if it separates an inner world from the outer as though they exist in disconnected spheres.

30. Bonhoeffer, *Barcelona, Berlin, New York*, 475.
31. Wieseltier, "Crimes against Humanities."

Nevertheless, Cavanaugh and I equally distance ourselves from reductive scientism because it not only undermines value and meaning, but as seriously it also undermines *the significance of matter* and our ability to understand it. For that reason, the two-state solution is an unsatisfactory way to relate science and theology, which is a view shared by many theologians and scientists engaged in the dialogue between the two disciplines.

Generally, in the contemporary dialogue between science and theology they are related under the rubric of "critical realism." Critical realism, as Ian Barbour, who first articulated the approach, writes, "can point to both the extraordinarily abstract character of theoretical physics and the necessity of experimental observation which distinguishes it from pure mathematics."[32] Critical realism, as distinct from "naive realism," means that the real is what is intelligible and logical but not necessarily what is observable and empirically verifiable. This is as true for the social sciences, the humanities, and theology as it is for natural science, even if in different degrees.

Disciplinary methodologies vary according to their subject, but they all claim to be "scientific" (at least in the German sense of *Wissenshaftlich*) in their approach. Not all philosophical or theological explanations can be empirically verified, but they can all be critically evaluated within their respective disciplinary communities and the humanist enterprise whether Christian or otherwise. The key issue is the explanatory power of a particular discipline within its own guild and in dialogue with others.[33] Of course, as it is always possible and often likely that there will be different approaches and answers between and within disciplinary communities, relying on explanatory power for evaluating claims within a discipline is not foolproof. But there is no alternative.

Neither Cavanaugh nor I, as Cavanaugh puts it, "settle for a recognition of the autonomy of science in the realm of fact, while leaving theology only to provide the values that help to make sense of the facts." But my rejection of the "two-state solution," according to Cavanaugh, goes deeper than claiming "that science errs when it crosses borders into theological or philosophical territory, or pretends to explain all, rather than part, of reality." I am not simply challenging the notion that science is only a neutral descriptor of principles and procedures, or that "empirical research is the only way of knowing the truth." I am saying that such scientific reductionism is

---

32. Barbour, *Issues in Science and Religion*, 172.
33. See Russell and Wegter-McNelly, "Science," 513–16.

untrue. This, says Cavanaugh, has a "profoundly unsettling effect on the two-state solution." As he summarizes my position, "Science, then, does not reveal reality, to which mystery is then superadded." Rather, mystery is "beneath the real," it "transcends empirical reality," and "seems to indicate that reality without this transcendence is not reality at all." If that is so, science *"without transcendence does not reveal reality; it is not merely incomplete but untrue."*[34] The truth, I believe, is that only those who are willing to face reality will discern mystery, and only those who are open to mystery will discover reality.[35] Reality is mystery laden. A meaningful relation between science and theology is therefore contingent on a recognition that there is more to reality than meets the eye whether aided by the microscope and telescope or not.

SCIENCE WITHOUT TRANSCENDENCE IS UNTRUE

Physical reality is fundamental to all reality. That is why physics is the foundational science—beginning with particle physics, on which is built atomic physics, physical chemistry and up the hierarchy of structure and causation to cosmology. But physical reality is not the sum total of reality. In fact, Ellis speaks of four worlds of reality. The first is the physical world of matter and forces; the second, that of individual and communal consciousness; the third, that of Aristotelian possibilities, namely, "the ontological status of the laws of physics," which is unknown, but real; and the fourth, the Platonic worlds of abstract realities: mathematics, logic, and algorithms, each of which is represented in the brain but is independent of human existence.[36]

The thoughts we have are real (they exist), but even though they are processed by the brain, they are not physical; mathematical equations or beauty, truth, and goodness are similar. These are ontologically real irrespective of how they are neurologically explained or physically embodied, and they are so because we can demonstrate that they have a causal effect on physical entities. If this is so, then any transcendental Idea actually or potentially *un*related to physical reality is *un*real.

But then so is reductive materialism, for in not acknowledging mystery it becomes a closed system impervious to critical reflection except on its own terms, thereby excluding possibilities of reality that mystery

34. Cavanaugh, "Science and Theology" (italics added).
35. See de Gruchy, *Led into Mystery*, 44, 115–20.
36. Ellis, "True Complexity."

discloses. As Cavanaugh puts it, "A purely immanent materialism . . . is not a true appreciation of the material but an evacuation from matter of the only thing that truly makes it matter, which is its link to something beyond itself." In this sense, all material things "are not self-sufficient but constantly receive being, and therefore meaning, from a transcendent source beyond themselves." To grasp something means "to situate it within the larger telos or end of all creation, which has been sent forth from God and is returning to God. Matter only matters, in other words, when it is related to a transcendent cause larger than itself."[37] Whereas mystery encounters us always in the penultimate, mystery is rooted in the ultimate, and therefore it never ceases to be mystery; its character as mystery only deepens as we are led deeper into it.[38] But reality remains located for us in the penultimate where it confronts faith. Science and faith do not exist in separate silos because physical reality is foundational for both. God is unknowable apart from worldly reality and only becomes known to faith through our participation in such reality.

Dumas, as I have previously noted, referred to Bonhoeffer as a "theologian of reality (*Wirklichkeit*)," because he responded to "the alternatives, whether they be a dogmatic and unreal transcendence or a nihilistic and tragic denial of truth . . . not from the standpoint of naïve realism but on the basis of a christological ontology, insisting that the truth of God is hidden in the reality of the world."[39] From a Christian perspective, the mystery that lies at the core of reality has been disclosed in Jesus Christ. This audacious claim is mythically expressed in the Epiphany narrative when sages, representing the wisdom of the east, acknowledge the incarnation of the *logos* or eternal wisdom. This will not satisfy secular reason or historical criticism, but that does not mean it has no explanatory or ontological significance as discerned by faith.

The incarnation is the presupposition of Christian faith precisely because the mystery of God is disclosed in material reality. Christianity is, for that reason, profoundly materialist, albeit in a nonreductive sense.[40] The mystery we name God is disclosed to faith by participating in matter. The incarnate Word is "truly God and truly human." To repeat Bonhoeffer's words: "In Jesus Christ the reality of God has entered into the reality of

---

37. Cavanaugh, "Science and Theology."
38. See Tietz, "Mysteries of Knowledge," 45.
39. Dumas, *Dietrich Bonhoeffer: Theologian of Reality*, 37.
40. Murphy, *Bodies and Souls*, 5–6, 52.

the world."⁴¹ God is not an eternal Idea, but self-giving or kenotic love embodied in and disclosed to us in historical reality. The transcendent Other is revealed in Jesus of Nazareth. The mystery of the Son of Humanity to which the Gospels bear witness is made evident to faith in the "signs" that "reveal his glory" in John, or in the "wonders and miracles" that abound in the Synoptics.

It is undoubtedly true that not everyone in the narrative sees the glory or has the faith to discern the significance of the miracles—that is, as a means of discerning the mystery of God present in Jesus as Messiah. In fact, many who witnessed the miracles soon turned away from following Jesus as the cost of doing so became more apparent. That is, when it became clear that the mystery being revealed was not an escape from reality but an engagement with reality, not least political reality, that might require suffering and even death. Christian faith, then, takes empirical reality as fundamental to critical reflection, but in doing so recognizes that there is more to reality than meets the eye. This is the reason why Christianity rejects both dualism in any unqualified form and positivist realism, and why Bonhoeffer rejects "thinking in two realms"—not just with reference to the separation of church and state but also with reference to a wider "range of dualisms."⁴² Among these is the separation of "body and soul."

RECOVERING SOUL

The human person is not a disembodied soul but a complex psychosomatic whole in relation to God, the other, and the world. A surgeon may treat her patient on the operating table as a purely physical, mechanical entity, but good surgeons respect the person as person, that is, in traditional language, as body and soul. Just as there is more to reality that we can see, there is more to being human than having a body; that is the mystery of our humanity. Respecting the psychosomatic reality of being human, and therefore respecting human dignity and rights is an acknowledgement of this reality that faith perceives and defends against dehumanizing forces that, in Bonhoeffer's words, "conquer the soul."⁴³ Human beings who are truly in touch with reality, then, are especially sensitive to the reality of human

---

41. Bonhoeffer, *Ethics*, 54.
42. Bonhoeffer, *Ethics*, 35.
43. Bonhoeffer, *Letters and Papers from Prison*, 500.

suffering and crimes against humanity. Science cannot get to the existential heart of our humanity in the way Job, Jeremiah, and Dostoevsky do.

But the mystery we name God and the enigma of being human must also always be considered in relation to each other. We cannot know God apart from knowing ourselves any more than we can know ourselves apart from knowing God. In naming ultimate mystery "God," theists personalize Transcendence or Ultimate Reality, to use Paul Tillich's term.[44] This distinguishes theistic and nontheistic mysticism even though otherwise they share similar characteristics. But the Christian reason for insisting on the personality of transcendence is precisely because it is mediated through "the other," and is best, even if inadequately, described (as Bonhoeffer described the relation) in "I-Thou" rather than "I-It" terms, but not in an individualistic way.[45] The soul is always embodied, a person *in relation to others*; it fact we cannot *meaningfully* relate to any other in any other way.

Personalizing ultimate reality and naming such reality God also creates a mythos or story in which mystery is related to the world and humanity in ways that give meaning and hope to us not just as individuals but as communities. This is of the essence of religion: its rituals, its sacramental life, and its ability to discern wisdom over time and place. To attack religion is not to attack God, as many assume; it is to debunk the framework within which the word *God* is explained and the experience of God is shared. Of course, in so far as theism is embedded in religious tradition it is vulnerable to debunking, in the process of which the word *God* often becomes unusable in expressing ultimacy. Idolatry is the obvious example because it is the attempt to collapse the ultimate in into the penultimate. This is evident within the Bible itself where concepts of God are continually challenged by the revelation of YHWH as beyond human grasp. Ultimate mystery does not exist as one entity among others waiting to be discovered in the gaps of our knowledge and then being excluded once the gaps have been filled or explained. Reality is not waiting to be discovered by empirical methods; reality confronts, questions, and unsettles us; reality makes moral demands on us precisely because it is the medium of mystery.

In his prison reflections on "religion in a world-come-of-age," Bonhoeffer does not encourage the demythologization of religion because for him, myth is the mediator of mystery, providing the narrative that enables us to relate to it. Instead, Bonhoeffer proposes interpreting biblical and

---

44. See Tillich, *Theology of Culture*, 127–32.
45. See Green, *Bonhoeffer*, 29, 129–44.

specifically Christian concepts central to the narrative, that is, the mysteries of faith, "in a way that does not make religion the condition for faith."[46] In other words, the various secular critiques of religion, whether scientific or philosophical, may be valid but generally miss the point when it comes to mystery. Christian faith in God as ultimate mystery is not dependent on religion. Religion is not the essence of faith; it provides the framework within which faith is expressed; in which meaning is sought and celebrated; in which community is fostered, identity affirmed, and convictions communicated from one generation to the next. Religion, for all its inadequacies and weaknesses, is a witness to mystery not by indulging in flights of fantasy but by virtue of its historical existence.

In seeking to respond to the reality that faces us, we therefore need to understand the spiritual and moral crisis facing civilization. In seeking to control the reality of the world, that is material reality, through science and technology, we have lost touch with the reality of God. Despite the explosion in our knowledge of the world, we lack the wisdom that derives from the "fear of God." In affirming and celebrating the secular, we have fallen prey to secularism and scientism; we have reduced reality to the mundane; in expanding the boundaries of our knowledge we have lost touch with the wisdom needed to live life responsibly "before God." That, says Bonhoeffer, "is the only genuine way to overcome stupidity."[47] And the Christian contribution to that task is participating with all who are committed to it, not by silencing the core convictions of the faith we confess but by affirming them. There is a hermeneutical as well as a practical task demanded of us, and they are inseparable.

The practical is obvious. Christians need to be involved in concrete ways with people of other faiths and those of none who are committed to working for the common good. They cannot contribute to the ethical discourse from outside the arena of moral action. Bonhoeffer's "ethics of free responsibility" was developed as he became more involved in the Resistance against Hitler alongside his secular humanist compatriots. But it was precisely this that also led him to his hermeneutical endeavors when, in prison, he began outlining his understanding of Christian faith and action in a world "come-of-age," not by surrendering core convictions but by restating them.

---

46. Bonhoeffer, *Letters and Papers from Prison*, 430.
47. Bonhoeffer, *Letters and Papers from Prison*, 44.

Christian theology and ethics cannot contribute to the pursuit of human well-being, of justice and peace in a world torn apart by religious fundamentalism, scientism, and secularism if it surrenders its core convictions. For it is these that make Christian faith liberating and humanist, and therefore able to participate with others in making the world a better, more humane place in which to live. This does not mean that we should thrust our faith convictions on others in a take-it-or-leave-it manner, but rather we must find the language we need to express them within the broader context of moral discourse. And that includes scientists who operate with a very different discourse.

To clarify, ethics has to do with critical and systematic thinking about moral agency, about the criteria for establishing what is good or moral. Scientists may be morally exemplary but are not trained qua scientists to engage in critical ethical reflection or even in the philosophy of science. They approach moral issues as human beings who are culturally located and therefore with perspectives that have been fashioned in a variety of ways, not least by social forces and even by religious traditions. Specifically, Christian ethics is critical and systematic thinking about "the good" in relation to Christian faith claims and the reality that confronts us—for example, abortion, racism, global warming, or war. For this reason, Christian ethics cannot ignore scientific knowledge that contributes to our understanding of the issues. But neither can atheist scientists be allowed to get away with moral conclusions based on scientific understanding alone without taking philosophical objections seriously into account.

Christian ethics links critical theological reflection on the mystery we name God, which we discern in Jesus, and the reality of the world. But in doing so it rejects both idealism and positivism. The good is not a set of principles to be applied, but a demand placed on us by the reality of the "other" through whom we are encountered by the mystery of "the Other." To repeat Bonhoeffer's words, "our relationship to God is a new life in 'being there-for-others' through participation in the being of Jesus. The transcendent is not the infinite, unattainable tasks, but the neighbor within reach in any given situation."[48] We are back in our discussion in chapter three on the meaning of transcendence. The Transcendent does not encounter us outside of worldly reality, but in the concrete claim and demand of the "other."

---

48. Bonhoeffer, *Letters and Papers from Prison*, 501.

A HUMANIST CONSENSUS WITHOUT COMPROMISING FAITH

Steven Pinker's claim is that the scientific approach to morality—including what he calls, but does not define, "liberalizing" religion—is espoused by all enlightened humanists today without any recourse to traditional religious values and norms. In critically responding to that claim, I do so as a Christian humanist who seeks to participate with humanists of other faith traditions as well as secular humanists in the struggle for the common good, but not on Pinker's terms.[49] Science is not our enemy, nor is theology his, but scientific understanding alone—even in tandem with Enlightenment humanism—cannot make our world more humane and just. Nor can theology, religion, and philosophy. What is necessary is the building of an overlapping mutually critical humanist consensus to guide and promote moral agency in seeking the common good. But as I have said, this does not mean compromising core Christian convictions in seeking a working consensus. Christian humanism is not humanism with a religious veneer attached; Christian humanism is an expression of the mystery revealed in Christ at the center of the world for the sake of its redemption.

In continuity with Bonhoeffer's project in prison, Wolfgang Huber suggests that faith in God's presence in mundane reality, along with the expectation of God's reign, opens up "a specific access to reality in three dimensions." These are gratitude and hope, a sober analysis of human fallibility, and respect for human dignity (something shared with all major religious traditions). In substance, this is what I understand by the Christian humanism that has its roots in Bonhoeffer's legacy:[50] a Christian humanism in which faith and reason, and theology and science critically engage one another in their exploration of reality and mystery for the sake of the common good. This is not the "liberalizing religion" to which Pinker refers, because that, according to his definition, has rejected both religious norms and values from the past and the attempt to critically retrieve them in the present; it has become secularized and therefore, in effect, has nothing distinctive to bring to the table. As Jens Zimmermann has cogently argued, secularism is exhausted because it has lost its roots in the religious tradition

---

49. See de Gruchy, ed., *Humanist Imperative in South Africa*.

50. See de Gruchy, "Dietrich Bonhoeffer as Christian Humanist"; de Gruchy, *Confessions of a Christian Humanist*.

that gave it birth.[51] The resulting vacuum, partially filled by scientism and fundamentalist religion, has had disastrous consequences.

To foster understanding and cooperation Zimmermann goes behind modernity to explore the theological origins of humanism, including secular humanism. He reminds us that its foundations were already laid in patristic Christology, and that it was Scholastic theology that later, on that foundation, gave birth to "the most important kind of humanism Europe has ever produced."[52] This laid the foundation for Western culture as expressed in education, art, and science, and led to the rise of modern science. But in the process, Scholastic theology lost the plot, undermined the synthesis of faith and reason, and prepared the way for secular humanism after the Enlightenment. Retrieving what was lost—that is, overcoming the dualisms that led to the antagonism between science and theology, and therefore reality and mystery—was what Bonhoeffer had in mind when, in prison, he wrote about the need to return to the Middle Ages to address the moral crisis in the modern world.[53]

Those of us who are seeking to critically retrieve Christian humanism today are not wanting to return to a previous age, but to contribute to the debate between religion and secular society in response to the current moral crisis. This does not mean jettisoning the moral values of Christian tradition in favor of a scientific understanding, but critically retrieving them—human dignity, freedom, hope and social responsibility—in a way that relates to the humanist trajectories in other faith traditions and to the scientific understanding in pursuit of a more humane, just, and compassionate world. This is a tough call, but there is no alternative whether practical or hermeneutical, for just as the two-state solution to the relationship between science and religion is untenable, so too is the notion that the secular and the religious, or the Christian and the Muslim (not to mention other faith traditions) can respond to reality from separate silos.

Being a Christian today means becoming more truly human. That means learning to live fully in the world by throwing "oneself completely into the arms of God," for this, Bonhoeffer says, "is how one becomes a human being, a Christian."[54] "Living without God" (that is, in worldly reality), we live "before God" (that is, embraced by mystery). Likewise, the church

51. Zimmermann, *Humanism and Religion*, 24–29.
52. Zimmermann, *Humanism and Religion*, 101.
53. Bonhoeffer, *Letters and Papers from Prison*, 319–20.
54. Bonhoeffer, *Letters and Papers from Prison*, 486.

must be "open to the world" by existing for others in the "real world," but in a way that remains deeply rooted in the mystery of its faith in Christ. That is why the church needs to protect the mysteries of the faith from profanation.[55] In the world, the church should be known by its "critical realism," its compassion and work for justice and peace—but if you probe deeper, you will see that hidden disciplines, prayer, and eucharistic praxis enable and sustain faith, hope, and love, and help the church tap into the wisdom of God disclosed in the mystery of Christ.

In other words, responding to the worldly reality that confronts us does not mean jettisoning the vast spiritual and moral resources that are available to us in our religious traditions, but rediscovering, reimagining, and re-embodying them in a new key. Indeed, "in a new language, perhaps quite nonreligious language, but liberating and redeeming like Jesus's language, so that people will be alarmed and yet overcome by its power—the language of a new righteousness and truth, a language proclaiming that God makes peace with humankind and that God's kingdom is drawing near."[56]

---

55. Bonhoeffer, *Letters and Papers from Prison*, 373.
56. Bonhoeffer, *Letters and Papers from Prison*, 390.

5

SOLIDARITY

&

the Palestinian Question

> I was hungry and you gave me food, I was thirsty and you gave me something drink, I I was a stranger and you welcomed me, I was naked and you gave me clothing, I was sick and you took care of me, I was in prison and you visited me.
>
> —Matthew 25:35–39

> Vicarious representative action (*Stellvertretung*) is the life-principle of the new humanity. True, I know myself to be in a guilty solidarity with the other person, but my service to the other person springs from the life-principle of vicarious representative action.
>
> —Bonhoeffer[1]

> *Vox victimarum vox Dei*—the cries of victims are the voice of God. The scandal of the Cross is the scandal of God identified with all the victims of history in the passion of Christ.
>
> —Lamb[2]

---

1. Bonhoeffer, *Sanctorum Communio*, 146.
2. Lamb, *Solidarity with Victims*, 1.

Those who are more influential, because they have a greater share of goods and common services, should feel responsible for the weaker and be ready to share with them all they possess. Those who are weaker, for their part, in the same spirit of solidarity, should not adopt a purely passive attitude or one that is destructive of the social fabric, but while claiming their legitimate rights, should do what they can for the good of all.

—Pope John Paul II[3]

If reality (*Wirklichkeit*) provided me with the first clue to understanding Bonhoeffer's theology, the second dawned on me as I was studying *Sanctorum Communio*, namely, *Stellvertretung* or "vicarious representative action," that is, living and acting in solidarity with "the other." This takes us to the heart of the significance of the death of Christ on behalf of the world, and what it means to act responsibly in correspondence to reality.[4] As Green sums it up, "Vicarious responsible action (*Stellvertretung*), grounded in the vicarious, responsible action of Christ for the world, is the paradigm of Christian action."[5] Such action not only is seen in individual relationships but also involves "people acting in responsibility for communities and nations, such as the biblical prophet and diplomat." This, Green adds, "includes Dietrich Bonhoeffer—and his family members and colleagues in the resistance movement—acting in responsibility for Germany."[6] Such action invariably means being willing to accept the guilt of one's nation, taking the side of and standing in solidarity with its victims, and even being prepared to be rejected as a traitor by one's own. In the end, such traitors prove to be the true patriots, the ones who loved their country most.[7]

PROPHETS AS TRUE PATRIOTS

The Hebrew prophets could be as wise as serpents, but diplomacy was not their forte. Their calling was to speak truth to power, and they sometimes did so in anger on behalf of the victims of corrupt politicians, religious

---

3. Pope John Paul II, *Sollicitudo Rei Socialis*.
4. See Green, Introduction to Bonhoeffer, *Ethics*, 13.
5. Green, *Bonhoeffer*, 314.
6. Green, *Bonhoeffer*, 314.
7. De Gruchy, "Confessing Guilt in South Africa."

leaders, and systems. Prophets ruffled feathers and, unsurprisingly, often became the victims of the powerful, not usually of foreign nations but of their own. As Jesus reminded his hearers, "Prophets are not without honour except in their own country and their own house" (Matt 13:57). Indeed, Jerusalem, not Babylon was singled out as the "city that kills the prophets and stones those who are sent to it" (Matt 23:37). The prophets were not interlopers; they were Jews who loved their nation. But that only made it worse for them, for it meant they were regarded as traitors. As Bethge wrote: "The patriot had to perform what in normal times is the act of a scoundrel. 'Treason' had to become true patriotism, and what was normally 'patriotism' had to become treason."[8] This was the reason for Bonhoeffer's martyrdom and lay behind the suffering of many others who endured ostracism and worse at the hands of the apartheid regime. Sadly, too often, the church has been party to their fate either through silence or complicity in the crime committed against them.

Archbishop Desmond Tutu (1931–2021) came to mind as I reflected on this tragic fate of prophets, for he died shortly before I completed this chapter, and no one more than Tutu "stirred up discussion" in apartheid society. Like Beyers Naudé, Tutu did not die a martyr, but both often received death threats because of their outspoken defense of the victims of injustice. And both were finally vindicated and even honored by some who had rejected and opposed them, and, remarkably, those who had persecuted them were not only shamed by history but often forgiven, for as Tutu put it, there is "no future without forgiveness."[9] Ironically, but not surprisingly there are those in post-apartheid South Africa whom Tutu helped to liberate who now reject him for being too forgiving, too bent on reconciliation and peace. But true prophets refuse to be co-opted even by their erstwhile supporters. Tutu stood in solidarity with and struggled for justice on behalf of the oppressed irrespective of who they were. True patriotism does not mean loving one's own at the expense of truth and justice; it may even require, as Jesus taught, "loving your enemies" (Matt 5:44).

After winning the Nobel Peace Prize in 1984, Desmond Tutu continued his prophetic ministry, and it went global. He was applauded in many countries but also vilified in some, especially when he declared that the Israeli occupation of Palestine reminded him of apartheid and was in some respects even worse. This did not go down well in either Jerusalem or New

---

8. Bethge, *Dietrich Bonhoeffer*, 675.
9. Tutu, *No Future without Forgiveness*.

York.[10] Yet I was with Tutu on one occasion when he was warmly welcomed at the Holocaust Centre in Cape Town, of which he was a patron, and where he spoke out strongly against anti-Semitism. Critics now accuse him of being patronizing and insincere in his anti-Semitism. But his criticism was aimed at the State of Israel, not at Jews; in the same way he had attacked the apartheid South African state, not Afrikaners or other Whites. He was equally critical of corrupt Black leaders and of Christians and the church when they supported injustice or remained silent when they should have spoken out.[11]

Prophets speak the truth, then, not only on behalf of the victims of oppression but also for the sake of the future of their oppressors. Whether they are Black or White, Jewish or Palestinian, does not matter; what matters is justice, peace, human dignity, and an end to violence. It was with this in mind that Tutu said that Israel had three options: to retain the status quo "bristling with tension, hatred, and violence"; "to perpetuate genocide and exterminate all Palestinians"; or "to strive for peace based on justice," and that required that the Palestinians must also be committed to such peace.[12] What mattered to Tutu was the rights and dignity of all, but it is true, the less powerful and more vulnerable they were, the more he took their side. This was the "Jesus' position," or "God's preferential option for the poor," as Latin American Catholic liberation theologians described it. Like the prophet Jeremiah, who was more scathing in his rebuke of Israel than he was of the surrounding nations, Tutu was a scourge to apartheid South Africa but also a "prophet to the nations" (Jer 1:5).

Bonhoeffer modeled his ministry on Jeremiah.[13] After his experience of racism in the US, which enabled him to see things from the perspective of the oppressed, he consistently took the side of victims irrespective of who or where they were, and was one of only a few theologians in Germany who condemned Nazi anti-Semitism from the outset. He would undoubtedly continue to condemn it today if he were alive. But I believe that if he were still with us, he would also condemn the occupation of Palestine by the State of Israel because of his solidarity with the victims of injustice. This is surely what he meant by "vicarious representative action," that

10. See Allen, *Rabble-Rouser for Peace*, 383–88.
11. See Tutu, *God Is Not a Christian*, 85–109.
12. Tutu, *God Is Not a Christian*, 107.
13. De Gruchy, *Bonhoeffer's Questions*, 60–66; de Gruchy, "Bonhoeffer among the 'Glorious Company of the Prophets.'"

is, responsible action that is appropriate to the reality facing faith in the Middle East.

But is it appropriate to ask what Bonhoeffer would say today given that he said nothing about the Palestinian question during his lifetime, even though he spoke about racism in the United States? After all, there is only one reference to Palestine in the whole of Bonhoeffer's works, namely, when he writes to Bethge about his resolve to travel there with him after the war.[14] That wish was never fulfilled. By the time the State of Israel was founded in 1948 Bonhoeffer had been dead for three years, though of course, the Balfour Declaration issued by the British government in 1917, had already promised a homeland for Jews in Palestine. This was a typical colonial action taken for the sake of Britain as much as it was for Jews. But there was little meaningful consultation with the Palestinians, and it was even rejected by many Zionists because they believed it favored the Arabs. The future of the Palestinians, among them many Christians, was not a matter of major concern. In the end, Britain capitulated to Zionism and could do little to prevent the Palestinian *Nakba*, which followed the formation of the State of Israel in 1948.

IS IT AN APPROPRIATE QUESTION?

At a conference on "Bonhoeffer for the Coming Generations" held in New York in November 2011, two sessions were devoted to public ethics, with presentations on Germany, South Africa, the United Kingdom, the United States, Brazil, and Japan.[15] Afterwards, someone asked whether it was appropriate to invoke Bonhoeffer's legacy in doing theology in contexts other than his own. It is a legitimate question. But few Bonhoeffer scholars have questioned the appropriateness of relating Bonhoeffer's legacy to the struggle against racism in the United States or apartheid in South Africa. However, there has been a reluctance to consider what he might say about the Palestinian-Israeli conflict that has been going on for such a long time at such terrible cost, posing a threat not only to stability in the Middle East, but to global peace. Indeed, what is the essential *moral*, to say nothing of the material, difference between the invasion of Ukraine by Russia to occupy and control the country, and the occupation of Palestine and the war on Gaza?

14. Bonhoeffer, *Letters and Papers from Prison*, 249.
15. Green and Carter, eds., *Interpreting Bonhoeffer*.

In any case, does the fact that the Palestinian question was not on Bonhoeffer's radar screen justify our silence on the subject? As Ruth Zerner, in an essay on Bonhoeffer and the "Jewish Question," observes, Bonhoeffer had, from early on, "displayed sensitivity towards the struggles of marginal groups in society . . . revealing his unwillingness to retreat from reality."[16] More directly to the point are the words of a rabbi, Albert Friedlander, who, in a lecture to the International Bonhoeffer Congress in Amsterdam in 1988, said, "The shadow of the Holocaust looms over all our lives. In Israel it is an anguished and dark presence added to the intolerable situation where the majority of Jews feel the pain of the Palestinians deeply." He went further: "Let it be quite clear that Judaism and most Jews cry out against the moral blindness and racism we see in one segment of the Israeli community."[17] Tragically that one segment is now the dominant power in the State of Israel, and the refusal to acknowledge that the oppression of Palestinians is a form of racism, as Friedlander states, is widespread not only in Israel itself but within large segments of the church under the sway of Christian Zionism.

However, let us not ignore what Jewish scholar Mark Braverman rightly points out: it is not only Christian Zionists who give their uncritical allegiance to the State of Israel; many mainstream Christian theologians and church leaders who are otherwise outspoken on racism remain mute on the Palestinian question.[18] How do we account for this? Undoubtedly, it derives largely from a justifiable sense of guilt for the Holocaust, but it also stems from a fear that criticism of the State of Israel will result in being charged with anti-Judaism and anti-Semitism.[19] But can such guilt, real as it is, and such fear justify silence?

Christendom was guilty for the persecution of the Jews long before Nazism; after all, the Holocaust was the climax of centuries of anti-Semitism, persecution, and pogroms. So, it is understandable that so-called Christian nations in the West have supported the State of Israel and been hesitant to express any criticism of its actions. Yet, hypocritically, after the Second World War these same nations, Britain, France, and the United States among them, were often unwilling to accept Jewish refugees and other victims of the Holocaust to any significant extent. For them, the solution

---

16. Zerner, "Church, State and the 'Jewish Question,'" 190.
17. Friedlander, "Israel and Europe," 115.
18. See Braverman, *Fatal Embrace*, 214–16.
19. See Shain, *Antisemitism*, 93–99; Achar; *Arabs and the Holocaust*.

lay in Palestine, despite what this would cost the Palestinians who now had to carry the burden of European and especially German guilt. But this did not lessen the guilt for centuries of European anti-Semitism; it only added guilt for the *Nakba* to the equation. In solidarity with its former victims, Germany became one of the main suppliers of sophisticated armaments to Israel,[20] something that would have horrified Bonhoeffer, for whom the path to peace was justice, not weapons of war.

So while it is true that I cannot speak for Bonhoeffer on the Palestinian question, I can speak about what I have learned from his legacy over the years, as well as from my own experience, about the reality that confronts Christian faith in Israel-Palestine today—a reality that also confronts all Christians who "pray for the peace of Jerusalem" and believe that the Israeli occupation of Palestine is unjust and will continue to foster hatred, resistance, repression, violence, and war.

A PERSONAL JOURNEY

My high school in Cape Town was roughly 50 percent Jewish, many of the students being the children of refugees from Eastern Europe and some of Holocaust victims, as was one of my teachers. Jewish family friends and neighbors were an important part of my youth. I knew that my Jewish fellow students were different, but so was I as far as they were concerned, and this was something we were taught to respect. Later when I went to study at the University of Cape Town there was a strong and distinguished Jewish presence both among faculty and students, many of them activists in opposing apartheid. But, despite this, I recall instances of anti-Semitism even within that environment, and if I had been Jewish, I would undoubtedly have experienced it much more acutely. Like racism, anti-Semitism seeps insidiously into the life of communities and institutions. So, the fact that many of my peers in the classroom and on the sports field were Jewish does not mean that I was immune from anti-Semitism. If racism is deeply embedded in the White psyche, so is anti-Semitism embedded in the Christian. And some worthy colonial institutions patronized by Christians in Cape Town, which certainly excluded Blacks, also prohibited Jews from membership. But just as my awareness of racism was heightened by my exposure to the Civil Rights Movement in the US, it was there too that I

---

20. Based on a Report of the US Congressional Research Service, 2007. See Achar, *Arabs and the Holocaust*, 267.

became more aware of the dangers of anti-Semitism when I was introduced to the post–World War II discussions on the Christian response to the Holocaust. Indeed, one of my teachers in Chicago (1963–1964) was Franklin Littell, a supporter of the Confessing Church in Germany and prominent participant in the post-Holocaust discussions between Jews and Christians. He was also a strong advocate of the State of Israel and a friend of Eberhard Bethge's. Years after my student days in Chicago, Littell invited me to participate in several Jewish-Christian conferences where I met some of the outstanding Jewish thinkers of that generation, and I was even asked to contribute to a Festschrift in his honor.[21] It pains me to say that today I no longer share either Littell's uncritical views of the State of Israel nor Bethge's reluctance to engage the Palestinian question. But I do understand where they were coming from.

Since I first met Bethge in 1970 he became my unofficial mentor in my research on Bonhoeffer's legacy—as he was to many other Bonhoeffer scholars of my generation. Eventually I wrote his biography with the support of the Bethge family.[22] Bethge spent a great deal of his time and energy in trying to change Christian attitudes towards Jews and Judaism in postwar Germany, a subject we often talked about.[23] He introduced me to Jewish scholars, and on one celebrated occasion I accompanied him to the Kaiser Wilhelm Kirche in Berlin for the first official meeting of reconciliation between the leadership of the German Protestant Church and the Jewish community.

As Bethge's passion was to redress Christian anti-Semitism and to establish a better relationship between Christians and Jews in Germany, I was hesitant to speak to him about the Palestinian question until towards the end of his life when I raised it with him on two occasions. I still have some personal hesitation to speak about it. Having visited the concentration camps at Auschwitz, Buchenwald, and Flossenbürg (where Bonhoeffer was put to death); Holocaust museums from Jerusalem to Washington DC, from Berlin and Prague to Cape Town; and having been involved in discussions with Jewish scholars about the issues, I am only too aware of the horrors unleashed by Christian anti-Semitism in the course of history. What, then, tipped the scale for me and led to my recognition that the Jewish question that concerned Bonhoeffer cannot be separated from the

---

21. Libowitz, ed., *Faith and Freedom*.
22. De Gruchy, *Daring, Trusting Spirit*.
23. See de Gruchy, *Daring, Trusting Spirit*: 181–204.

Palestinian question that confronts us today, especially if we take Bonhoeffer's legacy seriously?

I first became aware of the plight of the Palestinians when I visited the Holy Land in 1969 soon after the Six-Day War. I was delighted to have the opportunity and am still indebted to those Israelis (presumably supported by the State) who made my visit possible even though I am now more aware of their likely motives. For I soon discovered that the situation of the Palestinians was a taboo subject among those Israelis on our schedule, whether tour guides, kibbutz leaders, or army officers, or those who invited me to speak at meetings on my return to South Africa. Even my mentioning that I, as a Christian, had a special interest in the situation of Palestinian *Christians* caused anger in some Jewish circles where I was invited to speak. But what I saw and heard in Israel bothered me, as did my growing awareness of the increasingly cozy relationship between Israel and the apartheid regime, especially with regard to security and military technology.

Twenty years later, in 1990, I had the opportunity to revisit Israel, this time to attend a World Council of Churches (WCC) working group that met at Tantur, the Catholic conference center on the road between Jerusalem and Bethlehem. Prior to our arrival at Tantur, Isobel and I, together with an American friend, traveled by car through the West Bank, down the Jordan Valley, and then through East Jerusalem before reaching Tantur. We stayed on several kibbutzim, one heavily defended on the northern border with Lebanon. Our WCC working group also spent time in Bethlehem meeting with various church leaders and listening to the voices of Palestinian Christians. Although the WCC group's agenda had to do with matters relating to church unity, one evening we had the opportunity to listen to Jewish, Arab, and Christian leaders talking together with us about the situation in Israel-Palestine at that time when optimism had been raised by the Oslo Agreement. But daily as I walked in the grounds of Tantur, I could see how Israeli settlements were encroaching on land once owned and farmed by Palestinians.

In the years since then I have continued to listen carefully to the voices of Jews, among them distinguished scholars, rabbis, and public figures— some of whom were surprisingly critical of Israeli policy and actions, and supportive of the rights of the Palestinians. I cannot ignore this Jewish voice, which I first heard when as a student I began to read the writings of Martin Buber. If distinguished Jews could be critical of Israeli policies towards Palestine, and they could not be guilty of anti-Semitism, then the charge that being critical was anti-Semitic was fatuous. Indeed, from Buber I learned that the Zionist vision of Hebrew humanism was not Zionism as a nationalist ideology, something he lamented.[24] Some Jewish leaders, such as the first president of Hebrew University in Jerusalem, Judah Magnes, even argued that "the establishment of a Jewish state" would undermine "the moral purpose" of a Jewish homeland because it would be built on conquest and maintained by oppressing the Palestinian Arabs.[25] Concerned Jews whom I have met the world over, including in South Africa where I, as a deputy dean, was chair for a time at the Centre for Jewish Studies at the University of Cape Town as well as a consultant at the Holocaust Centre, continue to say this, and they do so out of a love for Israel, not hatred.

The truth is, Jews vary greatly in their religious and political opinions, and Israel is a very complex and ideologically divided state and society. This was well described by Baruch Susser of Bar-Ilan University, who in 2012 spoke in Cape Town about the "realignment in Israeli politics" since the Six-Day War. "Without becoming ideologically more radical," he said, "Israel's cleavages have become deeper and more threatening. It is hard not to fear that the worst is still to come."[26] That "fear" for the future is perfectly understandable in the light of the Shoah, as is the way it determines relationships with the Palestinians and the rest of the world.

Israel is a small nation surrounded by many hostile countries; its existence is contested, and its security is a matter of concern to citizens, who regularly become victims of Palestinian militants. So, it would be crass not to appreciate Israeli fears, especially in the light of past and current threats made against the right of Israel to exist at all. Given their history of persecution, Jews have good reason to be anxious and vigilant, and most Jews would argue that the State of Israel, with the indispensable support of the West, provides security from once again becoming victims on a mass scale. But from the Hebrew prophets onwards, there have been Jews who have insisted that the security of Israel cannot be assured by military might and alliances *if it surrenders its moral basis*. If it does so, then the State of Israel must be considered like any other, for its claim to have a God-given right to "possess the land", if still valid, is contingent on the divine obligation to "do justice and love mercy" to all, as it has always been. But can the State of

---

24. Buber, *Israel and the World*, 240–63.
25. See Ruether and Ruether, *Wrath of Jonah*, 70.
26. Susser, "Society Divided," 52.

Israel be held accountable to that high standard of social justice today when surrounded by hostile nations?

More than thirty years ago Larry Rasmussen, a leading ethicist among Bonhoeffer scholars, engaged an Orthodox rabbi and American scholar, Irving Greenberg, in dialogue with Bonhoeffer on the question of state power and moral accountability. He highlighted their consensus on the inevitable moral ambiguities that emerge in the exercise of power even in countries with a strong culture of moral accountability.[27] For this reason, the State of Israel cannot be expected to always act according to the high moral demands of Judaism; neither can it be judged differently because of its Jewish character. However, Israel is not being called to a higher morality or to empathize somewhat paternalistically with the Palestinians, but, as Greenberg urged, it is being called to the same morality as other nations that expropriate the land of indigenous people, oppress them in other ways, and turn many into refugees. To criticize this, as many Jews themselves do, "is not anti-Semitism but simply justice."[28]

Amid a widespread Israeli indifference to the plight of the Palestinians there are many Jews who have come to recognize Palestinian victimization, Jews whose sense of justice and commitment to human rights has been offended by the way Palestinians have been and still are being treated, and who see their compatriots becoming psychologically damaged, if not brutalized and killed, by the ongoing strife.[29] It is perhaps unsurprising then, that Marc Ellis, a Jewish theologian, has asked whether the time has not come "after the Holocaust and after Israel and its injustice to the Palestinians, to think through and embrace a costly Jewishness?" Or, as he put it more succinctly: "Do we need a Jewish Bonhoeffer?"[30] Only Jews can answer that question. But that does not mean that Christians must remain silent, especially if we take the Hebrew prophets and Bonhoeffer's witness seriously. Indeed, as Mark Braverman, another Jewish scholar, has passionately argued, Christians fail in their witness and responsibility if they stay silent. So, his call on the churches not to let Israel down by denying their own faith-commitments is compelling if uncomfortable.[31] As Braverman

---

27. See Rasmussen, with Bethge, *Dietrich Bonhoeffer*, 137.

28. Ruether and Ruether, *Wrath of Jonah*, 216.

29. See Achar, *Arabs and the Holocaust*; Ellis, *Toward a Jewish Theology of Liberation*; and Braverman, *Fatal Embrace*, and Brueggemann's Foreword, xiii–xx.

30. Ellis, "On Israel's Indigenous Prophetic," 82.

31. Braverman, *Wall in Jerusalem*, see especially 216–42.

rightly says, it is not only "fundamental Christian principles of equality and social justice that are at stake," but also at stake is "the Israeli dream of a secure homeland . . . because conquest is the fundamental barrier to peace."[32]

The fact that Israel is now a state among the nations, albeit a Jewish one but also one that claims to be a modern democracy, introduces issues that were not part of Bonhoeffer's reflections on the Jews as powerless victims. More to the point are Bonhoeffer's comments on what constitutes a just state, and on the state's responsibility towards the marginalized. After all, as Bernard Lewis acknowledged, "The Arab-Israeli conflict is a political one—a clash between states and peoples over real issues, not a matter of prejudice and persecution."[33]

There are many Christians around the world, as well as in South Africa, both Black and White, who, influenced by Christian Zionism, are uncritically committed to the State of Israel, and opposed to those who support the liberation of Palestine, including the South African government. Christian Zionism is not a new phenomenon: its roots can be traced back to the beginnings of Christendom and later to the Protestant Reformation when some European nations claimed a special relationship to God—chosen, like ancient Israel, to fulfill a divine mission.[34] If you study the liturgy for the coronation of British kings and queens, you will soon discover how it often reflects this theme, and how the hymns and anthems sung reinforce it. It is not surprising, then, that so much Christianity, especially in the United States, is strongly pro-Zionist because the ideology fits well into its national self-understanding of being specially favored and called by God to rule the world. What is surprising is when some claim Bonhoeffer's support for Christian Zionism and support for the State of Israel because of his solidarity with the Jews in Nazi Germany.

BONHOEFFER ON THE "JEWISH QUESTION"

Bonhoeffer's essay on "The Church and the Jewish Question"[35] was published in 1933 at the commencement of Hitler's reign of terror, well before the Wannsee Conference in January 1942 adopted Hitler's Final Solution

---

32. Braverman, *Wall in Jerusalem*, 16.

33. Lewis, *Semites and Anti-Semites*, 23, quoted in Achar, *Arabs and the Holocaust*, 262.

34. See Ruether, *Wrath of Jonah*, 174–91.

35. See Bonhoeffer, *Berlin 1932–1933*, 497–99; Bethge, *Dietrich Bonhoeffer*: 257–324.

to the "Jewish Problem." It was a response to the German Christians' concerted attempt to enforce Hitler's Non-Aryan laws in the life of the Protestant Church. This was, said Bonhoeffer, the "state's decisive challenge to the church."[36] But it was also, as Barnett has shown, related to an ongoing struggle in the German Protestant Church to deal with the relationship between Christianity, the Jews, and German national and ethnic identity.[37] The question was, could Jews be truly German even if they converted to Christianity? And, following that, if the Reich Church was the spiritual representative of the German nation, could Jewish-Christians be welcomed as members?

This latter question divided the Protestant Church and led to the formation of the Confessing Church at Barmen in 1934. Bonhoeffer's essay on the "Jewish Question," which anticipated this development, was not primarily about national politics but about Protestant ecclesiology even though that, in turn, had far-reaching political implications because it was also about German identity. But for Bonhoeffer and those who gathered in Barmen, if the church was to be not a Reich Church but the church of Jesus Christ, then, as Saint Paul said, there could be no distinction between "Jew or Gentile" (Galatians 2). The political implications were not stated in the Barmen Declaration, but they were implicit because national identity and church identity were so deeply connected as a result of Luther's Reformation.

Anyone with a knowledge of the debate about Afrikaner identity, race, and the Dutch Reformed Church (NGK) in South Africa will recognize the contours of that German church debate, for like the Protestant Church in Germany, the NGK was a *Volkskirche*; it was the spiritual home of the Afrikaner people. They will also recognize the significance of the 1982 Belhar Confession, drafted by Jaap Durand and his colleagues, based on the Barmen Declaration, which declared that the theological justification of apartheid was a heresy.[38] Like Barmen, its immediate significance was ecclesial, but its implications were politically far-reaching. If the church was to be the church of Jesus Christ, not the "National Party at prayer," then the church could neither be racially segregated nor, on that basis or any other, theologically justify apartheid in society. What was ecclesiologically

---

36. Schlingensiepen, *Dietrich Bonhoeffer*, 127. See Tödt, *Authentic Faith*, 111; Moses, *Reluctant Revolutionary*, 148–72.

37. Barnett, "Dietrich Bonhoeffer's 'Jewish Question.'"

38. Cloete and Smit, eds., *Moment of Truth*.

wrong could not be politically right. Bonhoeffer's essay on "The Jewish Question" must be read, then, in its historical and ecclesiastical context, which explains why on the specific question of the Jews in general or on the relationship between Judaism and Christianity in particular it was more ambiguous than has usually been assumed.[39] Indeed, viewed later from the perspective of Holocaust studies, Bonhoeffer's "words and actions appear small, tentative, restrained, and ambivalent."[40]

Those Jews who oppose including Bonhoeffer among the "righteous Gentiles" in Yad Vashem are sensitive to the ambiguities in his legacy.[41] Bonhoeffer's theology, they insist, perpetuates the notion that Christianity supersedes Judaism; his involvement in the Resistance was motivated more by his sense of national responsibility and moral outrage than concern for the Jews; and he was murdered by the Nazi regime because of his involvement in the July 20, 1944, plot to assassinate Hitler, not because he helped Jews escape the clutches of the Gestapo.

However, when seen from the perspective of the complicity of the Reich Church in its support of Nazism, and the silence even of the Confessing Church on the persecution of the Jews apart from those who were Jewish-Christians, Bonhoeffer's witness stands out as one of a few small, courageous lights in the encroaching darkness. And as the war dragged on, and he began to receive more information about what was happening in the concentration camps from his brother-in-law and fellow conspirator, Hans von Dohnanyi, who compiled a detailed dossier on the subject until his arrest along with Bonhoeffer, Bonhoeffer's solidarity with the Jews became more decisive. Certainly, he was not only thinking about Jewish-Christians when he wrote in 1940, that "driving out the Jews from the West must result in driving out Christ with them, for Jesus Christ was a Jew."[42] And the Jews were undoubtedly paramount in his thinking when he declared that the church had to confess its guilt for "the murder of the weakest and most defenseless brothers and sisters of Jesus Christ."[43] And it is surely correct to say that Bonhoeffer's sense of patriotic responsibility and moral outrage that led him to join the Resistance cannot be separated from his growing concern for the plight of the Jews. Moreover, his legacy, taken much further

---

39. See Clements, *Dietrich Bonhoeffer's Ecumenical Quest*, 72–77.
40. See Barnes, "Dietrich Bonhoeffer and Hitler's Persecution of the Jews."
41. See Gushee, *Righteous Gentiles of the Holocaust*.
42. Bonhoeffer, *Ethics*, 105.
43. See Bonhoeffer, *Ethics*, 139 and n. 25; cf. *Ethics*, 105.

and more decisively by Bethge and others, has undoubtedly had a positive influence in shaping contemporary Christian attitudes towards the Jews and Judaism.[44]

But irrespective of how we evaluate Bonhoeffer's "solidarity" with the Jews in Nazi Germany, events in the Holy Land since 1948 now make it problematic to consider his response to the Jewish question apart from the Palestinian question. The fates of Arabs and Israelis, of Jews, Muslims, and Christians in the Holy Land are inseparable, and the key issue it seems to me is whether Israel is an exclusively Jewish state or an inclusive, modern democratic society. The question is strikingly similar to the debate about German identity in Nazi Germany and about racial identity in apartheid South Africa, albeit it in very different though historically connected contexts. We cannot disconnect this debate about Israel today from the horrors of the Holocaust, but can we accuse Israel, as Tutu did, of having become an apartheid state? And the fact that some have brought Bonhoeffer into the discussion in support of the State of Israel prompts the further question: Can Bonhoeffer be included among those Western theologians who today, according to the *Kairos Palestine Document*, misuse the Bible in defense of the State of Israel, and thereby threaten the existence of both Christian and Muslim Palestinians?[45]

THE COMPETITION OF VICTIMS

In 2010 I was asked to write a brief article for an Australian journal in response to the use of Bonhoeffer's name by some Western politicians to justify their policies in the Middle East and their support for Israel. Opposition from certain unnamed quarters forced the editors to withdraw it, but it was later published in an abbreviated version in the *Ecumenical Review*.[46] Clearly gaining Bonhoeffer's imprimatur on the subject was important, but was this justified given present historical realities? For the critical issue is not simply how Bonhoeffer responded to the Jewish question in Germany, but how his evolving solidarity with social and political victims, which began when he first became aware of the plight of African Americans, would inform his response to the Palestinian question today. How would Bonhoeffer identify the victims in Israel-Palestine today, and how would he

44. Bethge, "Dietrich Bonhoeffer and the Jews."
45. *The Kairos Palestine Document,,* 2.3.4.
46. De Gruchy, "Bonhoeffer and the Palestinian-Israel Conflict."

express his solidarity with them? This highly emotive and contested subject in the narrative wars that accompany the Israeli-Palestinian conflict, is sometimes referred to as the "competition of the victims."[47]

Jews have unquestionably been victims over the centuries, largely at the hands of Christians. The Holocaust is not just a crime against humanity, but especially against Jews, and because anti-Semitism eventually led to Hitler's Final Solution, anti-Semitism must always he regarded as a threat to be condemned and opposed, as must the denial of the Shoah. But this does not mean that Palestinians who have suffered from the *Nakba* and the subsequent aggression of the State of Israel should not also be regarded as victims. From Bonhoeffer's perspective such an inference would be impossible. His solidarity with the oppressed or victims of injustice, whoever they might be, and his preparedness to speak out and act on their behalf, was unequivocal. To repeat his well-known words written shortly before his arrest in 1943:

> We have for once learned to see the great events of world history from below, from the perspective of the outcasts, the suspects, the maltreated, the powerless, the oppressed and reviled, in short from the perspective of the suffering.[48]

In saying this, Bonhoeffer was not oblivious to the suffering of many others, including his fellow Germans who were victims of the Nazis. His twin sister, Sabine, and his Jewish-Christian brother-in-law, Gerhard Leibholz, had to flee Germany, as did his best friend, Franz Hildebrandt. Many of his students, reluctant participants in the army, were killed on the battlefield, and his aged parents and other friends and relatives living in Berlin were in constant danger from Allied bombing while he was in prison. But Bonhoeffer would not have numbered them among "the maltreated, the powerless, the oppressed and reviled," whose cry in that context had to be heard. He was also aware of countless others—communists, homosexuals, the physically disabled, along with the conquered peoples of Eastern Europe—who were being exploited, tortured, and killed by the Gestapo and other agents of Nazi tyranny. When Bonhoeffer spoke out on behalf of the victims of Nazism, then, he had in mind all who were oppressed.[49]

---

47. See Achar, *Arabs and the Holocaust*.
48. Bonhoeffer, *Letters and Papers from Prison*, 52.
49. See Gushee, *Righteous Gentiles of the Holocaust*, 110–14, and 219 n. 128.

Already in a sermon preached in London, probably in 1934, on 2 Cor 12:9, Bonhoeffer unequivocally declared that Christianity by its very nature should always identify with those who "cannot help themselves but who have just to rely on other people for help, for love, for care."[50] He went on to say that "Christianity stands or falls with its revolutionary protest against violence, arbitrariness and pride of power and with its apologia for the weak." Indeed, he insisted that "Christianity should . . . take a much more definite stand for the weak than to consider the potential right of the strong."[51] This concluding sentence is critical. Bonhoeffer is making a distinction that is not often remembered when debating the Palestinian question. The strong have rights, potential or real, just as they can also become victims, both actual and potential, but their status and claims must always be evaluated in relation to the rights of the weak who are their victims. Pope John Paul II put it succinctly: those who are influential or have "a greater share of goods and common services, should feel responsible for the weaker and be ready to share with them all they possess." This remains so, even though the pope went on to say that the weaker should adopt "the same spirit of solidarity," so that "while claiming their legitimate rights" they also "do what they can for the good of all."[52]

The State of Israel may be vulnerable, but it is not weak. Even in its vulnerability it can depend on its own powerful military and the support of the United States, other Western powers, and some Arab nations. The Palestinians may have the support of Iran and other countries, and the militant among them undoubtedly pose a threat to Israeli citizens. But that does not alter the position of the majority of Palestinians, who are daily at the mercy of the Israeli occupation. Even if some are Israeli citizens and others have certain rights, all experience discrimination and often humiliation. And nothing illustrates their vulnerability more than the never-ending Gaza conflict as described in *The Goldstone Report*.[53]

Richard Goldstone, a respected South African judge, was pressured by Jewish organizations to retract some of the statements in his Report, but its substance remains well-documented and is reinforced by the expansion

---

50. Bonhoeffer, *London*, 401. See also Bonhoeffer, *Discipleship*, 285.

51. Bonhoeffer, *London*, 402–3.

52. Pope John Paul II, *Sollicitudo Rei Socialis*.

53. See Horowitz et al., eds., *Goldstone Report*. Despite some later retractions by Goldstone, the *Report* provides overwhelming evidence of the use of oppressive power against civilians.

of illegal settlements and the continual daily indignities of the occupation. Even the security wall that encircles much of Israel is built largely on confiscated Palestinian land. Israel can impose its will on Palestine even in the face of international protest. In short, the Palestinians at this historical moment are undoubtedly the victims whose voices must be heard above that of the spin doctors of the powerful.

This is the reality on the ground that confronts Christian faith as described in the *Kairos Palestine Document*, which concludes: "We see the upper hand of the strong, the growing orientation towards racist separation and the imposition of laws that deny our existence and our dignity. We see confusion and division in the Palestinian position."[54] At this historical moment, then, from a perspective shaped by Bonhoeffer's theology, the Palestinians are the primary victims, but whose voice among them should we listen to given what we have learned from Bonhoeffer?

THE VOICE OF KAIROS PALESTINE

My accumulation of experience and reflection led me to endorse the *Kairos Palestine Document* drafted by Palestinian Christians, based on the South African *Kairos Document* (1986), and supported by the patriarchs and heads of churches in Jerusalem in 2009.[55] Gaining such endorsement was no small achievement given the history of dissension and division within the Palestinian Christian community over the centuries, which has so badly compromised Christian witness. For the leaders of the Greek, Latin, Armenian, Coptic, Syrian, Maronite, Ethiopian Orthodox, along with the Greek, Syrian, and Armenian Catholic, and the Lutheran and Anglican Churches to express their support, and stand by its drafters "in their faith, their hope, their love and their vision for the future" is quite remarkable. Soon after, the *Kairos Palestine Document* was published in South Africa in English, Afrikaans, and Arabic, and endorsed by Archbishop Tutu and other South African church leaders and theologians.

Bonhoeffer's influence is clearly evident in the *Kairos Palestine Document*, just as it was in the original South African *Kairos Document* in 1986.[56] His personal example of resistance to oppression, his insistence that there can never be security without justice, and his ecumenical commitment to

---

54. *Kairos Palestine Document* 3.2.
55. *Kairos Palestine Document*.
56. Clements, *What Freedom?*, 61–62.

peace, immediately suggest that what he had to say on such issues during the 1930s remains of critical importance today.[57] So I am persuaded that Bonhoeffer would have listened above all to the voice expressed in the *Kairos Palestine Document*, which so clearly resonates with his legacy. It is, of course, the voice of a small and shrinking minority group within the Palestinian community, but it is a Christian voice that explicitly seeks to express the gospel in a way that might well speak to both Muslim and Jew. The document states at the outset:

> We, a group of Christian Palestinians, after prayer, reflection and an exchange of opinion, cry out within the suffering of our country, under the Israeli occupation, with a cry of hope in the absence of hope, a cry full of prayer and faith in a God ever vigilant, in God's providence for all the inhabitants of this land.[58]

Palestinian Christians acknowledge that they are few, but their message of faith is important, for, as they say, their land "is in urgent need of love. Our love is a message to the Muslim and to the Jew, as well as to the world." This is not the voice of politicians serving the interests of their constituencies; nor is it the voice of jet-setting diplomats engaged in pursuing their own agendas within the vortex of Middle Eastern politics, or Zionist-Christians awaiting the apocalypse and the final conversion of Jews. It is the voice of the brothers and sisters of Jesus who have been living in Jerusalem, Bethlehem, and Galilee since the beginning of the Christian era. It is a cry for justice born in pain but also in hope; it is an expression of love and concern about the welfare of all who live in and seek the welfare of the Holy Land whether Jew, Muslim or Christian; and it is a testimony to faith in Jesus Christ, who was born in the West Bank and died in the city that is at the heart of the conflict.

The *Kairos Palestine Document* is above all a faithful testimony to the gospel of the crucified and risen Christ. Despite the "destruction that looms on the horizon,"[59] it celebrates "signs of hope,"[60] which it links to the mission of the church in the Holy Land. It indicates a steadfast belief in the justice of the Palestinian cause, and the determination "to overcome the resentments of the past and to be ready for reconciliation once justice has

---

57. See the essays in the *Ecumenical Review*, vol. 63, no. 1, March 2011, see especially the comments by Rifat Odeh Kassis, 120–22.

58. *Kairos Palestine Document*, opening paragraph.

59. *Kairos Palestine Document* 3.2.

60. *Kairos Palestine Document* 3.3.

been restored."[61] This is not an expression of naïve optimism—quite the reverse, for the situation is dire—but an expression of biblical faith in the risen Christ, who is "the source of our hope,"[62] and the motivation for the Palestinian church to remain "a witnessing, steadfast and active church in the land of the Resurrection."[63]

Thus, without wanting to be separate from their Muslim brothers and sisters, Palestinian Christians believe they have a special contribution to make to the struggle for peace and justice as Palestinian Christians. It is not a mission to save themselves or even the church, but a vicarious task on behalf of all who live in the Holy Land, and all who pray and work for the peace of Jerusalem. "Our vocation" *Kairos Palestine* states, "is to bear witness to the goodness of God and the dignity of human beings . . . to pray and to make our voice heard when we announce a new society where human beings believe in their own dignity and the dignity of their adversaries."[64] But the document is also a call to the ecumenical church to repent of "unjust political options with regard to the Palestinian people" and to "stand alongside the oppressed and preserve the word of God as good news for all rather than turn it into a weapon with which to slay the oppressed."[65]

Surely the ecumenical church today cannot turn a deaf ear to this Palestinian cry for solidarity any more than when it heard the cries of the Jews in Nazi Europe and too often remained silent. In words that owe their origin to Bonhoeffer himself, even the authors of the *Kairos Palestine Document* confess that "as individuals or as heads of Churches, we were silent when we should have raised our voices to condemn the injustice and share in the suffering."[66] This is not only a cry for understanding and justice, but also for resistance in the struggle for justice and peace that resonates with Bonhoeffer's legacy. So we turn in conclusion to that part of his legacy for which he has become an ecumenical Christian icon.

---

61. *Kairos Palestine Document* 3.4.
62. *Kairos Palestine Document* 3.5.
63. *Kairos Palestine Document* 3.5.
64. *Kairos Palestine Document* 3.4.2.
65. *Kairos Palestine Document* 6.
66. *Kairos Palestine Document* 5.2. See Bonhoeffer, *Ethics*, 137.

REALITY, RESISTANCE, AND PEACEMAKING

Bonhoeffer was deeply involved in the ecumenical movement during the 1930s, a time when European nations were frantically engaged in re-armament. He purposefully chose to participate in the peace witness of the World Alliance for Promoting International Friendship through the Churches. Unless the churches cooperated in working for peace, he insisted, all talk about unity was theoretical. But even so, Bonhoeffer, with incisive theological motivation, took a more radical stance on the issues than either his fellow Germans or most ecumenical leaders, who did not want to alienate the German Reich Church any more than some do not want to labeled anti-Semitic today for standing in solidarity with the Palestinians.

Bonhoeffer's approach is evident in his lecture on "Christ and Peace," probably given in 1932, at a time when discussions on disarmament in Europe were faltering. He acknowledges that Christ does not give us "specific rules for our conduct in every possible complex political, economic, or other situation," but that does not compromise God's commandment to love the other and to work for peace.[67] Bonhoeffer's better-known contribution to the debate, however, was his address to the ecumenical conference in Fanø, Denmark, in 1934, on the responsibility of the churches among the nations.[68] He spoke about God's commandment to "make peace" and the twin temptations to avoid doing so. Blind obedience oblivious to reality was one; the questioning of the peace mandate itself was the other. It seems to me that such blindness and questioning continues to prevent the church today from addressing the issues with Bonhoeffer's prophetic boldness.

If blind obedience to party, ideology, or religion leads to irresponsible actions oblivious to reality on the ground, questioning the peace mandate leads to prevarication, compromise, and inaction. With the devil's words in paradise in mind Bonhoeffer asked, "Must God not really have said that we should work for peace, of course, but also make ready tanks and poison gas for security? . . . Did God say you should not protect your own people?" To ask such questions, Bonhoeffer insists, is already to deny God.[69] So the ecumenical church dare not be sidetracked in its witness but rather must speak God's word to the world "regardless of the consequences."[70] Peace is

---

67. Bonhoeffer, *Berlin 1932–1933*, 258–61.
68. Bonhoeffer, *London*, 307–10.
69. Bonhoeffer, *London*, 307–8.
70. Bonhoeffer, *London*, 307.

not achieved through treaties, economic investment, or arms, for peace is not security. "There is," Bonhoeffer says, "no peace along the way of safety. For peace must be dared."[71] This can only be done through developing trust and pursuing justice and the common good. The rest will follow.

Bonhoeffer's rejection of both radicalism and compromise in Christian witness to Jesus Christ in public life, reflected in his political realism yet decisive action in his own day, is critical.[72] He develops this at length in his *Ethics* where he insists that all responsible political action must correspond to reality: Christ must neither be used to sanction the status quo nor to bless every revolution.[73] "Responsible action is nourished not by an ideology but by reality, which is why one can only act within the boundaries of that reality."[74] Robin Lovin expresses this well with Bonhoeffer in mind: "The Christian realist shares the radical's dissatisfaction with injustice, but focuses on responsible choices amongst the concrete possibilities now available."[75] In the end, this meant that Bonhoeffer himself had to join the Resistance, help Jews escape from Germany into Switzerland, and participate in the plot to kill Hitler.

In describing "reality on the ground" as they experience it, the authors of the *Kairos Palestine Document* quote Jeremiah's critique of those who, in ancient Israel, "say: Peace, peace' when there is no peace" (6:14). In doing so, they identify the Israeli occupation of Palestine and all the consequences that flow from it as the main obstacle to peace. Resistance is a reaction to the occupation. If "there were no occupation, there would be no resistance, no fear and no insecurity." In saying this, the *Kairos Palestine Document* affirms nonviolence and rejects the "fanaticism and extremism" of some Muslims, but equally rejects the stereotyping of Muslims as terrorists.[76] Addressing the Jews, the *Kairos Palestine Document* declares, "Even though we have fought one another in the recent past and still struggle today, we are able to love and live together. We can organize our political life, with all its complexity, according to the logic of this love and its power, after ending the occupation and establishing justice."[77]

---

71. Bonhoeffer, *London*, 309.
72. Bonhoeffer, *Ethics*, 154–60.
73. Bonhoeffer, *Ethics*, 219–98.
74. Bonhoeffer, *Ethics*, 22.
75. Lovin, *Christian Realism and the New Realities*, 5.
76. *Kairos Palestine Document* 5.4.1.
77. *Kairos Palestine Document* 5.4.3.

To the cynic all this sounds naïve, as it has done ever since Jesus of Nazareth spoke in these terms about the peace of Jerusalem (Luke 19:41–42). It is the path of nonviolent resistance to oppression, the way of loving rather than hating enemies and further entrenching the cycle of violence. This is precisely what Bonhoeffer advocated, as did Martin Luther King Jr. in his struggle against racism, and Mahatma Gandhi in opposing British colonialism.[78] It is the language of the Christian gospel. The *Kairos Palestine Document* is anything but naïve. Its description of "reality on the ground" indicates a thorough grasp of the problem and the reason why it is so difficult to resolve.

We should also heed its words to the international community "to stop the principle of 'double standards' and insist on the international resolutions regarding the Palestinian problem with regard to all parties." This is clearly indicative of the *Kairos Palestine Document*'s recognition of the role of political negotiation and diplomacy. What it is asking for is an application of international law which does not only understand "the logic of force." It therefore calls for nonviolent resistance (sanctions and boycotts) "to reach a just and definitive peace that will put an end to Israeli occupation . . . and will guarantee security and peace for all."[79] A call that is, significantly, expressed within the context of Jesus' commandment to love your enemies, and the Pauline and Petrine injunctions not to "repay anyone evil for evil" (Matt 5:45–47; Rom 12:12; 1 Pet 3:9):

> Love is seeing the face of God in every human being . . . However, seeing the face of God in everyone does not mean accepting evil or aggression on their part. Rather this love seeks to correct the evil and stop the aggression.[80]

Given the realities of the occupation, then, the only option is to resist. "Resistance is a right and a duty for the Christian. But it is a resistance with love as its logic. It is thus a creative resistance for it must find human ways that engage the humanity of the enemy."[81] This is the language of Bonhoeffer. To love the "other," especially the other who is enemy, is to follow Christ in costly obedience; it is not pursuing the path of cheap reconciliation but of doing justice in obedience to the divine commandment of making peace.

---

78. See Rasmussen, *Dietrich Bonhoeffer*, 213–17.
79. *Kairos Palestine Document* 7.
80. *Kairos Palestine Document* 4.2.1.
81. *Kairos Palestine Document* 4.2.3.

6

RESPONSIBLE FREEDOM

&

the Threat to Bodily Life

It is God's gift that all should eat and drink and take pleasure in all their toil.

—Ecclesiastes 3:13

I became a doctor to save lives, not to play God, having to choose between those who I can keep alive and those I must leave to die.

—A Young Doctor's Cry[1]

He knew that the tale he had to tell could not be one of final victory. It could only be the record of what had to be done, and what assuredly would have to be done again in the never-ending fight against terror ... [W]hile unable to be saints, but refusing to bow down to pestilences, [they must] strive to their utmost to be healers ... [for] the plague bacillus never dies or disappears for good.

—Albert Camus[2]

---

1. The cry of a young doctor posted on Twitter during the coronavirus pandemic.
2. Camus, *Plague*, 252.

FAITH FACING REALITY

> Those who act out of free responsibility are justified before others by dire necessity; before themselves they are acquitted by their conscience, but before God they hope only for grace.
>
> —Bonhoeffer[3]

Albert Camus concludes *The Plague* (1947) on a sobering note. After the pandemic in Oran ends, the virus goes into hiding waiting for another opportune moment to wreak havoc. Camus was a member of the French Resistance in Algeria during the Second World War. He knew that after the defeat of Nazism, virulent nationalism would resurface, and as a victim of tuberculosis he knew there was no escape from the long-term consequences of disease. So, the plague is a metaphor for the relentless recurrence of war-mongering ideologies and their inevitable consequences, famine and disease among them. And those on the front lines, those who care for the bodily life of others, whether in the trenches or intensive care units, like Camus's Dr. Rieux, must make decisions that affect the destiny of many. That is the reality that confronts faith in our time, the time of COVID-19 and the invasion of Ukraine when the threat to bodily life faces us on every side, and those in authority, whether they are medics or politicians, bishops, or school principals, must provide leadership and seek solutions.

As the pandemic spread during 2020 and spilled over into 2021, many of us became more aware of the complex ethical dilemmas facing governments, public health authorities, medical practitioners, and concerned citizens.[4] How do they, and we, choose between saving the lives of the sick, many of them aged and chronically ill (and also increasingly many younger people in the prime of life), and saving the economy and the livelihood of the poor, chronically ill, undernourished, and unemployed? How do we exercise our responsibility without losing our freedom or denying that freedom to others in protecting our own?

The many public protests that have erupted to defend freedom against government measures to control the spread of the pandemic have highlighted the age-old problem of relating freedom and responsibility. But it is not a problem confined to the lecture hall; it is being fought over on the streets and in hospital wards. How do we respond to the need to make

---

3. Bonhoeffer, *Ethics*, 282.
4. See Williams, "Choices We Make."

responsible decisions about lives and livelihoods, about caring for the seriously ill and making triage decisions? Who should live and who be left to die? Theoretically it may be the same philosophical conundrum, but whereas the first—protest in defense of democratic freedoms—is characterized by personal self-interest clothed in political rhetoric, the second is about exercising responsibility on behalf of the sick and in the interests of the common good. "Playing God" in this way is not an act of hubris but an awesome responsibility for anyone, but especially for those medics who believe, with Bonhoeffer, that even where there is "the smallest responsible possibility of allowing the other to stay alive, then the destruction of this life would be arbitrary killing—murder."[5]

Every person has the right to bodily life, but does everyone have the same right? What if we choose not to follow COVID protocols, and thereby endanger the lives of others? What if we must choose between saving the life of some at the cost of the lives of others? What if some choose to die rather than stay alive? What if necessity demands that we play God? Such questions force us to face the reality of our responsibility and the limits to our freedom on the boundary between life and death. And, as Bonhoeffer well knew, there are seldom, if ever, final, or categorical answers to such borderline moral dilemmas which have perplexed ethicists over the centuries, and all of them have to do with our bodily existence. Are there ever circumstances in which we can legitimately kill another person—for example during a war—despite the commandment that we should never do so? Is it ever right for those living with excruciating pain to take their own lives, or for those who love them to assist them in doing so? Is it ever right to take the life of someone in order that another might live?

Not only does Bonhoeffer's *Ethics* show us *how* he wrestled with such questions, but his reflections provide us with *perspectives*, if not answers, that help us to do the same in making such decisions ourselves. Bonhoeffer reminds us that we cannot evade our responsibility on the pretext that we are free to do so, nor can we exercise it without the humility to acknowledge our limitations and the possibility, even inevitability, of a compromised conscience and a sense of guilt.

---

5. Bonhoeffer, *Ethics*, 190–91.

PLAGUE ON BOARD SHIP

One of the most dramatic moments that captured global headlines soon after the COVID-19 pandemic erupted was the rapid way it spread on cruise liners. The first to gain attention was *World Dream* on a journey from Guangdong in China to Da Nang in Vietnam in January 2020. There were seven thousand people on board, including some from Wuhan, the Chinese city where the virus was first detected, whatever its actual origins. Soon after, at the beginning of February, the pandemic was confirmed on the *Diamond Princess*, which had docked in Yokohama in Japan and was then quarantined at sea the next day. Within a few days the liner had more than half of the reported infections outside China in the rest of the world. Other cruise ships, it was then reported, were also affected, and passengers and crew found themselves isolated from the world as countries woke up in panic to the reality of the pandemic as it spread from one country and town to the next.

Medical scientists had long warned governments about the possibility of a global pandemic, but it took time to understand the epidemiology of COVID-19 and to find ways to treat it, let alone to prevent it from spreading. And, as it spread, so too did fears and rumors. Reports of overcrowded hospitals, exhausted medical workers, and daily bulletins of infections and deaths, added to the anxiety as governments introduced lockdowns, wearing masks became mandatory, and scientists searched for cures and tested vaccines. That was the context in which I was asked to write my essay on Bonhoeffer for the *Ecumenical Review*. And what I wrote was prompted by the cry of a young doctor in South Africa: "I became a doctor to save lives, not to play God, having to choose between those who I can keep alive and those I must leave to die."

On hearing this cry, I recalled a section in Bonhoeffer's *Ethics* where he writes about the "Right to Bodily Life" and asks whether it is ever justifiable to kill "innocent sick life . . . for the benefit of the healthy." What is more, in seeking to answer the question, Bonhoeffer refers to a "borderline case" that echoed the headlines of our time. He wrote: what if "a plague broke out on a ship that had no facilities for isolation and, by human reckoning, the healthy could be saved only by the death of the sick?" His conclusion? "In this case the decision would have to remain open."[6] Without reference to the word, Bonhoeffer was talking about triage, or the prioritizing of medical

---

6. Bonhoeffer, *Ethics*, 195.

treatment to victims of war, disaster, or disease, according to the likelihood of survival, given the lack of resources to treat all. But the underlying issue that bothered Bonhoeffer was not the plague; it was the sinister practice of euthanasia in the Third Reich and, implicitly, the possibility and legitimacy of tyrannicide—that is, the assassination of Adolf Hitler. Did not Hitler have to die so that the many could be saved?

Since the time Bonhoeffer wrote about euthanasia in his *Ethics*, the debate on the subject has developed further, given advances in medical science as well as demographics—notably the rising age profile in the West. This, as Paul Clarke indicates, has strengthened the pressure to permit active euthanasia and has focused attention on "the allocation of health care resources measured against the quality of life."[7] The utilitarian calculation to establish the quality of a person's life (Quality for Adjusted Life Year or QALY) has become a way of measuring its value. On this basis an "economically active young person scores higher . . . than an economically inactive elderly person who is consuming large resources." In a time of limited resources, the conclusion seems obvious. Yet can any person's life be evaluated in this way, especially if life is not simply understood in individualistic terms but also in terms of relationships? What if the measurement of value shifts from the purely utilitarian to the possible contribution that the wisdom of age may contribute to the well-being of society? Personally, as an octogenarian, I am fully aware of the problem, for even though I still live what seems to be a productive life, my need for medical resources has grown considerably, and what my medical aid can provide is far greater than what many others need simply to live. At the same time, the preoccupation of earlier generations with death has shifted to a concern about living without the acute pain that accompanies the process of dying. I will reflect further on this in the Epilogue. For now, I return to the German context in which Bonhoeffer was reflecting on euthanasia.

EUTHANASIA, STATE MURDER & TYRANNICIDE

Already in 1929, Hitler had proposed to his followers at a rally in Nuremberg that there should be a yearly culling of the "weakest Germans" to improve the vitality of the *Volk*.[8] Ten years later, on September 1, 1939, Hitler began to implement his plan by targeting children and then adults

---

7. Clarke, "Euthanasia," 340.
8. See Barnett, *For the Soul of the People*, 106–10,

in state and church institutions who were physically challenged. This "led to the gassing of over one hundred thousand men, women, and children who did not fit the image of healthy racial Aryans."[9] These included those "classified as incurably sick, insane, crippled, or otherwise possessed of lives deemed 'not worth living.'"[10] They were murdered "in gas chambers disguised as shower rooms or in mobile vans into which carbon monoxide was pumped."[11] Their bodies were then cremated.

The rationale used by defenders of this ghastly program, trying to put the best possible spin on its goal, was that just as young, healthy, and virile Germans were giving their lives on the battlefield in defense of the Reich, so the sacrifice of the chronically ill and physically deformed was necessary for the well-being of the *Volk*.[12] Although the program was meant to be kept secret, word soon leaked out, resulting in considerable protest, including from some church leaders. But by then Hitler had achieved his immediate goal, having perfected the methods he would soon use to exterminate the Jews in a mass act of state-controlled murder. Victims were graded like cattle; the only distinction made was between those who were fit enough for slave labor until they died and those who should be eliminated.[13] It was left to the Gestapo officers on duty to "play God" and decide the fate of each.

Now we return to Bonhoeffer's allusion to the cruise liner carrying passengers infected by the plague. Sacrificing the sick for the sake of saving the healthy, he thought, was the only possible exception that could justify "mercy killing." But that would be, at best, a "borderline case," a "necessity" to preserve the life of many at the cost of some. But even then, it was problematic. Could this ever be justified? What was Bonhoeffer's reasoning? William Peck has helped us see how Bonhoeffer's discussion of euthanasia must be read at different levels. A "surface reading" would recognize that his treatment of euthanasia follows the traditional argument that rejects any arbitrary killing of innocent people except on the grounds of unconditional necessity. On those grounds, he rejects euthanasia in principle, as he also does abortion, clearly having in mind the Nazi program of eliminating undesirable elements (Jews, the disabled, homosexuals) from "polluting"

9. Fischer, *Nazi Germany*, 195,
10. Peck, "Euthanasia Text," 146.
11. Fischer, *Nazi Germany*, 389.
12. See Barnett, *For the Soul of the People*, 110.
13. Barnett, *For the Soul of the People*, 104.

society.[14] However, a "depth reading" of Bonhoeffer's text must take account that at the time he wrote this, Bonhoeffer was already involved in the plot to assassinate Hitler. Naturally, it would have been foolish to mention this, but that it was daily on his mind is evident in him saying that the "single, sufficient, and inescapable reason" such killing is permissible would be tyrannicide.[15]

Bonhoeffer's approach to ethics was not simplistically situational or contextual, but he did take reality seriously, namely, the catastrophic situation in Europe and the necessity to eliminate Hitler to save millions of lives. For Bonhoeffer, this could never be used as a pretext for violence more generally; nor did it necessarily compromise his commitment to a "peace ethic."[16] What was at stake, for him, was the need to exercise responsible freedom in the face of concrete reality. To discern God's will in doing so required considering all possibilities and consequences, and even then, there could be no absolute certainty.[17]

Bonhoeffer did not resolve to his satisfaction the "borderline case" of the outbreak of the plague on board a cruise liner, so he left that case open. But it clearly anticipated his "borderline" decision to participate in the assassination of Hitler because his discussion of euthanasia and mercy killing in his *Ethics* cannot be extracted from the reality of the Resistance in which he was involved, and specifically the attempt to kill Hitler. If the "ship of state" was about to sink into oblivion and drag the world with it because of the Nazi virus, then it was necessary, indeed, obligatory, to quarantine or eliminate the person who was infecting and threatening to destroy not only the nation but Europe as a whole. Bonhoeffer was fully aware that such an action on his part, this choice of "free responsibility," inevitably involved guilt, but he had to accept that possibility and throw himself on the mercy of God. As Green sums up his argument:

> Participating in a conspiracy to kill a tyrant involves guilt; it is contrary to the Decalogue and the Sermon on the Mount. Rather than trying to justify his involvement in the conspiracy by appealing to some principle or casuistry, Bonhoeffer saw it instead as an act

---

14. See Bonhoeffer, *Ethics* 190–91, 206–7; see also Peck, "Euthanasia Text," 147; and Green, Introduction to Bonhoeffer, *Ethics*, 24–25.

15. See Peck, "Euthanasia Text," 152.

16. See Green, Introduction to Bonhoeffer, *Ethics*, 14–16.

17. Bonhoeffer, *Ethics*, 324.

of repentance and was willing to take the guilt of his action upon himself.[18]

This was a classic case of "vicarious responsible action" in "correspondence with reality."

Bonhoeffer went further. Because he was not seeking to play the martyr for his own sake but willing to accept the guilt of Germany and the church by acting freely and responsibly on their behalf, he acknowledged he was a sinner dependent on God's mercy and grace. So, in a passage which is undoubtedly autobiographical in character, Bonhoeffer writes that whenever we are faced with the difficult choice of keeping our consciences clear or exercising our responsibility and therefore getting our hands dirty in obeying Christ, then our "conscience is set free by responsibility." So, he writes: "Those who in acting responsibly take on guilt—which is inescapable for any responsible person—place this guilt on themselves" and "take responsibility for it." And they do so "in the knowledge of being forced into this freedom and of their dependence on grace in its exercise." Which leads Bonhoeffer to make his celebrated comment: "Those who act out of free responsibility are justified before others by dire necessity; before themselves they are acquitted by their conscience, but before God they hope only for grace."[19]

The question to put to Bonhoeffer, then, is simply this: Is he not "playing God" not only by deciding that Hitler must be assassinated but also by committing the deed freely as an act of responsibility before God? And, if so, does this not provide us with some insight into the very difficult triage decisions that doctors have to make between which of two chronically ill patients should live and which should die?

TRUTH, TRIAGE, AND MORAL RESPONSIBILITY

Bonhoeffer's father, Karl, was a distinguished medical doctor, a professor of psychiatry and neurology at the University of Berlin, and director of its neurological clinic at the Charité Hospital. The fact that Dietrich was profoundly influenced by his father also meant that he imbibed something of the scientific and medical paternal ethos in his home environment. Certainly in prison Bonhoeffer showed his interest in the medical care of

---

18. Green, Introduction, 13.
19. Bonhoeffer, *Ethics*. 282.

prisoners, a subject on which he wrote a report; he also read a book on medical research and studied the medical corps handbook in the hope that on his release he could join the medical service.[20] But even previously, in writing about the ethics of responsibility and Christian vocation, he took the calling of a medical doctor as his example to show how the vocation of a Christian extends beyond the narrow boundary of any particular calling. A medical doctor not only serves a patient but also scientific knowledge, and knowledge of truth more generally. As Bonhoeffer writes: "Although in practice I render this service in my concrete situation—for example, at a patient's bedside—I nevertheless remain aware of my responsibility toward the whole, and only thus fulfill my vocation." But he also acknowledges that:

> it may come to the point that in a particular case I must recognize and fulfill my concrete responsibility as a physician no longer only at a patient's bedside, but, for example, in taking a public stance against a measure that poses a threat to medical science, or human life, or science in general.[21]

Given the context within which Bonhoeffer was writing, and the subjects that he was considering, among them euthanasia, he clearly had in mind that medical doctors in the Third Reich had a responsibility not only to practice medicine, but to do so ethically and therefore be responsible to the truth about what was happening in society. You could not be a medical doctor, and certainly not a Christian one, if you participated in medical practices that were immoral, or turned a blind eye to them as many did in the service of the state or to save their own skins. "Vocation," he wrote, "is responsibility, and responsibility is the whole response of the whole person to reality as a whole." Bonhoeffer continues:

> This is precisely why a myopic self-limitation to one's vocational obligations in the narrowest sense is out of the question; such a limitation would be irresponsibility. The nature of free responsibility rules out any legal regulation of when and to what extent human vocation and responsibility entail breaking out [*Durchbrechen*] of the "definite field of activity." This can happen only after seriously considering one's immediate vocational obligations, the dangers of encroaching on the responsibilities of others, and finally the total picture of the issue at hand. It will then be my free

---

20. Bonhoeffer, *Letters and Papers from Prison*, 140, 212, 286, 343–47, 424.
21. Bonhoeffer, *Ethics*, 293.

responsibility in response to the call of Jesus Christ that leads me in one direction or the other. Responsibility in a vocation follows the call of Christ alone.[22]

In normal situations, doctors make life-and-death decisions after consulting families, peers, and patients where possible. But in frontline military hospitals during battle, overcrowded ICU wards, or rural hospitals during a pandemic, making such decisions, even when guided by triage protocols,[23] is much more difficult for overworked and exhausted medics often working on their own. They find themselves having to "play God" not by choice but by default.

In a different and generally less traumatic way, political leaders too often end up playing God by default—even if they are more eager to and adept at doing so—deciding how to respond to a pandemic affecting millions of people. How should resources be distributed, especially when unjust policies and practices have long prevailed?[24] Should their country go into lockdown and, if so, for how long? When and how should they return to normal, and what are the norms that should govern the rebuilding of social life? Decisions like these are most difficult for those with moral sensitivity, not just political shrewdness, and with no desire to play God. Such public leaders, like frontline doctors, sometimes pay a heavy moral and psychological cost in doing so.

But often the decisions are made with political interests in mind, if not with a dose of cynicism—hence the charge that some indulge in what has come to be called "vaccine apartheid." Writing online, Kamau Mwangi of Taganza University College in Kenya puts the various sides of the argument succinctly. Acknowledging that some countries have done a great deal to distribute vaccines to more needy nations, he goes on to argue "that the action of pharmaceutical companies to patent the vaccines in order to maximize on profits is tantamount to apartheid and putting profits before people."[25] In addition, it could be said that in times of emergency like our own, serving the common good should be the primary factor that

---

22. Bonhoeffer, *Ethics*, 293.

23. See "Standard Operating Procedure (SOP) for Triage of Suspected COVID-19 Patients in non-US Healthcare Settings," published online by Centers for Disease Control and Prevention (CDC), Updated April 14, 2020; and "COVID-19 rapid guideline: critical care in adults," NICE (UK) guideline [NG159] 20 March 2020.

24. See Baldwin-Ragaven et al., eds., *Ambulance of the Wrong Color*; Baldwin-Ragaven, "Social Dimensions."

25. Mwangi, "Vaccine Apartheid?"

companies ought to refer to while making these decisions. Of course, the counterargument made by pharmaceutical companies and governments is that "forcing these companies to forgo patenting will result in stultifying creativity and industriousness"[26] and therefore curb research. Whether the label "vaccine apartheid" is appropriate may be a moot point, as Kamau Mwangi acknowledges, but it does highlight a serious moral issue. Do rich and powerful nations have the right to decide who should live and who should die elsewhere? Are the lives of the poor, the majority of whom are Black, of less value than the lives of the wealthy and White? If the wealthy and White are more valuable than the Black poor, then it would be a clear denial of what Bonhoeffer called "the right to bodily life." Indeed, just as the pseudoscience of eugenics was used to rationalize Nazi racial policy and its implementation, it would then mean that racist assumptions drive the policies of the powerful and the rich in responding to the COVID-19 pandemic.

In a thoughtful article on the moral costs involved in making and implementing triage decisions in medical practice (as distinct from political decisions of some governments), Joshua Parker and Mikaeil Mirzaali point out that the emerging utilitarian approach to the problem, which is fundamentally one of distributive justice, represents a paradigm shift from deontological to utilitarian ethics. Generally, in medical practice, the good of the majority now has priority over the inherent rights of individual patients. Doctors may not have to decide on such policy guidelines, but they must implement them and so shoulder the burden of responsibility. But there is a cost involved, for the inevitable risk is "moral injury," that is, "psychological harm caused by transgressing one's deeply held values" resulting in "feelings of guilt and remorse."[27] This was dramatically demonstrated in April 2020 by the tragic suicide of Dr Lorna Breen, a medical director of New York Presbyterian hospital, because she felt unable to save patients dying of COVID-19.[28]

GUILT AND GRIEF

I have no competency to comment on triage guidelines or the advice given by public health specialists, but my reflections may be helpful in dealing

---

26. Mwangi, "Vaccine Apartheid."
27. Parker and Mirzaali, "Moral Cost of Coronavirus."
28. Hauck, "'Brave, Compassionate, and Dedicated.'"

with the problem of moral responsibility and cost, and the feelings of guilt and grief that might incur. In sharing my thoughts, I am not suggesting a clear analogy between Bonhoeffer's situation and that which we now face. Nonetheless, his reflections on ethical decision-making in response to Nazi medical policies and in response to the plot to assassinate Hitler are helpful. Bonhoeffer was a moral and pastoral counselor to those military officers in the Resistance circle of which he became a part. This circle, located in the *Abwehr* (Military Intelligence), was where Bonhoeffer's brother-in-law Hans von Dohnanyi worked as a senior lawyer. And it was Dohnanyi who arranged for Bonhoeffer to serve in the *Abwehr* to avoid military service. However, his main reason for placing Bonhoeffer in the *Abwehr* was so that he could use Bonhoeffer's ecumenical contacts to gain Allied support for the Resistance. Thus the theologian became "an accessory" to the conspiracy.[29] But von Dohnanyi had another motive for involving Bonhoeffer, namely, his pastoral skills and theological insight. Evidently, on one occasion the brothers-in-law had discussed a question that was bothering others in Resistance circles: could they, in exceptional circumstances, commit murder? In response Bonhoeffer replied, "Murder is still murder, even when, as in the case of Hitler, it is absolutely necessary. Moreover, one must be prepared to take the guilt for this sin upon oneself." And, Bonhoeffer added, he would kill Hitler himself given the chance![30]

The military officers in the Resistance were increasingly aware that the war was lost. Their growing consensus was that they had to eliminate Hitler, and that the military leadership had to take control if anything was to be salvaged, including their own future.[31] Just thinking this out aloud was dangerous, but even if they agreed that it was necessary, they were not necessarily willing to act accordingly. Nonetheless, they were thoughtful men of conscience who debated ad nauseum the moral issues and possible consequences of their planned actions. They knew that the plot they were hatching was a denial of everything for which they stood: honor, duty, and obedience.[32] Not only were they planning to commit murder, an option rejected by some, such as Helmut von Moltke, out of Christian commitment, but also treason. Had they not taken an oath of obedience to Hitler

---

29. Bethge, *Dietrich Bonhoeffer*, 622–25.

30. Schlingensiepen, *Dietrich Bonhoeffer*, 274. See also Bonhoeffer, *Barcelona, Berlin, New York*, 367.

31. Bracher, *German Dictatorship*, 549–68.

32. See Rasmussen, *Dietrich Bonhoeffer*, 178–79.

as binding as the Hippocratic oath, even though they served vastly different purposes?

Bonhoeffer's role in the Resistance, then, was to encourage the increasingly pessimistic conspirators not to lose hope, and to help them deal with feelings of guilt about killing Hitler, which prevented them from acting decisively.[33] We get a taste of his counsel in "After Ten Years," his 1942 Christmas letter to them:

> Have there ever been people in history who in their time, like us, had so little ground under their feet, people to whom every possible alternative open to them at the time appeared equally unbearable, senseless, and contrary to life? Have there been those who like us looked for the source of their strength beyond all those available alternatives? Were they looking entirely in what has passed away and in what is yet to come? And nevertheless, without being dreamers, did they await with calm and confidence the successful outcome of their endeavor?[34]

This paragraph was, as Barnett puts it, "a synthesis of an ongoing and troubled conversation" between Bonhoeffer's inner circle of resisters, "as they wrestled with their consciences and the diminishing options open to those who sought the end of National Socialism."[35] "After Ten Years" captures the essence of what we find in in Bonhoeffer's *Ethics*, and his "observations about what happens to human decency and courage when a political culture disintegrates continue to resonate around the world today."[36]

Bonhoeffer's role in the assassination plot was not to pull the trigger. That task was eventually undertaken by the aristocratic Claus von Stauffenberg, an officer accustomed to decisive action, who became involved in the Resistance only after Bonhoeffer's imprisonment.[37] A Catholic by upbringing, Stauffenberg was a year younger than Bonhoeffer and in many respects a contrasting figure, yet he had the "civil courage" to undertake his fateful task on July 20th, 1944.[38] He did so under the influence of General Henning von Tresckow, a committed Protestant who had assumed leadership in the

---

33. See Tödt, *Authentic Faith*, 215.
34. Bonhoeffer, *Letters and Papers from Prison*, 38.
35. Barnett, ed., "After Ten Years," 4.
36. Barnett, ed., "After Ten Years," 4.
37. Venohr, *Stauffenberg*, 137–44. See Bethge, *Dietrich Bonhoeffer*, 803; Schlingensiepen, *Dietrich Bonhoeffer*, 286, 298, 321; Rasmussen, *Dietrich Bonhoeffer*, 192–96.
38. See Venohr, *Stauffenberg*, 144.

conspiracy and become its "moral core."³⁹ In convincing Stauffenberg of the legitimacy of killing Hitler, Tresckow used the same arguments and even language as Bonhoeffer, suggesting the latter's influence, possibly through his brother Klaus, who had contact with Treschow's circle.⁴⁰ But what was Bonhoeffer's argument and what has it to do with the ethics of playing God during this pandemic?

DARE WE PLAY GOD?

Bonhoeffer begins his *Ethics* by asserting that Christian ethics does not ask "how can I know the good?" but "what is the will of God?"⁴¹ Acting decisively does not result from endless discussions about the morality of some action, but from discerning "the will of God" and acting accordingly. But is this not a presumptuous, fanatical, and dangerous claim to make? Too many people claim to be doing the will of God when going to war, assassinating a politician, blowing up a car, or simply rejecting scientific evidence regarding the environment or disease, or in adopting unjust political policies. However, what if playing God is not determined by egotistic self-will and corrupt self-interest but motivated by the commandment to love our neighbor? That is, "the other"—whether enemy, foreigner, refugee, Jew, Muslim, homosexual, mentally disabled, or a patient gasping for breath?

In the section on "Natural Life" in his *Ethics*, where Bonhoeffer discusses euthanasia, he implicitly contrasts the protection of innocent life with the duty to take the life of Hitler.⁴² In conclusion he makes his passing, but remarkably prescient comment on the borderline question I earlier mentioned: "if a plague broke out on a ship that had no facilities for isolation and, by human reckoning, the healthy could be saved only by the death of the sick."⁴³ While he cannot provide a clear-cut answer, Bonhoeffer, as I have noted, was fully aware of the problem raised by the plague in relation to the conspiracy against Hitler. Indeed, in a novel he later wrote in prison, the only other place in his extensive works in which he mentions "the plague," he implicitly refers to the plot against Hitler and the pessimism of his co-conspirators:

39. Bracher, *German Dictatorship*, 557.
40. Bethge, *Dietrich Bonhoeffer*, 808.
41. Bonhoeffer, *Ethics*, 47.
42. Peck, "Euthanasia Text," 150.
43. Bonhoeffer, *Ethics*, 195.

> "And yet, boys," he [the major] continued, "one mustn't be discouraged by the seeming hopelessness of the struggle. Whoever has brought down even one of these petty tormentors can boast of saving many human lives. Such people are benefactors of humanity, even if no one else knows it. Many well-meaning people of our class have become accustomed to smiling about these petty tyrants and regarding as fools those who have declared total war on them.

But, continues Bonhoeffer,

> "Smiling about them is as foolish and irresponsible as smiling about the tiny size of bacteria and about the doctors who save this or that life during an epidemic and then fall victim to it themselves. To be sure, this war also needs both strategists and soldiers, as the war against an epidemic needs those who probe under the microscope for the cause of the disease, and others like doctors who attack the individual case. But woe to people who scorn those who sacrifice their lives in this war!"[44]

Bonhoeffer knew that the problem the conspirators faced in taking the decisive step could be traced back to their upbringing and training. They were programmed to act according to rational principles and a conscience determined by a sense of duty.[45]

In "After Ten Years," Bonhoeffer offers another perspective. Having given his critique of those virtues, he says that what is now needed is "civil courage." And that could "grow only from the free responsibility of the free human . . . founded in a God who calls for the free venture of faith to responsible action and who promises forgiveness and consolation to the one who on account of such action becomes a sinner."[46] The extent to which these insights may apply to frontline medics or politicians during a pandemic will have to be determined by them. But it must surely be the case that when it becomes a matter of necessity, they need to be encouraged to make decisive interventions, and to do so in a timely fashion with the assurance that there is a way to handle the inevitable moral cost that will be incurred.

---

44. Bonhoeffer, *Fiction from Tegel Prison*, 121–22.
45. See Bonhoeffer, *Ethics*, 78–80; Bonhoeffer, *Letters and Papers from Prison*, 38–40.
46. Bonhoeffer, *Letters and Papers from Prison*, 41.

THE UNCONDITIONAL NECESSITY
FOR CIVIL COURAGE

At the time he was writing his *Ethics*, Bonhoeffer was also reading Machiavelli's *The Prince*, where he noted the dictum that "a prince who wants to keep his authority must learn how not to be good, and use that knowledge, or refrain from using it, *as necessity requires*."[47] Bonhoeffer does not dismiss Machiavelli's counsel out of hand because, as he says, we cannot deny that "such necessities actually exist. To deny them would mean ceasing to act in accord with reality."[48] And to act "in accord with reality" was a necessary part of free responsible action. Nonetheless, such necessities, Bonhoeffer writes, "cannot be captured by any law and can never become laws themselves." They are "borderline cases." Therefore, in war "there is killing, lying, and seizing of property solely in order to reinstate the validity of life, truth, and property."[49] This grave breaking of the law cannot be cynically affirmed, but neither can we deny the possibility that such action is done out of a genuine sense of responsibility. Or even that although "the one who acts is not torn apart by destructive conflict," he "can with confidence and inner integrity do the unspeakable, namely, in the very act of breaking the law to sanctify it."[50] That is, to play God responsibly. Indeed, if Hitler pursued power because he and his supporters believed he was God's agent and therefore could do whatever he wanted for his own ends out of necessity, did not necessity also require that something normally considered immoral could be done to get rid of him? Thus, writes Bonhoeffer:

> The killing of another's life can only take place on the basis of unconditional necessity, and then it must be carried out even against any number of other reasons, even good ones. Never may the killing of another's life be one possibility among many, however well founded that possibility may be. Where there is even the smallest responsible possibility of allowing the other to stay alive, then the destruction of this life would be arbitrary killing—murder.[51]

---

47. Machiavelli, *Prince*, 52 (italics added); see Bonhoeffer, *Ethics*, 273n99.

48. See Bonhoeffer, *Ethics*, 89, 130, 239–40; Bonhoeffer, *Letters and Papers from Prison*, 475–76.

49. Bonhoeffer, *Ethics*, 272.

50. Bonhoeffer, *Ethics*, 297.

51. Bonhoeffer, *Ethics*, 190.

Sometimes, Bonhoeffer says, "the strict observance of the explicit law . . . entails a clash with the basic necessities of human life" whereas "civil courage" requires departing from laws because we are "confronted with the extraordinary situation of ultimate necessities that are beyond any possible regulation by law."[52]

Even so, Bonhoeffer insists, we must avoid two false ways of fulfilling our God-given responsibility: the "radical" way, and that of "compromise." In unpacking what this means, he contrasts the "ultimate" and the "penultimate," that is what may be regarded as absolute (whether absolute truth, love, or justice) with what can be done or achieved given the realities under which we live in the penultimate. So, he says, the "radical solution sees only the ultimate, and in it sees only a complete break with the penultimate."[53] This is fanaticism: a refusal to listen to reason, scientific evidence, political analysis, and the wisdom of tradition—a refusal to weigh the options before embarking on action.

Responsible political action, by contrast, must correspond to reality, and Christians must refrain from using Christ either to sanction the status quo or to bless every revolution.[54] "Responsible action," Bonhoeffer says, is not nourished by "an ideology but by reality, which is why one can only act within the boundaries of that reality."[55] Otherwise "it is the craziest Don Quixotry."[56] There is nothing morally responsible about "going down fighting like heroes in the face of certain defeat."[57] The plot on Hitler required a great deal of careful reflection and planning to be successful and not quixotic.[58] But the way of compromise goes to the other extreme by separating the ultimate from the penultimate. This leads to inaction because there is never a perfect time or plan to engage in necessary action in an extraordinary situation. To wait for perfect conditions—a fully functioning ICU with unlimited resources or a perfect, foolproof plan to assassinate a tyrant—is wishful and unrealistic. By contrast, to act responsibly out of necessity invariably means taking risks and doing so freely. In the penultimate, that cannot be avoided.

52. Bonhoeffer, *Ethics*, 272–73.
53. Bonhoeffer, *Ethics*, 153.
54. Bonhoeffer, *Ethics*, 219–98.
55. Bonhoeffer, *Ethics*, 22.
56. Bonhoeffer, *Ethics*, 51.
57. Bonhoeffer, *Ethics*, 51, 80.
58. Bonhoeffer, *Ethics*, 35.

THE VENTURE OF FREE RESPONSIBILITY

When the conspiracy began, not only did Hitler still have immense popular support, but the Allied leadership had also decided that Germany must surrender unconditionally. So, the plotters had no guarantees that even a successful coup led by the Resistance would be acceptable, end the war, and save millions of lives. However, it was increasingly apparent to those in the Resistance (as it was to most observers after the Battle of Stalingrad) that the situation on the warfront was seriously deteriorating just as it was in Germany itself. Hitler's opponents also knew that the possibility of passive resistance had long ceased to be an option when the likes of Bonhoeffer had publicly confronted evil from the pulpit or through lectures and conference statements. Now, in the shadowy world of the underground, Bonhoeffer had to discover how to confess Christ in secret when all other avenues were shut, ethical absolutes no longer applied, and even lying was justified. This was why he was open to the invitation to join the conspiracy, even though it appeared he was reneging on his commitment to the Sermon on the Mount. It was, for him, the necessary step of "civil courage" he had to take in solidarity with his fellow conspirators.

Significantly, as Barry Harvey remarks, Bonhoeffer did not try "to harmonize either theoretically or practically, the profound tension between his peace ethic and his cooperation with those who sought with all the means at their disposal to bring the regime to an end."[59] Obeying the will of God was no longer a matter of working out and applying principles based on philosophical reasoning and intellectual abstractions, or even gospel injunctions. The challenge was not to satisfy conscience or extricate oneself from the situation, but to act in ways that brought the Nazi catastrophe to an end and prepared the way for a world in which the coming generation could live in peace.[60] In such situations "shrouded in twilight," writes Bonhoeffer, we "must decide not simply between right and wrong, good and evil, but between right and right, wrong and wrong."[61] This means that we cannot work to the rule of purity of motive, favorable conditions, or "the meaningfulness of an intended action," hiding behind it or "appealing to its authority" in order to "be exonerated and acquitted." The courage to

---

59. Harvey, *Taking Hold of the Real*, 277.
60. Bonhoeffer, *Letters and Papers from Prison*, 42.
61. Bonhoeffer, *Ethics*, 283–84.

act, Bonhoeffer said, "can grow only from the free responsibility of the free man."[62]

But what, then, about the "sovereignty of God" and the biblical injunction that "vengeance belongs to God"? Dare we take this into our own hands? Bonhoeffer addresses this perplexing question in another brief paragraph in "After Ten Years":

> I believe that God can and will let good come out of everything, even the greatest evil. For that to happen, God needs human beings who let everything work out for the best. I believe that in every moment of distress God will give us as much strength to resist as we need. But it is not given to us in advance, lest we rely on ourselves and not on God alone. In such faith all fear of the future should be overcome.

Bonhoeffer then adds this faith conviction:

> I believe that even our mistakes and shortcomings are not in vain and that it is no more difficult for God to deal with them than with our supposedly good deeds. I believe that God is no timeless fate but waits for and responds to sincere prayer and responsible actions.[63]

I found these words particularly helpful following the Soweto uprising in South Africa in 1986 in trying to decipher the relationship between human agency in the struggle for justice and God's action in history.[64] But I recognized in them what Bethge told me at the time, namely, that Bonhoeffer struggled hard to understand the "providence of God": how divine action and human action correlate, and how God brings good out of evil. We see this time and again in his *Ethics* where he writes that because reality is not "built on principles" but rests "on the living, creating God," our decisions depend on God's guidance and trust that what we do is ultimately God's action. In this way our "venture of free responsibility" is a "divine necessity."[65]

Bonhoeffer well knew that what he was saying and planning to do could set a dangerous precedent, encouraging fanaticism in the name of God. To counter that danger, he said that those who are responsible and act

---

62. Bonhoeffer, *Letters and Papers from Prison*, 41.
63. Bonhoeffer, *Letters and Papers from Prison*, 46.
64. See de Gruchy, *Bonhoeffer and South Africa*, 47–65.
65. Bonhoeffer, *Ethics*, 284.

in their own freedom, even if they do so collectively, still have "to observe, judge, weigh, decide, and act on their own." Moreover, they "have to examine the motives, the prospects, the value, and meaning of their action." This is when the "simplicity of wisdom" comes into play because it is only the truly wise who seek "the best possible information about the course of events without becoming dependent on it" and know "the limits of principles when confronted by reality."[66] In any case, believing we are doing God's will does not mean that we will not make mistakes. On the contrary, the "God who calls for responsible action" also "promises forgiveness and consolation to the one who on account of such action becomes a sinner."[67]

But what could this mean for people who, like most of the conspirators, including his brother-in-law Hans von Dohnanyi, had lost faith in Christianity and the church and were agnostics or practical atheists? Or what can it mean for doctors who must play God without believing in God? This is the question that Bonhoeffer struggled to answer in prison. What does the "free venture of faith and responsible action" mean in a "world come of age," a world that "lives and manages its affairs in science, in society and government, in art, ethics, and religion" without recourse to the "working hypothesis: God"?[68]

We have encountered this question several times before in these pages, and necessarily so, because it is *the* question that bothered Bonhoeffer the most as he wrestled with what it means for faith to face reality. Inevitably we, too, come back to it again and again as if it were a constant refrain in facing reality today. How do people act morally yet freely and responsibly if in all honesty they no longer believe—indeed, when it is not faith facing reality, but reality confronting us in all our vulnerability as honest human beings, like those who were Bonhoeffer's companions in the Resistance?

Bonhoeffer said it is "pointless, ignoble, and unchristian" to argue or exploit the idea that people need "God, and the church and the pastor" to deal with "ultimate questions" such as death and guilt. He also knew from his own experience that Christians who claim to believe in God too often do not do "the will of God," while many secular humanists who make no such claims are often closer to following Christ in standing up for human dignity and justice.[69] Indeed, if you believe, as Tutu provocatively said, that "God

---

66. Bonhoeffer, *Ethics*, 284.
67. Bonhoeffer, *Letters and Papers from Prison*, 41.
68. Bonhoeffer, *Letters and Papers from Prison*, 476.
69. See Bonhoeffer, *Ethics*, 340–41.

is not a Christian," then you do not have to be religious or a Christian to do the will of God. Furthermore, to assume that God is a cosmic magician who saves the world independently of human agency is to deny not only our God-given responsibility as humans but also the incarnation, namely, that God became human for the very purpose of taking responsibility as a human being to save other human lives in a violent world.[70]

ACTING WITHOUT NECESSARILY BELIEVING

Whether we believe in God or not, when making moral, political, scientific, and medical decisions based on reason and evidence we must take responsibility for our actions *etsi deus non daretur*, that is, "as if there were no God."[71] To categorically and arrogantly claim that God told me to assassinate Hitler or to turn off a ventilator in the ICU is a misuse of God's name. But if I act in "free responsibility" (that is, having considered all possible options and evidence) and do so out of necessity, then, from Bonhoeffer's faith perspective, I am acting "before God" even if I do not believe And I am doing so because the "same God who makes us to live in the world without the working hypothesis of God is the God before whom we stand continually. Before God, and with God, we live without God."[72] If necessity demands that I must play God, then I must do so in "fear and trembling." Which brings to mind Kierkegaard's moving account of Abraham on Mount Moriah, for just as Abraham went out into the unknown by faith, when he had to sacrifice his own son, he knew what faith required even if he dreaded taking the step (Gen 22). Nobody ever wants to be in the position to make such a decision, but the father of biblical faith did, and so the story of faith did not end on Mount Moriah but continued to Mount Calvary.[73]

Acting out of free responsibility, then, is a penultimate action, something we decide to do out of necessity in the here and now, the messy world of ambiguity and contradiction in which we live and must act freely, responsibly, but also out of necessity. We do so without invoking God to condone or justify what we choose to do, for we know that in the end (ultimate) we remain, as Jesus said, "unworthy servants," that is, compromised to some lesser or greater degree (see Luke 17:7–10). Nevertheless, we live and act

---

70. Bonhoeffer, *Letters and Papers from Prison*, 476–82.
71. Bonhoeffer, *Letters and Papers from Prison*, 476. See also 476n23.
72. Bonhoeffer, *Letters and Papers from Prison*, 478–79.
73. Kierkegaard, *Fear and Trembling*, 48.

"before God," in the light of the ultimate, God's final word of forgiveness and justification by grace. We cannot naively justify what we do as the "will of God," but we can say that we have acted in the knowledge that God will not ultimately hold us guilty for doing what we believed we had to do out of necessity.

Bonhoeffer traced back to their upbringing, education, or what he refers to as their formation (*Bildung*), the inability of people to act out of free responsibility when necessity required. That is why he speaks of Christian ethics as *formation*. Following Saint Paul, for Bonhoeffer, this formation requires *metanoia* or a fundamental change of mind, without which we cannot begin to know the "mind of Christ" and therefore the "will of God" (see, inter alia, Rom 12:2; Phil 2:5). And this starts with the recognition that in Christ the reality of the world and the reality of God meet. So in his *Ethics*, Bonhoeffer writes that it is not by ideals or programs, conscience, duty, responsibility, or virtue that we meet and overcome reality, but only by "the consummate love of God." This is not accomplished "by a general idea of love, but by the love of God really lived in Jesus Christ," a love of God that "does not withdraw from reality into noble souls detached from the world, but [that] experiences and suffers the reality of the world at its worst."[74] That is why I quoted Kierkegaard at the beginning of Chapter 1, who says that the love of God cannot be measured by any common standard; it is greater than reality itself.

Discerning the will of God revealed in Christ "does not happen as we strive 'to become like Jesus'"; rather, it occurs "as the form of Jesus Christ himself so works on us that it molds us, conforming our form to Christ's own (Gal. 4:9)."[75] This means that if faced with "absolute necessity" in extraordinary situations when the accepted norms of ethics do not provide clear-cut answers and even prevent responsible action, we must act freely in conformity to the Incarnate, Crucified, and Risen Christ. This means being involved fully and vicariously in the life and struggles of the world, identifying with the suffering of the victims and being in solidarity with the oppressed, and living and acting in hope for the sake of future generations.[76] In this way, "Christ's love moves the world to reconciliation and unity" not just during a pandemic such as we have experienced, but also at this time in world history when enmity and discord have once again become rampant.

74. Bonhoeffer, *Ethics*, 82–83.
75. Bonhoeffer, *Ethics*, 47, 93.
76. Bonhoeffer, *Ethics*, 82–83.

What Bonhoeffer did, then, became a necessity that he embraced freely and responsibly, and in doing so paid the cost with his own life. But even though much of his life and martyrdom speak to our times and challenge us as individuals, we should not turn his example into a principle, precedent, or rule to guide all action in every situation. That would be contrary to his intention. In seeking to express the love of Christ amid our present-day pandemic, we are called to act freely and responsibly, discerning the "will of God" for ourselves in accordance with reality and answering the question, "Who is Jesus Christ for us, today?"[77] But whether as doubting disciples or as seeking agnostics who are willing to give faith in God a chance, our answer to this question can never be reduced to an intellectual inquiry. It has to do with loving our neighbor both now and when the pandemic is over, or when confronted by a militant nationalism that endangers global peace—hence the need to be vigilant and mindful that the viruses which cause both war and disease are waiting, as Camus knew only too well, to strike again.

---

77. See de Gruchy, *Bonhoeffer's Questions*, 39–96.

EPILOGUE

LIVING IN HOPE

&

the Inevitability of Dying and Death

What use is life to me, when doomed to certain death?

—Job[1]

An excessive concern with dying is part of the inauthentic response to facing up to death. But Death is Life's other. To embrace one is to embrace the other: it is the one that makes the other possible. By contrast to be overly concerned with dying is to be overly concerned with living rather than with Life.

—Paul Clarke[2]

Being able to face dying doesn't yet mean we can face death. It's possible for a human being to manage dying, but overcoming death means resurrection. It is . . . through Christ's resurrection that a new and cleansing wind can blow through our present world . . . If a few people really believed this and were

---

1. Job 6:11 Jerusalem Bible.
2. Clarke, "Euthanasia," 345.

> guided by it in their earthly actions, a great deal would change. To live in the light of the resurrection—that is what Easter means.
>
> —Bonhoeffer[3]

Earlier in the week I began this Epilogue, I had another sudden blackout, which the doctor later diagnosed as vasovagal syncope, and fell unconscious in the passage. I was whisked away in an ambulance and spent some hours in the emergency ward. The tests were all good. But as I had had a new heart valve inserted by operation a few weeks earlier, I immediately assumed that something had somehow gone wrong. No, said the cardiologist later in the week, it was the searing heat and the fact that I had walked up the hill to our house twice that day. But certainly, it had to do with my blood pressure. My heart had missed a beat. Then, a week later, I had another blackout, this time more serious, for my fall down the stairway was life-threatening. Fortunately, I live to tell the tale. But since then both Isobel and I had COVID-19 Omicron while visiting our daughter in England. Although vaccination undoubtedly helped mitigate the severity of the illness, it was an unpleasant experience and, especially at our age, also life-threatening.

Let's face it, at eighty-three, death stares you in the face and challenges faith to the limit. As close friends and companions on the journey of life pass away, I know my turn is coming even as it did for my parents, who lived long lives, and Steve, who died in the prime of life, as did Suellen Shay, Steve's contemporary, who died of cancer this year aged sixty-one, to whom this book is also dedicated. Suellen sat beside me on the rocks above the place where two days previously Steve had drowned in the Mooi River, and where his body still lay trapped. She heard me cry out in anguish as I struggled to face reality. She sat silently for hour after hour, and then we walked slowly and silently together back up the hill to the cottage where Steve, her close friend, had been staying. Suellen and her husband, Don, had come to South Africa from the United States in 1988 to work in the church and wider community. They never returned except for brief sabbaticals. Suellen eventually became a professor of higher education at the University of Cape Town. Over the years, Suellen, Don, and their children became part of our extended family. Each year at the Steve de Gruchy Memorial

---

3. Bonhoeffer, *Letters and Papers from Prison*, 333.

Lecture Suellen would offer a prayer that helped to enter the mystery of God's presence afresh. Her devotion was profoundly simple, her life one of joyful compassion, and when she was diagnosed with cancer in 2018, she became an example of courageous and uncomplaining hope.

Seasons come and go more swiftly now, so do days and nights. As I observe the birth and death of nature, the rise and setting of the sun, I know that I cannot escape the rhythm of life that ends in death. I must face death along with everyone, from the most vulnerable to the seemingly imperishable. That is the inescapable reality that stares all of us in the face. I pray for courage to face it honestly, and to do so without too much complaint, though I fear I will be good at neither. At such a time when faith fluctuates between conviction and doubt, I depend less on the youthful confidence of faith and more on the grace that helps me, to say, week by week with millions of Christians around the world, "I believe in the resurrection of the dead and the life of the world to come." But can I say it with the confidence that Bonhoeffer did as he faced the gallows aged thirty-nine: "for me, this is the beginning of life"?[4]

It must suffice for me to say that I stand by what I wrote in *Led into Mystery*, but I also know even more surely that it is a confession of faith—no more and no less—and that faith continually struggles with doubt. It is not something that can be proved and triumphantly asserted, at least, not for me. If I could prove it, I would not need to believe. And when I have my doubts, and honesty requires that I admit them, then I am carried along by the faith of generations of Christians who have, together, confessed "*we*" not just "*I*" believe. That number includes Bonhoeffer, despite his moments of doubt and acute depression. Yet, we must remember that he also said that it is only "when one loves life and the earth so much that with it everything seems to be lost and at its end may one believe in the resurrection of the dead and a new world."[5]

The truth is that it is not just you or I who face death; the world in which we live is also living toward extinction. That will mean the end of every dream, the sudden conclusion of the genealogical line now dependent on grandchildren and whatever children they may have, or those who might remember us in one way or another. After all—quite literally—whatever our legacy, it is dependent on the future of memory, on those who can remember. If memory ceases, then everything is forgotten; we are

---

4. Bethge, *Dietrich Bonhoeffer*, 927.
5. Bonhoeffer, *Letters and Papers from Prison*, 213.

remembered no more. That, too, is the reality we, each one of us, must face: not only our own death but the death of those who may remember us. But I prefer not to think about that. More importantly is to think about how future generations can live and remember, and how we can still help them do so. Faith means not simply shrugging our shoulders and resigning ourselves and others to fate, but continuing to give a more hopeful shape to the future. That is the only way I can answer my granddaughter Kate's searching question: "Gramps, do you believe there is life after death?"

I have been reading a draft of Larry Rasmussen's *The Planet You Inherit: Letters to My Grandchildren*, in which he tells them that the only thing that is certain is uncertainty. Larry's book is beautifully crafted and a joy to read. It is an ode to embracing life and living in hope while fully facing tragedy. Larry, who has spent the latter years of his life fighting climate denial and challenging faith to face the reality of a planet facing extinction, is fully alert to the fact that his grandchildren must learn how to live in a world that is falling apart. Our generation, his and mine, at least if White and privileged, have generally had it good. But now we are all together on Noah's ark, and instead of it providing unending security it has sprung multiple leaks and the pumps are failing. I cannot look my grandchildren in the face and glibly say with Julian of Norwich, "All will be well, and all manner of things will be well." That may be true, as their grandmother has taught us all. But we must give them some reason for hope and therefore a task to do that might help them fulfil their dreams. Larry helps me put this into words that encourage concrete deeds:

> So dream a world and lace it with a little utopia. That's a world that levels the standard of living, with a steady-state economy attentive to Earth's regeneration. A world of jobs and health care for all in need of them. A world where quality of life for household and community are the economy's purpose and focus, not the profits of big firms and corporations. A world of widespread public transportation in and between green cities. A world of clean renewable energy sources.

Larry goes on to speak of a "world where spiritual well-being replaces gaudy consumerism. A world where diversity plays out as strength, not inequity, and where colonialist and environmental debt is settled with reparations on the way to liberty and justice for all. A world attentive to the *whole* community of life and its glory . . . a world full of music."[6] To stir up discussion

---

6. Rasmussen, *Planet You Inherit*, n.p.

on these critical issues, to live that dream and seek to be an agent in its fulfilment is what it means for faith to work itself out in the world in love and justice. This is what it means to live in Christian hope, a hope that lifts optimism to a new level because it does not deny or avoid the deadly realities that confront us. Bonhoeffer lived this hope, so I give him the last word to help us live by faith as we face reality, and therefore live in hope:

> There are people who think it frivolous and Christians who think it impious to hope for a better future on earth and to prepare for it. They believe in chaos, disorder, and catastrophe, perceiving it in what is happening now. They withdraw in resignation or pious flight from the world, from the responsibility for ongoing life, for building anew, for the coming generations. It may be that the day of judgment will dawn tomorrow; only then and no earlier will we readily lay down our work for a better future.[7]

---

7. Bonhoeffer, *Letters and Papers from Prison*, 51.

BIBLIOGRAPHY

Achar, Gilbert, *The Arabs and the Holocaust: The Arab–Israeli War of Narratives*. Translated by G. M. Goshgarian. London: Saqi, 2011.
Allen. John. *Rabble-Rouser for Peace: The Authorized Biography of Desmond Tutu*. London: Rider, 2006.
Baldwin-Ragaven, Laurel. "Social dimensions of COVID-19 in South Africa," *Wits Journal of Clinical Medicine* 2 (2020) (SI) 33–38.
Baldwin-Ragaven, Laurel, et al., eds. *An Ambulance of the Wrong Colour: Health Professionals, Human Rights and Ethics in South Africa*. Cape Town: Juta, 1999.
Barbour, Ian G. *Issues in Science and Religion*. Study ed. London: SCM 1972.
Barnes, Kenneth C. "Dietrich Bonhoeffer and Hitler's Persecution of the Jews." In *Betrayal: German Churches and the Holocaust*, edited by Robert P. Ericksen and Susannah Heschel, 110–28. Minneapolis: Fortress, 1999.
Barnett, Victoria, ed. *"After Ten Years": Dietrich Bonhoeffer and Our Times*. Minneapolis: Fortress, 2017.
———. "Dietrich Bonhoeffer's 'Jewish Question': New Approaches to Old Complexities." In *Polyphonie der Theologie: Verantwortung und Widerstand in Kirche und Politik*, edited by Matthias Grebe, 135–48. Stuttgart: Kohlhammer, 2019.
———. *For the Soul of the People: Protestant Protest against Hitler*. New York: Oxford University Press, 1992.
Barrow, John D., et al., eds. *Science and Ultimate Reality: Quantum Theory, Cosmology, and Complexity*. Cambridge: Cambridge University Press, 2004.
Barth, Karl. *Anselm: Fides Quarens Intellectum: Anselm's Proof of the Existence of God in the Context of His Theological Scheme*. 1960. Reprint, Pittsburgh: Pickwick Publications, 1975.
———. *Church Dogmatics I/2: The Doctrine of the Word of God, Part II*. Edited by G. W. Bromiley and T. F. Torrance. Translated by G. T. Thomson and Harold Knight. Edinburgh: T. & T. Clark, 1956.
———. *Church Dogmatics III/4: The Doctrine of Creation, Part 4*. Edited by G. W. Bromiley and T. F. Torrance. Translated by A. T. MacKay et al. Edinburgh: T. & T. Clark, 1961.
———. *Church Dogmatics IV/3.1: The Doctrine of Reconciliation, Part 3, First Half*. Edited by G. W. Bromiley and T. F. Torrance. Translated by G. W. Bromiley. Edinburgh: T. & T. Clark, 1961.
———. *Ethics*. Edited by Dietrich Braun. Translated by G. W. Bromiley. Edinburgh: T. & T. Clark, 1981.
———. *Ethics*. 1981. Reprint, Eugene, OR: Wipf & Stock, 2013.

---. *Protestant Theology in the Nineteenth Century*. London: SCM, 1972.
---. *Wolfgang Amadeus Mozart*. Grand Rapids: Eerdmans, 1986.
---. *Wolfgang Amadeus Mozart*. 1986. Reprint, Eugene, OR: Wipf & Stock, 2003.
Battle, Michael. *Desmond Tutu: A Spiritual Biography of South Africa's Confessor*. Louisville: Westminster John Knox, 2021.
Beasley-Murray, G. R. *Jesus and the Kingdom of God*. Grand Rapids: Eerdmans, 1986.
Begbie, Jeremy S. *Redeeming Transcendence in the Arts: Bearing Witness to the Triune God*, Grand Rapids: Eerdmans, 2018.
Begbie, Jeremy S., and Steven R. Guthrie, eds. *Resonant Witness: Conversations between Music and Theology* Grand Rapids: Eerdmans, 2011.
Bergsten, Gunilla. "Musical Symbolism in Thomas Mann's "Doktor Faustus." *Orbis Litterarum*, 14.2-4 (September 1959) 206-14.
Bethge, Eberhard. *Bonhoeffer: Exile and Martyr*. Edited with an essay by John W. de Gruchy. London: Collins, 1975.
---. "The Challenge of Dietrich Bonhoeffer's Life and Theology." *Chicago Theological Seminary Register* 51/2 (February 1961) 1-45.
---. "Dietrich Bonhoeffer and the Jews." In *Ethical Responsibility: Bonhoeffer's Legacy to the Churches*, edited by John D. Godsey and Geffrey B. Kelly, 43-96. Toronto Studies in Theology 6. Toronto: Mellen, 1981.
---. *Dietrich Bonhoeffer: A Biography.* Revised Edition. Revised and Edited by Victoria J. Barnett. Minneapolis: Fortress, 2000.
---. *Friendship and Resistance: Essays on Dietrich Bonhoeffer*. Geneva: WCC Publications, 1995.
---. "The Nonreligious Scientist and the Confessing Theologian: The Influence of Karl-Friedrich Bonhoeffer on His Younger Brother Dietrich." In *Bonhoeffer for a New Day*, edited by John W. de Gruchy, 39-56. Grand Rapids: Eerdmans, 1997.
Boesak, Allan Aubrey. "Church, Racism, and Resistance: Bonhoeffer and the Critical Dimensions of Theological Integrity." In *Luther, Bonhoeffer, and Public Ethics: Reforming the Church of the Future*, edited by Michael P. DeJonge and Clifford J. Green, 137-50. Lanham, MD: Lexington Books/Fortress Academic, 2018.
Bonhoeffer, Dietrich. *Act and Being: Transcendental Philosophy and Ontology in Systematic Theology*. Edited by Wayne Whitson Floyd Jr. DBWE 2. Minneapolis: Fortress 1996
---. *Barcelona, Berlin, New York 1928-1931*. Edited by Clifford J. Green. DBWE 10. Minneapolis: Augsburg Fortress, 2008.
---. *Berlin: 1932-1933*. Edited by Larry L. Rasmussen. DBWE 12. Minneapolis: Fortress, 2009
---. *Conspiracy and Imprisonment: 1940-1945*. Edited by Lisa E. Dahill and Douglas W. Stott. DBWE 16. Minneapolis: Fortress, 2006.
---. *Creation and Fall: A Theological Exposition of Genesis 1-3*. Edited by John W. de Gruchy. DBWE 3. Minneapolis, Minnesota: Fortress 1997.
---. *Discipleship*. Edited by Geffrey B. Kelly and John D. Godsey DBWE 4. Minneapolis: Fortress 2001.
---. *Ecumenical, Academic and Pastoral Work: 1931-1932*. Edited by Victoria J. Barnett et al. DBWE 11. Minneapolis: Fortress, 2012.
---. *Ethics*. Edited by Clifford J. Green. DBWE 6. Minneapolis: Fortress, 2005.
---. *Fiction from Tegel Prison*. Edited by Clifford J. Green. DBWE 7. Minneapolis: Fortress, 1999.

———. *Letters and Papers from Prison*. Edited by John W. de Gruchy. DBWE 8. Minneapolis: Fortress, 2010.

———. *Fiction from Prison*. Edited by Clifford J. Green. DBWE 7. Minneapolis: Fortress, 2000.

———. *Life Together, and Prayerbook of the Bible*. Edited by Geffrey B. Kelly. DBWE 5. Minneapolis: Fortress, 1996

———. *London: 1933–1935*. Edited by Keith Clements. DBWE 13. Minneapolis: Fortress, 2007.

———. *Sanctorum Communio: A Theological Study of the Sociology of the Church*. Edited by Clifford J. Green. DBWE 1 Minneapolis: Fortress, 1998.

———. *Theological Education at Finkenwalde: 1935–1937*. Edited by Gaylon Barker and Mark S. Brocker. DBWE 14. Minneapolis: Fortress, 2013.

———. *Theological Education Underground*. Edited by Victoria Barnett. DBWE 15. Minneapolis: Fortress, 2011.

———. *The Young Bonhoeffer 1918–1927*. Edited by Paul Duane Matheny et al. DBWE 9. Minneapolis: Fortress, 2002.

Bonhoeffer, Dietrich, and Maria von Wedemeyer. *Love Letters from Cell 92*. London: HarperCollins, 1994.

Bosch, David. "Nothing but a Heresy." In *Apartheid Is a Heresy*, edited by John W. de Gruchy and Charles Villa-Vicencio, 24–38. Grand Rapids: Eerdmans, 1983.

Bracher, Karl Dietrich. *The German Dictatorship: The Origins, Structure and Consequences of National Socialism*, London: Penguin, 1973.

Braverman, Mark. *Fatal Embrace: Christians, Jews, and the Search for Peace in the Holy Land*. Austin: Synergy, 2010.

———. *A Wall in Jerusalem: Hope, Healing, and the Struggle for Justice in Israel and Palestine*. New York: Jericho Books, 2013.

Brueggemann, Walter. *A Theology of the Old Testament*. Minneapolis: Fortress, 1997.

Bryson, Bill, ed. *Seeing Further: The Story of Science and the Royal Society*. London: Harper, 2010.

Buber, Martin. *Israel and the World: Essays in a Time of Crisis*. 2nd ed. New York: Schocken, 1963.

Burridge, Richard A. *Imitating Jesus*. Grand Rapids: Eerdmans, 2007.

Busch, Eberhard. *Karl Barth: His Life from Letters and Autobiographical Texts*. Translated by John Bowden. 1976. Reprint, Eugene, OR: Wipf & Stock, 2005.

Buthelezi, Manas. "Six Theses on Evangelism." *Journal of Theology for Southern Africa* 3 (June 1973) 55–56.

Campbell, James T. *Songs of Zion: The African Methodist Episcopal Church in the United States and South Africa*. New York: Oxford University Press, 1995.

Camus, Albert. *The Plague*. Translated by Stuart Gilbert. London: Penguin, 1966.

Carr, William. *A History of Germany 1815–1945*. London: Arnold, 1969.

Carter, Guy, et al., eds. *Bonhoeffer's Ethics: Old Europe and New Frontiers*. Kampen: Kok/Pharos, 1991.

Cavanaugh, William T. "Science and Theology: Questioning the 'Two-State Solution.'" *BioLogos* (blog), October 14, 2017. https://biologos.org/articles/science-and-theology-questioning-the-two-state-solution/.

Chua, Daniel K. L. "Music as the Mouthpiece of Theology." In *Resonant Witness: Conversations between Music and Theology*, edited by Jeremy S. Begbie and Steven R. Guthrie, 137–61. Grand Rapids: Eerdmans, 2011.

Clarke, Paul Barry. "Euthanasia." In *Dictionary of Ethics, Theology, and Society*, edited by Paul Barry Clarke and Andrew Linzey, 336-42. London: Routledge, 1996.
Clarke, Paul Barry, and Andrew Linzey, eds. *Dictionary of Ethics, Theology, and Society*. London: Routledge, 1996.
Clements, Keith W. *Dietrich Bonhoeffer's Ecumenical Quest*. Geneva: World Council of Churches, 2015.
———. *Faith on the Frontier: A Life of J. H. Oldham*. Edinburgh : T. & T. Clark, 1999.
———. Introduction to *Bonhoeffer, London: 1933-1935*, edited by Keith Clements, 1-17. DBWE 13. Minneapolis: Fortress, 2007.
———. *What Freedom?* Bristol, England: Bristol Baptist College, 1990.
Cloete, G. D., and D. J. Smit, eds. *A Moment of Truth: The Confession of the Dutch Reformed Mission Church, 1982*. Grand Rapids: Eerdmans, 1984.
Cochrane, James R. *Servants of Power: The Role of the English-Speaking Churches in South Africa, 1903-1930*. Johannesburg: Ravan, 1987.
Cochrane, James R., et al., eds. *Living on the Edge: Essays in Honour of Steve de Gruchy, Activist & Theologian*. Pietermaritzburg, South Africa: Cluster, 2012.
Cohen, Stuart A., and Milton Shain. *Israel: Culture, Religion, and Society, 1948-1998*. Cape Town: Kaplan Centre for Jewish Studies and Research, University of Cape Town, 2000.
Comaroff, Jean, and John Comaroff. *Of Revelation and Revolution*. Vol. 1, *Christianity, Colonialism, and Consciousness in South Africa*. 2 vols. Chicago: University of Chicago Press, 1991.
Cone, James H. *Speaking the Truth: Ecumenism, Liberation, and Black Theology*. Grand Rapids: Eerdmans, 1986.
Congressional Research Service. "Germany's Relations with Israel: Background and Implications for German Middle East Policy." CRS Report for Congress. RL33808. Washington, DC: January 19, 2007. https://www.everycrsreport.com/files/20070119_RL33808_0b24fa1e714b11b6a65685f68e639e2d2ab7a807.pdf/.
Conradie, Ernst, and Christo Lombard, eds. *Discerning God's Justice in Church, Society and Academy: A Festschrift for Jaap Durand*. Stellenbosch: Sun Press, 2009.
Cunningham. Conor. *A Genealogy of Nihilism*. Radical Orthodoxy Series. London: Routledge, 2002.
Dabrock, Peter. "Responding to 'Wirklichkeit': Reclaiming Bonhoeffer's Approach to Theological Ethics between Mystery and the Formation of the World." In *Mysteries in the Theology of Dietrich Bonhoeffer*, edited by Ulrik Nissen et al., 49-80. Forschungen zur systematischen und ökumenischen Theologie 119. Göttingen: Vandenhoek & Ruprecht, 2007.
Dawkins, Richard. *The God Delusion*. Boston: Houghton Mifflin, 2008.
Deane-Drummond, Ceila E. *Creation through Wisdom: Theology and the New Biology*. Edinburgh: T. & T. Clark, 2000.
De Gruchy, Isobel. *Making All Things Well: Finding Spiritual Strength with Julian of Norwich*. Norwich, UK: Canterbury, 2012.
De Gruchy, John W. *Being Human: Confessions of a Christian Humanist*. London: SCM, 2006.
———. "Beyers Naudé: South Africa's Bonhoeffer? Celebrating the Centenary of the Birth of Beyers Naudé—1915-2015." *Stellenbosch Theological Journal* 1.1 (2015) 78-98.

———. "Bonhoeffer among the 'Glorious Company of the Prophets'—Bonhoeffer as Prophetic Theologian." In *Engaging Bonhoeffer in a Global Era*, edited by Philip G. Ziegler and Christiane Tietz. Göttingen: Vandenhoeck & Ruprecht, forthcoming.

———, guest ed. "Bonhoeffer Centenary. (1906–2006)" Special issue, *Journal of Theology for Southern Africa* 127 (March 2007)

———. "Bonhoeffer and Public Ethics: South African Notes." In *Interpreting Bonhoeffer: Historical Perspectives, Emerging Issues*, edited by Clifford J. Green and Guy C. Carter, 15–24. Minneapolis: Fortress, 2013.

———. "Bonhoeffer and the Palestinian-Israel Conflict: South African Reflections." *Ecumenical Review* (22 March 2011) https://doi.org/10.1111/j.1758-6623.2010.00100_2.x.

———. "Bonhoeffer, Apartheid, and Beyond: The Reception of Bonhoeffer in South Africa." In *Bonhoeffer for a New Day*, edited by John W. de Gruchy, 353–65. Grand Rapids: Eerdmans, 1997.

———. "Bonhoeffer in South Africa." In *Bonhoeffer: Exile and Martyr*, by Eberhard Bethge, 26–42. Edited with an essay by John W. de Gruchy. London: Collins, 1975.

———. *Bonhoeffer and South Africa: Theology in Dialogue*. Grand Rapids: Eerdmans, 1984.

———, ed. *Bonhoeffer for a New Day*. Grand Rapids: Eerdmans, 1997.

———. "Bonhoeffer's Legacy and *Kairos-Palestine*." *Journal of Theology for Southern Africa* 143 (July 2012) 67–80.

———. *Bonhoeffer's Questions: A Life-Changing Conversation*. Lanham, MD: Fortress Academic, 2019.

———. "Can a White South African Male Enter the Kingdom of God?" Steve de Gruchy Memorial Lecture, Rondebosch United Church, Cape Town, South Africa, March 2019.

———, ed. *The Cambridge Companion to Dietrich Bonhoeffer*. Cambridge Companions to Religion. Cambridge: Cambridge University Press, 1999.

———. *Christianity and the Modernisation of South Africa, 1867–1936: A Documentary History*. Vol. 2. Hidden Histories Series. Pretoria: University of South Africa Press, 2009.

———. *Christianity, Art and Transformation*. Cambridge: Cambridge University Press, 2001.

———. "Christianity, Democracy and New Realities: Bonhoeffer's Political Witness Then and Now." In *A Spoke in the Wheel: The Political in the Theology of Dietrich Bonhoeffer*, edited by Kristen Busch Nielsen et al., 432–44. Gutersloh: Gütersloher, 2013.

———. "Confessing Guilt in South Africa Today in Dialogue with Dietrich Bonhoeffer." *Journal of Theology for Southern Africa* 67 (June 1989) 37–45.

———. *Confessions of a Christian Humanist*. Minneapolis: Fortress, 2006

———. *Daring, Trusting Spirit: Bonhoeffer's Friend Eberhard Bethge*. London: SCM, 2005.

———. "Dietrich Bonhoeffer and the Transition to Democracy in the German Democratic Republic and South Africa." *Modern Theology* 12 (1996) 345–66.

———. "Dietrich Bonhoeffer as Christian Humanist." In *Being Human, Becoming Human: Dietrich Bonhoeffer and Social Thought* edited by Jens Zimmerman and Brian Gregor, 3–24. Princeton Theological Monograph Series 146. Eugene, OR: Pickwick Publications, 2010.

———. *Icons as a Means of Grace*. Wellington, South Africa: Lux Verbi, 2008.

———. *I Have Come a Long Way*. Eugene, OR: Cascade Books, 2016.

———. *Led into Mystery: Faith Seeking Answers in Life and Death*. London: SCM, 2013

———. "Playing God during the Pandemic: Courage, Responsibility, and the Ethics of Necessity." *Ecumenical Review* 72.3 (July 2020) 660–72.

———. "Providence and the Shapers of History." In *Bonhoeffer and South Africa: Theology in Dialogue*, 47–66. Grand Rapids: Eerdmans,1984.

———. "Reality and Mystery: Scientific Understanding, Christian Humanism, and Defining Moral Imperatives." *Journal of Theology for Southern Africa* 157 (March 2017) 59–70.

———. "The Dynamic Structure of the Church: An Exposition and Comparative Analysis of the Ecclesiologies of Karl Barth and Dietrich Bonhoeffer, and an Interpretation Based on This Exposition and Analysis of the Basic Principles Which should Determine the Structure of the Church in our Situation Today." DD diss., University of South Africa, 1972.

———. *The End Is Not Yet: Standing Firm in Apocalyptic Times*. Dispatches. Minneapolis: Fortress, 2017.

———, ed. *The Humanist Imperative in South Africa*. Stellenbosch: Sun Press, 2011.

———. "The Liberation of the Privileged." In *Bonhoeffer and South Africa: Theology in Dialogue*, 67–90. Grand Rapids: Eerdmans, 1984.

———. "The Local Church and the Race Problem in South Africa." MTh thesis, Chicago Theological Seminary, 1964.

———. "The Search for Transcendence in an Age of Barbarism: Bonhoeffer, Beethoven, Mann's *Dr Faustus*, and the Spiritual Crisis of the Present Time." In *Polyphonie der Theologie: Verantwortung und Widerstand in Kirche und Politik*, edited by Matthias Grebe, 195-208. Stuttgart: Kohlhammer, 2019.

———. *This Monastic Moment: The War of the Spirit & the Rule of Love*. Eugene, OR: Cascade Books, 2021.

De Gruchy, John W., and Charles Villa-Vicencio, eds. *Apartheid Is a Heresy*. Grand Rapids,: Eerdmans, 1983.

De Gruchy, John W., and Isobel de Gruchy. *The Volmoed Journey*. 30th ann. ed. Cape Town: Methodist Publishing House, 2016.

De Gruchy, John W., and Steve de Gruchy. *The Church Struggle in South Africa*. 25th ann. ed. London: SCM, 2004.

De Gruchy, John W. et al. *Dietrich Bonhoeffer's Theology Today: A Way between Fundamentalism and Secularism?* Gütersloh: Gütersloher, 2009.

De Gruchy, Steve. "Human Being in Christ: Resources for an Inclusive Anthropology." In *Aliens in the Household of God*, edited by Paul Germond and Steve de Gruchy, 233–69. Cape Town: Philip, 1997.

———. *Keeping Body and Soul Together: Reflections by Steve de Gruchy on Theology and Development*. Edited by Beverley Haddad. Pietermaritzburg, South Africa: Cluster, 2015.

———. "Not Liberation but Justice: An Analysis of Reinhold Niebuhr's Understanding of Human Destiny in the Light of the Doctrine of the Atonement." ThD diss., University of the Western Cape, 1992.

Dumas, André. *Dietrich Bonhoeffer: Theologian of Reality*. Translated by Robert McAfee Brown. New York: Macmillan, 1971.

Durand, Jaap. *Evolusie, Wetenskap en Geloof*. Wellington, South Africa: Bybel-Media, 2013.

———. *The Many Faces of God*. Stellenbosch: Sun Press, 2007.

Eagleton, Terry. *Culture*. New Haven: Yale University Press, 2016.

Eco, Umberto. *Faith in Fakes: Essays.* Translated from the Italian by William Weaver. London: Secker & Warburg, 1986.

Ecumenical Review 63.1 (March 2011).

Ellis, George F. R. "On Rationality and Emotion, Faith and Hope: Being Human in a Scientific Age." In *The Quest for Humanity in Science and Religion: The South African Experience*, edited by Augustine Shutte, 1–28. Pietermaritzburg, South Africa: Cluster, 2006

———. "True Complexity and its Associated Ontology." In *Science and Ultimate Reality: Quantum Theory, Cosmology, and Complexity*, edited by. John D. Barrow et al., 607–36. Cambridge: Cambridge University Press, 2004.

Ellis, Marc, H. "On Israel's Indigenous Prophetic: A View from a Jewish Theology of Liberation." *Journal of Theology for Southern Africa* 143 (July 2012) 81–89.

———. *Toward a Jewish Theology of Liberation: The Challenge of the 21st Century.* 3rd expanded ed. Radical Traditions. Waco: Baylor University Press, 2004.

Elphick, Richard. *The Equality of Believers: Protestant Missionaries and the Racial Politics of South Africa.* Reconsiderations in Southern African History. Charlottesville: University of Virginia Press, 2012.

Elphick, Richard, and Rodney Davenport, eds. *Christianity in South Africa: A Political, Social & Cultural History.* Oxford: Currey, 1997.

Feil, Ernst. *The Theology of Dietrich Bonhoeffer.* Translated by Martin Rumscheidt. Philadelphia: Fortress, 1985.

Ferguson, Niall. *Doom: The Politics of Catastrophe.* London: Allen Lane 2021.

Fischer, Klaus P. *Nazi Germany: A New History.* New York: Continuum, 1998.

Flew, Antony, with Roy Abraham Varghese. *There Is a God.* New York: HarperOne, 2007.

Floyd, Samuel A., Jr. *The Power of Black Music: Interpreting its History from Africa to the United States.* New York: Oxford University Press, 1995.

Fredrickson, George M. *Black Liberation: A Comparative History of Black Ideologies in the United States and South Africa.* Oxford: Oxford University Press, 1995.

Frenssen, Gustav. *Peter Moors Fahrt Nach Südwest: Ein Feldzugsbericht.* (First published in 1906) London: Forgotten Books, 2011.

Frick, Peter. "Friedrich Nietzsche's Aphorisms and Dietrich Bonhoeffer's Theology." In *Bonhoeffer's Intellectual Formation*, edited by Peter Frick, 175–200. Religion in Philosophy and Theology 29. Tübingen: Mohr Siebeck, 2008.

———, ed. *Bonhoeffer's Intellectual Formation.* Religion in Philosophy and Theology 29. Tübingen: Mohr Siebeck, 2008.

Friedlander Albert H. "Israel and Europe." In Bonhoeffer's *Ethics*: Old Europe and New Frontiers, edited by Guy Carter et al., 112–20. Kampen: Kok/Pharos, 1991.

Fowler, James W. *Stages of Faith: The Psychology of Human Development*, San Francisco: HarperCollins, 1981.

Furlong, Patrick J. *Between Crown and Swastika: The Impact of the Radical Right on the Afrikaner Nationalist Movement in the Fascist Era.* Johannesburg: Witwatersrand University Press, 1991.

Germond, Paul, and Steve de Gruchy, eds. *Aliens in the Household of God: Homosexuality and Christian Faith in South Africa.* Cape Town: Philip, 1997.

Gill, David. "Technology." In *Global Dictionary of Theology: A Resource for the Worldwide Church*, edited by William A. Dyrness and Veli-Matti Kärkkäinen, 870–74. Downers Grove, IL: IVP Academic, 2008.

Gilson, Etienne. *Reason and Revelation in the Middle Ages*. The Scribner Library. New York: Scribner, 1966.
Gleick, James. *Chaos: The Amazing Science of the Unpredictable*. New York: Vintage, 1998.
Godsey, John D., and Geffrey B. Kelly, eds. *Ethical Responsibility: Bonhoeffer's Legacy to the Churches*. Toronto Studies in Theology 6. Toronto: Mellen, 1981.
Gopal, Priyamvada. *Insurgent Empire: Anticolonial Resistance and British Dissent*. London: Verso, 2019.
Green, Clifford J. *Bonhoeffer: A Theology of Sociality*. Rev. ed. Grand Rapids: Eerdmans, 1999.
———. "Dietrich Bonhoeffer's Letter to Mahatma Gandhi." *Journal of Ecclesiastical History* 72 (2021) 113–21.
———. Introduction to *Barcelona, Berlin, New York 1928-1931*, by Dietrich Bonhoeffer, edited by Clifford J. Green, 1–50. DBWE 10. Minneapolis: Augsburg Fortress, 2008.
———. Introduction to *Ethics*, by Dietrich Bonhoeffer, 1–44. Edited by Clifford J. Green. DBWE 6. Minneapolis: Fortress, 2005.
Green, Clifford J., and Guy C. Carter, eds. *Interpreting Bonhoeffer: Historical Perspectives, Emerging Issues*. Minneapolis: Fortress, 2013.
Gushee, David, P. *Righteous Gentiles of the Holocaust: Genocide and Moral Obligation*, Minneapolis: Paragon House, 2003.
Hauck, Grace. "'Brave, Compassionate and Dedicated': ER Doctor Who Treated Coronavirus Patients Dies by Suicide." News. Nation. *USA Today*, April 28, 2020. Updated April 29, 2020. https://www.usatoday.com/story/news/nation/2020/04/28/new-york-coronavirus-emergency-room-doctor-lorna-breen-dies-suicide/3038704001/.
Hansen, Len, ed. *The Legacy of Beyers Naudé*. Beyers Naudé Centre Series on Public Theology 1. Stellenbosch: Sun Press, 2005.
Harari, Yuval N. *Homo Deus: A Brief History of Tomorrow*. London: Harvill-Secker, 2015.
Hartman, Tim. *Theology after Colonization: Kwame Bediako, Karl Barth, and the Future of Theological Reflection*. Notre Dame Studies in African Theology. Notre Dame, IN: University of Notre Dame Press, 2020.
Harvey, Barry. *Taking Hold of the Real: Dietrich Bonhoeffer and the Profound Worldliness of Christianity*, Eugene, OR: Cascade Books, 2015.
Haynes, Stephen R. *The Bonhoeffer Phenomenon: Portraits of a Protestant Saint*. Minneapolis: Fortress, 2004.
Heschel, Abraham. *The Prophets*. New York: Harper & Row, 1969.
Horowitz, Adam, et al., eds. *The Goldstone Report: The Legacy of the Landmark Investigation of the Gaza Conflict*. New York: Nation Books, 2011.
Jay, Martin. *The Dialectical Imagination: A History of the Frankfurt School and the Institute of Social Research 1923–1950*, London: Heinemann, 1976.
Jenkins, Willis, and Jennifer M. McBride, eds. *Bonhoeffer and King: Their Legacies and Import for Christian Social Thought*. Minneapolis: Fortress, 2010.
John Paul II, Pope. *Sollicitudo Rei Socialis*. Papal Encyclical. 30 December 1987, no. 39. https://www.vatican.va/content/john-paul-ii/en/encyclicals/documents/hf_jp-ii_enc_30121987_sollicitudo-rei-socialis.html/.
Jung, Carl J. *The Collected Works*. Vol. 5, *Symbols of Transformation*. 20 vols. 2nd ed. London: Routledge & Kegan Paul, 1968.

Karis, Thomas G., and Gail M. Gerhart. *From Protest to Challenge: A Documentary History of African Politics in South Africa.* Vol. 5, *Nadir and Resistance, 1964–1979*. Bloomington: Indiana University Press, 1997.

Kassis, Rifat Odeh. "A Moment of Truth": The Kairos-Palestine Document." *Ecumenical Review* 63.1 (March 2011) 120–22.

Kee, Alistair. *Nietzsche against the Crucified.* London: SCM, 1999.

Kierkegaard, Søren. *Fear and Trembling, The Sickness unto Death.* Translated with introductions and notes by Walter Lowrie. A Doubleday Anchor Book. New York: Doubleday, 1954.

Lamb, Matthew L. *Solidarity with Victims: Toward a Theology of Social Transformation,* New York: Crossroad, 1982.

Leech, Kenneth. "Racism." In *Dictionary of Ethics, Theology, and Society,* edited by Paul Barry Clarke and Andrew Lindzey, 709–11. Routledge Reference. London: Routledge, 1996.

Lewis, Bernard. *Semites and Anti-Semites: An Inquiry into Conflict and Prejudice.* New York: Norton, 1999.

Lewis, Sinclair. *It Can't Happen Here.* London: Penguin, 2017.

Libowitz, Richard, ed. *Faith and Freedom: A Tribute to Franklin H. Littell.* Oxford: Pergamum, 1987.

Lovin, Robin W. *Christian Realism and the New Realities.* Cambridge: Cambridge University Press, 2008.

MacIntyre, Alasdair. *After Virtue: A Study in Moral Theory.* Notre Dame, IN: University of Notre Dame Press, 1981.

Mann, Thomas. *Doctor Faustus.* Translated by John E. Woods. London: Vintage, 1999.

———. *Letters of Thomas Mann, 1889–1955.* Vol. 1, *1889–1942*. Selected and translated from the German by Richard and Clara Winston. Introduction by Richard Winston. London: Secker & Warburg 1970.

———. *Letters of Thomas Mann, 1889–1955.* Vol. 2, *1942–1955*. Selected and translated from the German by Richard and Clara Winston. Introduction by Richard Winston. London: Secker & Warburg 1970.

———. *Pro and Contra Wagner.* Translated by Allan Blunden, with an introduction by Erich Heller, Chicago: University of Chicago Press, 1985, (German 1932–1933).

———. *The Sorrows and Grandeur of Richard Wagner.* Translated by Allan Blunden. Chicago: University of Chicago Press, 1985.

———. *The Story of a Novel: The Genesis of "Doctor Faustus."* Translated from the German by Richard and Clara Winston. New York: Knopf, 1961.

Mannheim, Karl. *Ideology and Utopia,* New York: Harcourt, Brace & World, 1956.

Marsh, Charles, *Reclaiming Dietrich Bonhoeffer: The Promise of His Theology,* New York: Oxford University Press, 1994.

McBride, Jennifer. "Bonhoeffer and Feminist Theologies." In *The Oxford Handbook of Dietrich Bonhoeffer,* edited by Michael Mawson and Philip Ziegler, 365–82. Oxford Handbooks. Oxford: Oxford University Press, 2019.

McGilchrist, Iain. *The Master and His Emissary.* New Haven: Yale University Press, 2009.

McGrath, Alister. *Why God Won't Go Away.* London: SPCK, 2011.

Merton, Thomas. *Contemplation in a World of Action,* Garden City, NY: Doubleday, 1973.

Moltmann, Jürgen. *The Crucified God: The Cross of Christ as the Foundation and Criticism of Christian Theology.* Translated by R. A. Wilson and John Bowden. London: SCM, 1974. Reprint, Minneapolis: Fortress, 1994.

Moodie, T. Dunbar. *The Rise of Afrikanerdom: Power, Apartheid, and Afrikaner Civil Religion*. Berkeley: University of California Press, 1975.

Morris, John. *Culture and Propaganda in World War II: Music, Film and the Battle for National Identity*. International Library of Twentieth-Century History 64. London: Taurus, 2014.

Moses, John A. "Rejecting Kultur: Thomas Mann's and Dietrich Bonhoeffer's Reaction to Wilhelminism, National Socialism and the USA—an Historian's Perspective." In "The Bonhoeffer Legacy." Special issue, *Australasian Journal of Bonhoeffer Studies* 4.2 (2016) 23–40.

———. *The Reluctant Revolutionary: Dietrich Bonhoeffer's Collision with Prusso-German History*. New York: Berghahn, 2009.

Mumford, Lewis. *Technics and Civilization*. London: Routledge, 1934.

Murphy, Nancey. *Bodies and Souls, or Spirited Bodies? Current Issues in Theology*. Cambridge: Cambridge University Press, 2006.

Mwangi, Kamau. "Vaccine Apartheid?" *I Am Kamau Mwangi* (blog), Philosophy & Culture, December 3, 2021. https://www.kamaumwangi.co.ke/vaccine-apartheid/.

Newell, Waller R. *Tyrants: A History of Power, Injustice, and Terror*. Cambridge: Cambridge University Press, 2016.

Niebuhr, Reinhold. *An Interpretation of Christian Ethics*. Rauschenbusch Lectures 1934. London: SCM, 1936.

Nietzsche, Friedrich. *Beyond Good and Evil*. Translated by R. J. Hollingdale ; with an introduction by Michael Tanner. Penguin Classics. London: Penguin, 1973.

———. *The Gay Science*. Translated, with commentary, by Walter Kaufmann. New York: Vintage, 1974.

———. *The Will to Power*. A new translation by Walter Kaufmann and R. J. Hollingdale. Edited, with commentary, by Walter Kaufman. New York: Vintage, 1968.

Nissen, Ulrik, et al., eds. *Mysteries in the Theology of Dietrich Bonhoeffer*. Forschungen zur systematischen und ökumenischen Theologie 119. Göttingen: Vandenhoeck & Ruprecht, 2007.

Oldham, J. H. *Christianity and the Race Problem*. London: SCM, 1926.

Ott, Heinrich. *Reality and Faith: The Theological Legacy of Dietrich Bonhoeffer*. Translated from the German by Alex A. Morrison. London: Lutterworth, 1971.

Pangritz, Andreas. "Point and Counterpoint—Resistance and Submission: Dietrich Bonhoeffer on Theology and Music in Times of War and Social Crisis." In *Theology in Dialogue*, edited by Lyn Holness and Ralf K. Wüstenberg, 28–42. Grand Rapids: Eerdmans, 2002.

———. *The Polyphony of Life: Bonhoeffer's Theology of Music*. Edited by John W. de Gruchy and John Morris, Eugene, OR: Cascade Books, 2019.

———."The Understanding of Mystery in the Theology of Dietrich Bonhoeffer." In *Mysteries in the Theology of Dietrich Bonhoeffer*, edited by Ulrik Nissen et al., 9–26. Forschungen zur systematischen und ökumenischen Theologie 119. Göttingen: Vandenhoeck & Ruprecht, 2007.

Parker, Joshua, and Mikaeil Mirzaali. "The Moral Cost of Coronavirus." *Journal of Medical Ethics*, March 16, 2020. https://blogs.bmj.com/medical-ethics/2020/03/16/the-moral-cost-of-coronavirus/.

Pauck, Wilhelm, and Marion Pauck. *Paul Tillich: His Life and Thought*. Vol. 1. London: Collins, 1977.

Paul, Diane, B. "Darwin, Social Darwinism, and Eugenics." In *The Cambridge Companion to Darwin*, edited by Jonathan Hodge and Gregory Radick, 214–39. Cambridge Companions to Religion. Cambridge: Cambridge University Press, 2003.

Peck, William J. "The Euthanasia Text." In *New Studies in Bonhoeffer's "Ethics,"* edited by William J. Peck, 141–66. Toronto: Mellen, 1987.

Pelikan, Jaroslav. *Bach among the Theologians*. Minneapolis: Fortress, 1986.

Pinker, Steven. *Rationality*. London: Lane, 2021.

———. "Science Is Not Your Enemy: An Impassioned Plea to Neglected Novelists, Embattled Professors, and Tenure-less Historians." *New Republic*, August 6, 2013. https://newrepublic.com/article/114127/science-not-enemy-humanities#:~:text=The%20mindset%20of%20science%20cannot,meaning%2C%20purpose%2C%20and%20morality/.

Plaatjies–Van Huffel, Mary-Anne, and Robert Vosloo eds. *Reformed Churches in South Africa and the Struggle for Justice: Remembering 1960–1990*. Stellenbosch: SunMedia, 2013.

Plato. *The Republic*. Oxford: Clarendon, 1955.

Prideaux, Sue. *I Am Dynamite: A Life of Friedrich Nietzsche*. Paperback ed. London: Faber & Faber, 2019.

Prior, Andrew, ed. *Catholics in Apartheid Society*. Cape Town: Philip, 1982.

Raheb, Mitri. *Faith in the Face of Empire: The Bible through Palestinian Eyes*. Maryknoll, NY: Orbis, 2014.

Rasmussen, Larry L., with Renate Bethge. *Dietrich Bonhoeffer—His Significance for North Americans*. Minneapolis: Fortress, 1990.

———. *Dietrich Bonhoeffer: Reality and Resistance*. Nashville: Abingdon, 1972.

———. *Earth-Honoring Faith: Religious Ethics in a New Key*. Oxford: Oxford University Press, 2013

———. *The Planet You Inherit: Letters to My Grandchildren; When Uncertainty's a Sure Thing*. Minneapolis: Broadleaf, 2022.

Rayson, Dianne. *Bonhoeffer and Climate Change: Theology and Ethics for the Anthropocene*. Lanham: Lexington Books/Fortress Academic, 2021.

Rees, Martin. "Conclusion: Looking Fifty Years Ahead." In *Seeing Further: The Story of Science & the Royal Society*, edited by Bill Bryson, 467–87. London: Harper, 2010.

Rosenbaum, Ron. *Explaining Hitler: The Search for the Origins of His Evil*. New York: Macmillan, 1998.

Ross, Alex. *Wagnerism: Art and Politics in the Shadow of Music*. New York: Farrar, Straus & Giroux, 2020.

Ruether, Rosemary Radford, and Herman J. Ruether. *The Wrath of Jonah: Religious Nationalism and the Quest for a Just Peace between Israel and the Palestinians*. San Francisco: Harper & Row, 1989.

Russell. Robert John, and Kirk Wegter-McNelly. "Science." In *The Blackwell Companion to Modern Theology*, edited by Gareth Jones, 511–26. Blackwell Companions to Religion. Oxford: Blackwell, 2004.

Sachs, Harvey. *The Ninth: Beethoven and the World in 1824*. London: Faber & Faber, 2010.

Schleiermacher, Friedrich. *On Religion: Speeches to Its Culture Despisers*. Translated by John Oman, with an introduction by Rudolf Otto. New York: Harper & Row, 1958.

Schlingensiepen, Ferdinand. *Dietrich Bonhoeffer, 1906–1945: Martyr, Thinker, Man of Resistance*. Translated by Isabel Best. London: T. & T. Cark, 2010.

Scruton, Roger. *Wagner's "Parsifal": The Music of Redemption*. London: Penguin, 2020.

Shain, Milton. *Antisemitism*. Bowerdean Briefings. London: Bowerdea, 1998.

———. *The Roots of Anti-Semitism in South Africa*. Reconsiderations in Southern African History. Johannesburg: University of Witwatersand Press, 1994.

Snyder, Ross. *The Ministry of Meaning*. RISK1.3-4. Geneva: World Council of Churches, 1965.

Soelle, Dorothee, *The Silent Cry: Mysticism and Resistance*. Translated by Barbara and Martin Rumscheidt. Minneapolis: Fortress, 2001.

Staats, Reinhart. "Editor's Afterword to the German Edition." In *Barcelona, Berlin, New York 1928/1931*, edited by Clifford J. Green, 605-33. DBWE 10. Minneapolis: Fortress, 2008.

Susser, Baruch. "A Society Divided." In *Israel: Culture, Religion, and Society, 1948-1998*, edited by Stuart A. Cohen and Milton Shain, 38-52. Cape Town: Kaplan Center for Jewish Studies, University of Cape Town, 2000.

Teilhard de Chardin, Pierre. *The Phenomenon of Man*. Translated by Bernard Wall. New York: Harper, 1959.

Terblanche, Sampie. *Western Empires: Christianity, and the Inequalities between the West and the Rest, 1500-2010*. Johannesburg: Penguin, 2014.

The Kairos Document, Johannesburg: Institute for Contextual Theology, 1986.

The Kairos Palestine Document: A Moment of Truth: A Word of Faith, Hope and Love from the Heart of Palestinian Suffering, Jerusalem, Palestine, 2009.

The Road to Damascus: Kairos and Conversion. Johannesburg: Skotaville, 1989.

Tietz, Christiane. "The Mysteries of Knowledge, Sin and Shame." In *Mysteries in the Theology of Dietrich Bonhoeffer*, edited by Ulrik Nissen et al., 27-48. Forschungen zur systematischen und ökumenischen Theologie 119. Göttingen: Vandenhoeck & Ruprecht, 2007.

Tillich, Paul. "Art and Ultimate Reality." In *Art, Creativity, and the Sacred*, edited by Diane Apostolos-Cappadonna, 219-35. New rev. ed. New York: Continuum, 1996.

———. *Biblical Religion and the Search for Ultimate Reality*. Chicago: University of Chicago Press, 1955.

———. *Perspectives on 19th and 20th Century Protestant Theology*. Edited and with an introduction by Carl E. Braaten. London: SCM, 1968.

———. *Systematic Theology*. Vol. 1. London: Nisbet, 1953.

———.*Systematic Theology*. Vol. 2, London: Nisbet, 1953.

———. *A Theology of Culture*. A Galaxy Book. New York: Oxford University Press, 1964.

Tödt, Heinz Eduard. *Authentic Faith: Bonhoeffer's Theological Ethics in Context*. Translated by David Stassen and Ilse Tödt; English ed. Edited by Glen Harold Stassen. Grand Rapids: Eerdmans, 2007.

Tötemeyer, Andree-Jeanne. "Die Problematik der Kinder- und Jugendliteratur Namibias: Gestern und heute." *Afrikanischer Heimatkalnder* (1990) 55-66.

Travers, Martin. *Thomas Mann*. Macmillan Modern Novelists. London: Macmillan, 1992.

Tutu, Desmond Mpilo, comp. *An African Prayer Book*. Selected and with introductions by Desmond Tutu. New York: Doubleday, 1995.

———. "God Is God's Worst Enemy." In *Living on the Edge: Essays in Honour of Steve de Gruchy, Activist & Theologian*, edited by James R. Cochrane et al., x-xv. Pietermaritzburg, South Africa: Cluster, 2012.

———. *God Is Not a Christian: Speaking Truth in Times of Crisis*. London: Rider, 2011.

———. *No Future Without Forgiveness*. London: Rider, 1999.

Vaget, Hans Rudolf. "'Politically Suspect': Music on the Magic Mountain." In *Thomas Mann's "The Magic Mountain,"* edited by Hans Rudolf Vaget, 123–41. New York: Oxford University Press, 2008.

Venohr, Wolfgang. *Stauffenberg: Symbol of Resistance; the Man Who Almost Killed Hitler.* Barnsley, UK: Frontline, 2019.

Villa-Vicencio, Charles. *Living between Science and Belief: The Modern Dilemma.* Eugene, OR: Cascade Books, 2021.

———. *Trapped in Apartheid: A Socio-theological History of the English-Speaking Churches.* Maryknoll, NY: Orbis, 1988.

West, Cornel. *Prophetic Fragments.* Grand Rapids: Eerdmans, 1988.

West, Gerald. "White Theology in a Black Frame: Betraying the Logic of Social Location." In *Living on the Edge: Essays in Honour of Steve de Gruchy, Activist & Theologian,* edited by James R. Cochrane et al., 60–78. Pietermaritzburg, South Africa: Cluster, 2012.

Wieseltier, Leon. "Crimes against Humanities: Now Science Wants to Invade the Liberal Arts. Don't Let It Happen." *New Republic,* September 3, 2013. https://newrepublic.com/article/114548/leon-wieseltier-responds-steven-pinkers-scientism/.

Williams, Reggie L. *Bonhoeffer's Black Jesus: Harlem Renaissance Theology and an Ethic of Resistance.* Waco: Baylor University Press, 2014.

Williams, Zoe. "The Choices We Make about Coronavirus Are Way More Complex than 'Lives v the Economy.'" *Guardian,* Tuesday 14 April 2020. https://www.theguardian.com/commentisfree/2020/apr/14/coronavirus-lives-economy-lockdown-left-right/.

Wilson Edward O. *Consilience: The Unity of Knowledge.* London: Abacus, 1998.

Young, Josiah Ulysses, III. *No Difference in the Fare: Dietrich Bonhoeffer and the Problem of Racism.* Grand Rapids: Eerdmans, 1998.

Zerner, Ruth. "Church, State and the 'Jewish Question.'" In *The Cambridge Companion to Dietrich Bonhoeffer,* edited by John W. de Gruchy, 190–205. Cambridge Companions to Religion. Cambridge: Cambridge University Press, 1999.

Zimmermann, Jens. *Humanism and Religion: A Call for the Renewal of Western Culture.* Oxford: Oxford University Press, 2012.

INDEX

abortion, 132, 100
Abwehr (German Military Intelligence), 138, 150
Abyssinian Baptist Church, Harlem, 44
Achar, Gilbert, 109–10, 114–5, 119
Adorno, Theodor W., 66
aesthetic
    desire, 87
    existence, 18, 63
    judgment, 18, 72
African National Congress, 37
African
    Christianity, 44
    Americans, 44, 64, 118
    slaves, 77
Afrikaner, 38–39, 50, 116
    nationalism, 38–39
    republics, 36, 42
"After Ten Years" (Bonhoeffer), 61, 73, 86, 139, 141, 145
All Quiet on the Western Front (Remarque), 43
American
    Christianity, 43–45, 49
    culture, 44
    empire, 77
    racial schism, 49
American Academy of Religion, 51
anti-Semitism, 19, 38, 44, 68, 107, 109–12, 114, 119–20
    and apartheid, 39
    in South Africa, 39
anti-Judaism, 109, 114
apartheid, 10–11, 37, 39–43, 47, 49–51, 63, 106

beneficiaries of, 55
exiles, 66
justification of, 49, 116
legacy of, 49–50
and Palestine, 108, 110, 112, 118
post-apartheid, 35–36, 106
struggle against, 4, 17, 25, 32, 34–35, 54
vaccine apartheid, 136–37
(*see also* South Africa, church struggle, Dutch Reformed Church)
Aryan Legislation, 116
Auschwitz, 73, 111
Ayer, A. J., 21

Bach, Johann Sebastian, 61–62, 74
Balfour Declaration, 108
baptism, 14, 45
Barbour, Ian G, 94
Barmen
    Declaration, 4, 47
    Synod of, 48, 116
Barth, Karl, 4, 15, 24–25, 31, 47, 62, 65–66, 74
beauty, 62, 67, 95
    Apollonian, 63
    death of, 71
    Dionysian, 63
Beethoven, Ludwig von, 56, 60–2, 67–74
Begbie, Jeremy, 75
Belhar Confession, 47, 116
Bell, George, 48
Berlin, 66, 88, 111, 119
    University of, 134

INDEX

Bethge, Eberhard, 18, 51, 63, 66, 106, 108, 111, 118, 145
Bethge, Renate, 18
Bible, 5, 17, 19–21, 23, 28, 53, 58, 76, 98, 118
   infallibility of, 80
   interpretation of, 5
Biko, Steve, 40
Bismarck, Otto von, 42
Black consciousness, 34, 40–41
Black Lives Matter, 41
Black suffering, 44
Black theology, 32
Boesak, Allan Aubrey, 41
Bonhoeffer, Dietrich
   and American church, 44–45
   on christology, 5, 27, 58, 74, 88
   on colonialism, 13, 52, 111
   conversion of, 64–65
   death of, 13, 52, 111
   ethics of, 117, 125–33, 140, 142–48
   on faith, 6, 85, 101
   and German Resistance, 52, 66, 99, 105, 117, 124–25
   as humanist, 6
   and the Jews, 113, 117–8, 125
   in London, 47–8, 64, 119
   and music, 59, 61, 64–5, 67–9
   in New York, 11, 13, 18, 30, 32, 43–44, 46, 61, 54, 64–65, 92
   and Palestine, 108
   on racism, 44, 107–8
   as radical, 124, 143
   in Rome, 46
   on science, 6, 85, 101
   on suffering, 28–29, 32, 76, 119
   on theology, 5–6, 9, 12–15, 18, 25–26
   on technology, 84–85, 89
   on transcendence, on, 15, 27, 58–59, 75–76, 96
   and victims, 107, 118–9, 129, 131–2
   and violence, 13, 64, 120, 126, 133
Bonhoeffer, Karl, 62, 134
borderline moral cases, 129–30, 132–33, 140, 142
Braverman, Mark, 109, 114
Breen, Lorna, 137

Brueggemann, Walter, 20
Buber, Martin, 112–13
Buchenwald, 111
Buthelezi, Manas, 50, 53

cantus firmus, 6, 74
Cavanaugh, William T., 90, 93–6
Chicago, 3, 40, 46, 111,
Chikane, Frank, 41
Christ
   center of history, as, 88, 101
   cosmic, 88
   crucified and risen, 46, 122, 148
   death of, 26, 46, 29, 105
   as church community, 46,
   faith in, 103, 122, 123
   following, 126, 146
   love of, 149
   mind of, 148
   mystery of, 103
   passion of, 104
   and peace, 124
   Stellvertreter/ung, 105
   vicarious action of, 105
   witness to, 125
   (*see also* Christology, God, Jesus of Nazareth)
Christendom, 21–22, 28, 40, 45, 50, 71, 72, 76, 109, 115
   Post-Christendom, 74, 77
Christian formation, 148
Christology, 5–6, 27
Chua, Daniel, 57,
church/es, 17, 24
   American, 44–45, 49
   Catholic, 46, 49
   and colonialism, 50
   as community, 46–47
   Confessing, 24, 47–48, 111, 117
   Dutch Reformed, 38, 47, 49, 51, 116
   ecumenical, 35, 123–24
   for others, 4, 47
   German, 46, 111, 115–17, 124, 134
   and the Jews, 115–17
   music, 65
   as new humanity, 46
   and Palestine, 111–12
   Palestinian, 122–23

INDEX

political witness, 14, 32, 35
prophetic, 35, 124
Protestant, 46–47, 115–16
and racism, 45–47, 49, 52, 116
in South Africa, 4, 32, 35, 40, 51, 116
and state, 97
as site of struggle, 50
White, 47, 49, 52, 54
and world, 102–3
and Zionism, 109
(*see also* America, Confessing Church, German, South Africa)
civil courage, 142–44, 151
Civil Rights Movement, 3, 11, 35, 110
Clarke, Paul, 131, 150
Clements, Keith, ix
colonialism, 7, 33–43, 51, 126
British, 36
Christianity and, 33–34
German, 43
legacy of, 30, 34, 41
and racism, 42, 48, 50
Comaroff, Jean and John, 34
compromise, 125, 133, 143
Communism, 40
Cone, James H., 32, 35, 41
Congress on Mission and Evangelism, 50
conversion (*see metanoia*), 51–2, 72
of Anthony Flew, 81–82
of Beyers Naudé, 51–52, 55
of Dietrich Bonhoeffer, 39, 44
conscience, 40, 61, 67, 128–29, 134, 138–39, 141, 144, 148
conspiracy against Hitler (*see* German resistance)
COVID-19, 2, 11–12, 16, 19, 35, 51, 41, 80, 83–84, 86, 128, 130, 137
protocols, 129 (*see also* plague, pandemic, triage)
creation, 20, 83, 87, 88, 96
and evolution, 83
critical realism, 94, 103

Dawkins, Richard, 81–82,
de Gruchy, Steve, 2, 5, 11, 35, 40, 51–55, 151,
de Gruchy, Isobel ix, 112, 151

death, 2, 7, 18, 59, 62, 131, 146, 150–53
of beauty, 71
of God, 71, 76
(*see also* euthanasia, triage)
dignity, 25, 97, 101–2, 107, 123, 146
Dohnanyi, Christoph von, 68
Dohnanyi, Hans von, 117, 138, 146
dualism, 97, 102
(*see also* thinking in two spheres, two-state solution)
Dumas, André, 13, 96
Durand, Jaap J.F., 2, 57, 116
Dutch East India Company, 35
Dutch Reformed Church (NGK), 38, 47, 49, 51, 116
duty, 22, 126, 138, 141, 148

Eagleton, Terry, 61
Eco, Umberto, 18
ecumenical movement, 124
Einstein, Albert, 85
Ellis, George F. R., 79–80
Ellis, Marc H., 114, 95
Enlightenment, the, 69, 91, 101
Post-Enlightenment, 70, 102
(*see also* humanism)
environmental crisis, 6, 42, 85, 87, 140, 153
epistemology, 21, 81
ethics
Christian, 100
of free responsibility, 99, 125, 135
of necessity, 128–33, 141–45, 147–49
euthanasia, 131–134, 140
exile/s, 66, 68

Fanø, Denmark, 124
Feminist theology, 4
Finkenwalde Seminary, 48, 65
Fischer, Franklin, 13, 44
Flew, Anthony, 81
forgiveness, 14, 89
Fowler, James, 16
Frankfurter Schule, 66
French Resistance, 128
Friedlander, Albert, 109
fundamentalism
Christian, 81

171

INDEX

religious, 12, 100
scientific, 80, 90
future generations, 12, 66, 73, 148, 153

Gandhi, Mahatma, 36–37, 48, 126
gender, 10, 46, 77
   justice, 54
   (*see also* violence)
German Christians (*Deutsche Christen*), 116
German Resistance, 73, 133, 138, 140, 144
Gestapo, 13, 119, 132
Gibbon, Edward, 60
Gleick, James, 91
God
   absence of, 74,
   belief in, 81
   biblical, 21
   of Christendom, 72, 76
   death of, 71
   grace of, 16, 134
   image of, 29
   kingdom of, 31, 63, 66
   knowledge of, 74
   living without, 27
   as love, 15
   as mystery, 33
   playing, 129, 134, 136, 140
   providence of, 145
   reality of, 1, 15–16, 20, 25–29, 58–59, 76, 81, 88–89, 96, 99, 148
   reality of God and world, 1, 20, 25, 28–29, 59, 76
   sovereignty of, 145
   suffering of, 28
   will of, 140, 144, 146–49
   word of, 27, 68, 123
Goethe, Johann Wolfgang von, 62, 66–67, 69, 71
Goldstone, Richard, 120
grace, 14, 75, 128, 152
   justification by, 148
Great Depression, 10
Green, Clifford J., 64, 76, 105, 133
Greenberg, Irving, 114
grief, 137–38
Grotius, Hugo, 28

Guangdong, China, 130
guilt, 133–34, 137–39, 146

Haber, Fritz, 85
Hartman, Tim, 50
Harvey, Barry, 15, 70, 144
Hildebrandt, Frans, 119
history
   Christ as center, 88
   revelation in, 15–16, 20, 26, 87
   twentieth century, 77
   world, 23, 26, 32, 119, 148
HIV/AIDS, 35
Hitler, Adolf, 115-7, 119, 131-4, 138–40, 142–144, 147
   (*see also* conspiracy, resistance)
Holocaust (Shoah), 109–11, 114, 118–19
   studies, 117
   museums, 107, 111, 113
Holy Land, 112, 118, 122–23
hope, 4, 9, 12, 87–88, 101–3, 123, 128, 134, 148
   cry of, 122
   losing, 18, 139
   living in, 150–54
   messianic, 19
   redemptive, 29, 68
   signs of, 122
   sustained by, 12, 20–21, 23
human
   agency, 145, 147
   being, 97–98
   dignity, 25, 97, 101–2, 107, 146
   lived experience, 17, 52, 54, 87, 89, 98
   rights, 66, 70, 114
   (*see also* freedom, responsibility, sin)
humanism/t, 25, 72–73, 90–91, 94, 102
   Bonhoeffer as, 6
   Christian, 25, 89, 100–102
   culture, 78
   and the Enlightenment, 91, 101
   Hebrew, 113
   origins of, 102
   Renaissance, 70
   secular, 25, 63, 66, 99, 102
   social, 65–66

INDEX

stoic, 73
values, 24, 65–767

icons, 75
Idealism, 21, 100
idolatry, 99–100
imperialism (*see* colonialism)
India, 10, 35–36, 39, 48
intellectual honesty, 22
International Bonhoeffer Society Congresses
  Amsterdam, 109
  Geneva, 4, 51
ISIS, 19
Israel
  ancient, 39, 87, 115, 125
  modern state of, 107–15, 118–21
  (*see also* Jews, Judaism)

Jeremiah, 98, 107
Jesus of Nazareth, 71–72, 74–76, 97, 100, 106–7, 122, 126, 136, 148
  (*see also* christology)
Jewish Question, 109, 111, 115–18
Jews, 44, 52, 68, 74, 85, 106–19, 123, 125
  Bonhoeffer and, 125
  persecution of, 109, 113, 115, 117, 132
  (*see also* anti-Semitism, Holocaust, anti-Judaism,)
John Paul II, pope, 106
Judaism, 50, 109, 111, 114, 117
  anti-Judaism, 109
  Christianity and, 117–18
Jung, Carl G., 69
justice
  distributive, 78
  economic, 42
  God's, 15, 20, 23, 52, 75, 106, 113, 126
  love and, 89, 154
  order and, 63
  peace and, 15, 19, 54, 77, 100, 103, 110, 123
  security and, 121
  struggle for, 2, 9, 25, 35, 41–42, 48, 52, 54, 64, 76, 83, 106–7, 122, 125, 145
  truth and, 106
  virtue, as, 87, 89
  kairos, 33

Kairos Document, 32–33, 50, 121
Kairos Palestine Document, 118, 121–23, 125–26
Kant, Immanuel, 21
Kierkegaard, Søren, 8, 148
King, Martin Luther Jr., 41, 90, 126
Kingdom of God, 31, 51, 54
Kirchenkampf, 3–4, 47–48, 66
Kreuzer, Leonid, 63
Kuruman Mission, 52

Lamb, Matthew L., 23, 104
Lasserre, Jean, 13, 43–44
Leech, Kenneth, 31
Lewis, Bernard, 115
Lewis, Sinclair, 71
life
  Christian, 29, 75
  meaning of, 93
  polyphony of, 6, 74
Littel, Franklin, 111
Lovin, Robin, 12, 125
love, 23, 77, 87, 103, 113, 120, 122, 126, 143
  agape, 59, 74, 89, 97
  commandment to, 14
  of enemies, 126
  eros, erotic, 59, 74
  of other, 75, 122, 124–25, 140
  of/for God, 8, 15, 27, 58, 74–75, 88, 148–49, 154
  of justice, 9
  of music, 61, 64, 67–68
  for the world, 75
Luther, Martin, 14, 61, 116

Machiavelli, Niccolò, 142
Magnes, Judah, 113
Mann, Thomas, 61–69, 73, 76
Mandela, Nelson, 40–41, 71

INDEX

materialism, 95–96 (*see also* matter, physical reality)
McGilchrist, Iain, 92
medical science, 2, 28, 131, 135
Mennonite peace tradition, 54
Merton, Thomas, 58, 77
metanoia, 33–34, 52, 55, 65, 77, 148 (*see also* repentance)
Michelangelo, 62
Middle Ages, 58, 82, 102
Middle East, 53, 108, 118, 122
Mirzaali, Mikaeil, 137
Moltke, Helmut von, 43, 138
Moltmann, Jürgen, 29
moral agency, 100, 101
Mozart, Wolfgang Amadeus, 61, 74,
Mumford, Lewis, 83–84
murder, 129, 131, 138, 142
music
   church, 65
   Classical, 62–62, 68–70, 76
   Romantic, 60, 62–63, 69–70, 73, 76
Mwangi, Kamau, 136–37
mystery, 95–96
   embraced by, 102
   language of, 54
   myth as mediator, 98
   of life, 68
   of God, 2, 33, 74–75, 96–100, 152
   of humanity, 97
   reality and, 95–96, 101–2, 114
   revealed, 101, 103
mysticism, 57–58, 62, 98

Nakba, 108, 110, 119
Namibia, 42–43
Natal Indian Congress, 36
National Party, 39
nationalism, 7, 19, 54, 128, 149
   Afrikaner, 38–9
   Christian, 77
   German, 13, 44, 52, 64
   Right-wing, 11
Nazism (National Socialism), 128
Niebuhr, Reinhold, 11, 44, 83
Niebuhr, Ursula, 64
Nietzsche, Friedrich, 21, 59–60, 62, 67, 69, 71–72, 81

nihilism, 71–72

Oldham, Joe, 48
Opus 111 (Beethoven), 68
Ott, Heinrich, 13

Palestine/Palestinian, 107, 110
   and apartheid, 106, 115
   Christians, 126
   Occupation of, 108, 110, 125
   Oslo Agreement, 112
   suffering, 122–23
   (*see also* Kairos Palestine Document, *Nakba*)
pandemic (*see* COVID-19, plague)
Parker, Joshua, 137
patriotism, 19, 52, 106
Peck, William J., 132
penultimate, 2, 12, 16, 58, 62, 96, 98, 143, 147 (*see also* ultimate)
Pilgrimage of Hope, 53
Pinker, Steve, 22–24, 90–93, 101
plague, 7, 127–28, 130–33, 140 (*see also* COVID, 19)
The Plague (Camus), 127–28
Platonic, 95
Prideaux, Sue, 60
politics/cal, 48, 59, 116, 125, 136, 139–40, 147
   analysis, 143
   diplomacy, 126
   gangsterism, 59–60
power, 76
   realism, 14, 97, 125, 143
   responsibility, 125, 143
polyphony of life, 6, 74
poor/poverty, 6, 11, 18, 23, 107, 128, 137
Pretoria, 10, 39

racism, 19, 23, 30, 100, 110
   in America, 44, 110
   brutality of, 40
   in the church, 44–50
   colonialism and, 30–38, 42, 126
   conversion from, 41, 54
   and land dispossession, 36
   not scientific, 39
   as sinful, 52

INDEX

systemic, 11, 13, 30–39, 41, 46–50
(*see also* apartheid, Palestine)
radical/ism, 16
  and compromise, 143
  divine commandment as, 16
  gospel as radical demand, 76
Raheb, Mitri, 8
rape, 59
Rasmussen, Larry L., 9, 87–88, 114, 153
rationality
  limits of, 22, 79, 89
  necessity of, 23–24, 86-87
  power of, 22
  (*see also* reason)
reason, 17, 70
  appeal to, 86
  faith and, 21–5, 27, 80, 82, 101–2
  fallibility of, 22–3, 79
  fanaticism and, 143
  (*see also* rationality, stupidity, wisdom)
reality (*Wirklichkeit*), 96, 46, 105
  knowledge of, 81
  as sacrament, 12
religion
  Christianity as, 27, 59
  essence of, 98
  faith and, 99
  fundamentalist, 79, 102
  liberalizing, 91, 101
  persistence of, 81
  revelation and, 46
  science and, 92, 102
  in secular society, 102
  wars of, 22
  as witness to faith, 99
  in world come of age, 98
Remarque, Erich Maria, 43
repentance (*see* conversion, *metanoia*)
resistance
  non-violent, 48, 126
  (*see also* conspiracy, Germany, Kairos Document, Palestine, South Africa, struggle,)
Rhodes, Cecil John, 37
Roman Catholic (*see* church)

Sachs, Harvey, 70
science
  faith, and, 23, 58, 69, 79–82, 88–93, 96
  fallible, 23, 79–81, 91–94, 98, 99
  foundation in physics, 95
  medical, 22, 28, 135
  mistrust of, 86
  morality, and, 92–93, 109
  and mystery, 95
  natural, 28
  promise of, 91
  as religion, 92
  and secularism, 18
  theology and, 83, 90, 93–94, 101
  technology and, 1, 80, 82–85, 91, 99, 102
  transcendence and, 95–97
scientific method, 21
scientism, 80, 90, 92
Scruton, Roger, 68, 75
secularism, 18, 71, 81, 99–101
Sermon on the Mount, 13, 48, 133, 144
sexuality, 59
Shain, Milton, 39
Sharpeville Massacre, 51
Shay, Suellen, 151
Shoah, *see* Holocaust
silence, 72, 74, 106, 109
sin, 9–10, 23, 31, 38, 52, 59, 69
Sobukwe, Robert, 40
Soelle, Dorothee, 58
Song of Songs, 74
soul, 56
  dark night of, 57
  embodied, 97–98
  loss of, 77
  recovery of, 97–98
  restless, 58
solidarity
  with Palestinians, 119, 123–24
  with victims, 55, 104–7, 110, 119–20, 148
  with Jews, 113, 117–18
  (*see also* vicarious action, suffering)
South Africa/n
  Anglo-Boer War, 37–38, 42–43
  amaXhosa, 36
  amaZulu, 36
  armed struggle, 40

INDEX

Cape Colony, 36–37
Christian Institute, 50–51
Cottesloe Consultation, 51
Council of Churches (SACC), 3, 40
South Africa/n *(continued)*
  French Huguenots, 36
  Indian laborers, 36
  Jewish refugees, 38
  Khoi, 35, 39
  Land Act (1913), 37
  Natal, 36
  Natal Indian Congress, 36
  San, 35, 39
  Soweto Uprising (1976), 40
  Union (1910), 37, 39
  Visit of Royal family (1947), 39
spirituals, 76
Stalingrad, battle of, 144
Stauffenberg, Klaus von, 139–40
stupidity, 85–86, 89
  (see also wisdom)
suicide, 71–72
suffering, 17, 19, 21, 29, 32, 13, 68, 76, 97–98, 119
  (see also God, Blacks, Jews, Palestinians)
Susser, Baruch, 113
Switzerland, 65, 125

Taizé Community, 53
Tantur, 112
technology, 2, 80, 82–85, 99
  destructive, 23, 79, 84, 91
  loss of soul, 83–84, 89
  medical, 78, 84
technological organization, 84–85, 89
Terblanche, Sampie, 34
theology, 11, 25–26, 29
  doing, 4–5, 52, 108
  method, 4–5
  survival of, 50
  White, 52
  (see also Black, Bonhoeffer)
Teilhard de Chardin, Pierre, 57, 88
thinking in two spheres, 93
Tillich, Paul, 66, 98
transcendence, 58
  demonic, 69, 72
  desire for, 10, 16, 55, 59–60, 69, 75–78
  of God, 15, 98
  and the other, 76
  and reality, 95–96, 98
  and silence, 72
  transformative, 75–76
  as will-to-power, 69, 77
  (see also God, mystery)
transcendentalism, 58
  Christian, 58–59
treason, 138
  patriotic, 52, 108
Tresckow, Henning von, 139–40
triage, 136, 140
Trump, Donald J., 71
truth
  and error, 17
  God of, 96
  Jesus Christ as, 27, 29
  knowing the, 94, 135
  as ontological, 95
  and reality, 14, 96
  and reason, 22
  speaking, 73, 105, 107
Tutu, Desmond Mpilo, 2, 41, 53, 106–7, 118, 121, 146
two-state solution, 92–95, 102
tyrannicide, 131

ultimate, the, 12, 58, 62, 96, 98, 143, 148
  reality, 2, 16
  questions, 18, 146
  (see also penultimate)
United States of America, 3, 45, 65, 71, 108–9
  and Israel, 115, 120
Union Theological Seminary, 26, 32, 43, 54, 64, 81, 92
University of Berlin,
University of Cape Town, 54, 110, 151
  Center for Jewish Studies, 113

vaccine apartheid, 136–37
Verwoerd, Hendrik, 49
vicarious action (*Stellvertretung*), 104–5, 107, 123, 134, 148

INDEX

victims
    competition of the, 118–19
    of Holocaust, 109–10, 119
    Jews as, 113, 115, 119
    solidarity with, 54, 104–7
    Palestinians as, 110, 121
    prophets as, 106
Villa-Vicencio, Charles, 81
virtues, 87, 91, 141
violence
    criminal, 60
    gender-based, 6, 11, 35, 51, 54–55
    perpetuation of, 23, 60, 110, 126
    rejection of, 13, 64, 107, 120
vocation
    sense of, 135

Wagner, Richard, 60, 62, 67–70
war
    Anglo Boer, 37–38, 41–42
    First World War, 10, 43, 65
    in Ukraine, 2, 12, 60, 84, 108, 129
    Second World War, 10, 35, 38, 43, 109, 128
West, Cornel., 32, 41
West, Gerald, 52
White
    being, 13, 38–40, 52–53
    liberation, 40, 51
    privilege, 53
    theology, 52
Wieseltier, Leon, 90, 93
will-to-power, 69, 77
    (*see also* transcendence)
Wilson Edward O., 92

Wirklichkeit, see reality
wisdom, 22, 79, 89, 98
    biblical, 87
    Christ as, 88
    false, 87
    gaining, 86
    fear of God, 99
    God of, 30, 88, 103
    as insight, 89
    and knowledge, 86
    of non-violence, 89
    redemptive, 88–89
    science and, 92
    simplicity of, 146
    true, 87
    of the world, 86
    (*see also* stupidity)
Wittgenstein, Ludwig, 21
Wolterstorff, Nicholas, 23
World Alliance for Promoting International Friendship, 14, 124
world come of age, 63
World Council of Churches, 41, 51, 112
    China, 130

Yad Vashem, 117
Yokohama, Japan, 130

Zerner, Ruth, 109
Zimbabwe, 37
Zimmermann, Jens, 25, 101–2
Zionism, 108, 113
    Christian, 109, 115
Zuma, Jacob, 71

www.ingramcontent.com/pod-product-compliance
Lightning Source LLC
Chambersburg PA
CBHW020850160426
43192CB00007B/856